Donald Clark

All or *Nothing* at *All*

A Life of Frank Sinatra

Fromm International / New York

First Fromm International paperback, 2000

Copyright © 1997 by Donald Clarke

All rights reserved under International and Pan-American copyright convention.
First published in hardcover in the United States by Fromm International
Publishing Corporation, New York, in 1997. Originally published in Great
Britain by Macmillan Publishers Ltd., London, in 1997.

LIBRARY OF CONGRESS CATALOGING-IN-PUBLICATION DATA

Clarke, Donald, 1940–
    All or nothing at all: a life of Frank Sinatra / Donald Clarke.--1st ed.
      p.   cm.
    Originally published: London : Macmillan, 1997.
    Includes Index.
    ISBN 0-88064-224-6
    1. Sinatra, Frank, 1915–   .   2. singers--United States--Biography.
I. Title.
    ML420.S565C53   1997
    782.42164'092--dc21
      [B]   97-21885
                                                                           CIP
                                                                           MN

10   9   8   7   6   5   4   3   2   1
Manufactured in the United States of America

For Lisa and Jenny
And for David

Contents

All or Nothing at All

F rank Sinatra made his first records with Harry James shortly before I was born, and I began listening to the radio as soon as I could reach the dial, so I guess it's safe to say that I've been listening to him all my life.

In the 1950s I was buying the wonderful albums he was making, but apparently there were two Frank Sinatras. There was the one who'd been singing on the radio since I could remember, and who made terrific albums with Nelson Riddle; and there was the other Frank, who was gossiped about, always in some kind of trouble or controversy, who led a Clan and behaved like a troubled adolescent. I heard the gossip about Hollywood, Palm Springs and Las Vegas from a considerable remove; there wasn't much trouble where I came from, but music was the most important thing in the world to me: I was listening to everything, and Sinatra was in the mix. I heard the loneliness and the understated passion; I heard the great American songs interpreted so that I understood why they were great songs. There's a story about a drunk in a bar, listening to Sinatra on the jukebox singing "One for My Baby": When the record is over, the drunk sighs and says, "I wonder who *he* listens to." Sinatra didn't have to listen to anybody. Somehow he knew how to live part of our lives with us.

Those of us who were born white, male and American at exactly the right time have been surfing all our lives on a tidal wave of postwar prosperity. I was not a Catholic or a Jew or an African-American; my name ended in a vowel, but it was a silent vowel, so I blended easily into the woodwork. My people being the kind of people who pretty much kept their heads down, I finally understood that what Sinatra (and Duke Ellington and Shostakovich and Ray Charles) did for me was to allow me to live vicariously: I could hear the pain and the joy in the music, and begin to understand it from the sidelines. They also prepared me for the real world, which was not as safe (or as boring) as I had been led to believe. America was in fact a restless place, never as sure of itself as it pretended to be; one kept bumping into people who were not so lucky, or who refused to believe in their own luck; eventually there were grown-up disappointments, and loneliness, while in the wider world our century has been an incredibly violent one, and finally we have no leaders: there is no one to look up to, no one to vote for. The greatest loneliness is in disillusion, which is one reason why we need art. Sinatra has been fighting against disillusionment all his life.

He brought to his struggle whatever he had from his background; having no apparent talent at all, he drove himself to become a singer, and in the end he interpreted the songs so that his struggle became that of his generation. In his personal life, as Humphrey Bogart put it, he was "a kind of Don Quixote, tilting at windmills, fighting people who don't want to fight." In fact he fought with himself, unable to harness his own undoubted charm for his own good; he often chose friends who were unworthy of him. But the honesty and the vulnerability came out in the songs. If he had not needed to tilt at windmills, he would have become a successful plumber in Hoboken, and we would never have heard of him; but as the chivalric fool Don Quixote was the center of one of the best-loved novels ever written, so Sinatra has reflected the anxiety of our century, and resolved it in his music.

There has been a lot of reporting about his bad behavior and, separately, millions of words about his music. In a curious way we have taken the two Sinatras for granted. Yet he became perhaps the most famous man of the century because the great singer and the troublemaker were in fact the same guy, and as he sang about love and marriage (which he tried four times), you can't have one without the other. A great artist comes from a certain time and place to transcend it with his or her work; what I have tried to do here is to paint a rounded picture of a man who became part of the soundtrack of our lives.

For this excuse to listen to all of Frank Sinatra's records, I am grateful to my agent, Clare Conville, to my editor at Macmillan, Georgina Morley, and to my wife, Ethne. I hope the book is worthy of them, and that it will be of value to all the Sinatra fans I haven't met yet.

Chapter One

The Kid from Hoboken

E ven as it began, it must have been obvious that the twentieth century would be an American century: the lusty, brawling, violent and sentimental United States was an irrepressible teenager of a nation. The Columbian Exposition in Chicago in 1893 had already been an enormous celebration of Americanism (the extermination of Native American cultures being virtually complete by then), and Independence Day observations in those years were marked by immigrant groups singing patriotic songs (except for those whose ancestors had come from Africa), while the nineteenth century had already decided what kind of nation the U.S.A. would become. Immigration had reached a crescendo after 1880: Protected by a Constitution, a Bill of Rights and an unquenchable optimism, the young nation's doors were open, and, of all the immigrant groups of the period, the Jewish and the Italian ultimately had the most profound influence on American culture.

We must qualify that, and say "popular culture": In Italy, for example, the barrow boys in the marketplace whistled the tunes from the newest operas, but in the U.S.A. (though it was supposed to be a classless society) there was already a gulf between the highbrow and the lowbrow. It was in the commercial marketplace that the riches and the fame lay, and hearts and souls were to be won.

The achievement of the Jews is obvious: the inventors of the dream machine itself, the Hollywood film industry, were all Jewish, as were many of the greatest songwriters of a golden age, and many of the greatest entertainers. But the accomplishment of second-generation Italian-Americans was hardly less impressive; in particular, they quickly became proficient at American music.

Harry Warren (Salvatore Guaragna) was one of the most prolific of all the great songwriters ("You're Getting to Be a Habit with Me"); Eddie Lang (Salvatore Massaro) virtually invented jazz guitar, and was Bing Crosby's favorite accompanist. Here is a partial list of the sons of Italy who played for only one bandleader, Benny Goodman: Toots Mondello, Art Rollini, Vido Musso, Lee Castle (Castaldo), Louis Bellson (Bellasano), Remo Palmieri, Conrad Gozzo, Gene Bertoncini, Johnny Guarnieri, Bucky Pizzarelli, and Buddy Greco (there were many more). And the Italian-American vocalists were more famous than the musicians: Al Martino (Cini), Dean Martin (Crocetti), Jerry Vale (Vitaliano), Tony Bennett (Benedetto), Vic Damone (Farinola), Frankie Laine (LoVecchio), Johnny Desmond (DeSimone), and many others. There were a few who didn't change their names: Julius LaRosa, Perry Como, and the biggest star of all. Those who sing a nation's songs must be among its greatest heroes, and the singer who would be named by most people as the single greatest interpreter of America's best songs is Frank Sinatra, a star of such magnitude that he became the virtual king of show business.

Between 1876 and 1914 over 7.6 million Italians crossed the Atlantic. Some of them went to South America, and some returned to Italy when they'd saved some money; but the U.S.A. was the land of opportunity. Until 1890 the majority of American immigrants had come from northern Europe, but from 1891 until 1915 more Italians came to the U.S.A. than any other national group. In earlier decades, California had more Italian immigrants than any other state, mostly working in agriculture, but by the end of the century they were settling in the northeastern U.S.A., looking for urban and industrial opportunities. Between 1900 and 1910 the Italian-born population of New Jersey increased by over 73,000, and that figure does not include those who landed there and left, or who came there after they arrived in the U.S.A.

By 1924 the Italians had become the largest foreign-born group in the state.

Italian families brought with them strong traditions of personal and familial pride and honor, yet they were often seen as dirty and ignorant, suspected of political radicalism and a tendency to pauperism and criminality. By 1925 a study had been made in New York City courts of over 2,000 criminal cases classified by nationality, and it was found that, relative to their numbers, native-born Americans committed more crimes than immigrants. Among immigrants who did get in trouble with the law, those from southern Europe were most likely to commit crimes of passion, but those from northern Europe were overwhelmingly more likely to be thieves, burglars and embezzlers—in other words, to choose crime as a way of making a living. In every study in every state, when the ratio in the population of each immigrant group was taken into consideration, the Italians turned out to be more law-abiding than average: if seventeen groups were included, the Italians would typically rank twelfth on the list of those contributing to criminal statistics. Yet American newspapers and periodicals were inclined to make much of "black-hand societies and cammorista bands."

In 1915–16, New York City had done a survey of its schools, classifying absenteeism according to nationality, and the Italian children were found overwhelmingly the most likely to be truant. This surprised some New Yorkers, who expected the worst miscreants to be Irish, as they probably would have been twenty years earlier: a long-standing New York prejudice against the Irish had not yet been transferred to the Italians. But in each generation, the children who are least likely to value education are those at the bottom of the social ladder, who perceive the establishment as treating them badly anyway and see no reason why they should submit to it. One interesting fact emerging from the studies of the period is that crime went up in the *second* generation of immigrant families: the children of the immigrants, more fully American and having no direct connection with the old country, were more likely to commit crimes. Yet against all the evidence, native-born Americans saw themselves as law-abiding, and foreigners—the "others"—more likely to be criminals.

Most of the Italian emigrants to the U.S.A. were from the south; Italy was one of the most densely populated countries in Europe, and then as now, the south was less prosperous than the north. Over 80 percent of the emigrants from the south were unskilled laborers, and over half of them were illiterate. Frank and Rose Sinestro brought their son Anthony Martin Sinestro to the U.S.A. from Sicily, as far south as you can get in Italy; but Natalie Della Garavanti had emigrated from Genoa in the northwest, an important and historic port which once had colonies of its own. Blonde-haired and blue-eyed, Natalie was spoiled by her family, and was called Dolly from an early age. They all came to Hoboken, on the Hudson River.

From Bayonne in the south, through Jersey City, Hoboken, Union City and North Bergen, to Englewood in the north, the New Jersey side of the Hudson River stretches for twenty miles or so, urbanized and densely populated. Hoboken had once been a resort of wealthy New Yorkers, but had long since become a factory town, with jobs for immigrants. There is an American irony here. From being a place where the nobs and nabobs of Manhattan gathered to relax and play croquet on their lawns, Hoboken then became the "wrong" side of the river, where the working class was quarantined. As commuter railways were built it was possible to live farther out of town; Manhattan became more glamorous in the twentieth century, and even as bridges were built, the distance across the river seemed to grow in sociological terms.

Hoboken had its Germans, its Irish and its Italians, in that order of respectability, and the Italians had their own pecking order. Marty's father is said to have worked in a pencil factory for eleven dollars a week; Natalie's father was a lithographer's stonecutter; no doubt they both breathed a lot of dust, but Natalie's father had a skilled trade. Marty's mother ran a small grocery store, so at least there was always enough food. Marty was apprenticed to a shoemaker, but then took up prizefighting, calling himself Marty O'Brien, because the fight game did not welcome Italians in those days. Two of Dolly's brothers were also fighters; when Marty fought her brother Champ, it was typical of her that she dressed up as a boy and sneaked in to see the match:

boxing was considered disreputable, but Dolly always did as she pleased. (The fight was an exhausting draw; neither of the boys managed to knock the other down, but for the rest of their lives they argued about who had won.)

Just as African-Americans have been prejudiced against the darker members of their community, and as the uptown Irish looked down at their poorer brethren, so the northern Italians considered themselves superior to the southerners. Marty was a quiet man, never strong; in fact he was asthmatic. He never spoke unless it was necessary, while Dolly was noisily gregarious; Marty had never held a steady job and could not read or write, while Dolly had at least finished elementary school. When they began seeing each other, Dolly's parents naturally did not understand what she saw in Marty, who was not even a very good boxer. But perhaps he was simply a good and decent man; and perhaps their different personalities allowed Dolly a rest from herself, a source of calm that she must have needed. And maybe she knew instinctively that she needed a man who would allow her to do as she pleased.

Dolly's parents refused to give them a wedding, so they eloped to Jersey City, on Valentine's Day 1914. The pressure to become Americanized was very strong, and nobody admitted to being an immigrant if they could avoid it; immigrants avoided brushes with authority anyway, some even believing that any policeman could send them back to the old country on a whim. So it is not surprising that Marty and Dolly fibbed when they obtained a marriage license in Jersey City, stating that they had been born there; but they were married until Marty died nearly fifty-five years later, for most people stayed married in those days.

The newlyweds moved into a flat in Hoboken at 415 Monroe Street. The area later became a slum, but in 1914 the building was not very old; in their cold-water flat with the toilet in the hall, Marty and Dolly were already better off than many of their neighbors, and that is where their only child was born, on December 12, 1915. He was the first grandchild on either side of the family, and the excitement must have been great, helping to heal the family differences. The boy who became known as Francis Albert Sinatra was a large baby, over thirteen pounds, and it was a long and difficult breech delivery: the doctor had to use forceps, and the baby's ear was torn, the side of his face scarred and his eardrum punctured. The family story is that the doctor thought he was dead, turning his attention to Dolly, and that Dolly's mother Rosa held him under the cold-water tap, shocking him into life. (Many years later, Dolly's sister cast doubt on this story, maintaining that Rosa had not even been present, whereupon Dolly never spoke to her again.) At any rate, twenty-year-old Dolly was unable to have any more children.

Dolly was apparently so long recuperating that it was not until the following April that Frank was baptized. She probably surprised some people by choosing an Irish godfather, Frank Garrick, a crony of Marty's whose uncle was a Hoboken police captain. There is another family story that the priest made a mistake and named the baby after Garrick instead of Marty, but his birth had been registered on December 17, and, whether he was named after his godfather or his grandfather, the name on the birth certificate is Frank Sinestro. The certificate states that Anthony Sinestro had been born in the U.S.A., and "Dollie Garaventi" in Italy.

We do not know why the family changed the spelling to Sinatra. "Sinestro" means nothing in modern Italian, but is close to the words for *left* and *sinister*; no doubt they wanted to Americanize and neutralize the spelling so that it was easier to remember and carried no connotations at all. Some other members of the family may already have made the change; Ray Sinatra, a distant relative, became a well-known radio bandleader in New York City. Also, there does not seem to be any record of their entry into the United States, nor of Dolly or Marty ever becoming naturalized; again, like many immigrants, they may simply have wished to avoid drawing that sort of attention to themselves. At any rate, in May 1945, when Frank Sinatra was already world-famous, Dolly had corrections made to the birth certificate: the original surname was spelled wrong, but "Frank Sinastro" officially became Francis A. Sinatra, and "Dollie Garaventi" became Natalie Garavanti. Her nickname had long been spelled "Dolly."

Married and with a child, and knowing that she would never have any more children, Dolly was set loose. She had chosen a husband who would not get in her way, and with her mother to look after little Frank she set out to conquer Hoboken. Even before she became a mother she had made traditional Italian pastry sweets and passed them out to the neighbors; she could speak every dialect in Little Italy, and she now concentrated on bettering the family's social position any way she could.

A cousin of Marty's came over from Italy and joined the household; Dolly found him a job, and he turned his paycheck over to her. (She kept Vincent under her thumb, and he never married.) At one point she worked on Saturdays dipping chocolates in a candy store, but her main occupation was that of midwife, and she also performed abortions. This was not only scandalous in a Catholic community, but got her in trouble with the law several times; her skill at ignoring such difficulties and getting away with it was developed early. And it was the Catholic community itself which banished its own daughters if they were unlucky enough to get caught by a man without being married, and the laws against abortion simply didn't work (a fact that is inconvenient for today's single-issue fanatics).

Dolly also became a ward-heeler. In those days (and still today, in some places) American cities were run by political machines; a rough-and-ready corruption saw to it that poor people were looked after in exchange for their votes, while the most successful wheeler-dealers could get rich through political influence. One of the most fascinating documents in American political history is *Plunkitt of Tammany Hall*, written down in 1905 by a journalist: it records the frank revelations of an unusually garrulous politician, George Washington Plunkitt, an Irishman who orated from his "office" (a bootblack's stand at the New York County Courthouse). Plunkitt proposed his own epitaph: "He seen his opportunities and he took 'em." He became a millionaire, and when he died full of honors in 1924 *The Nation* summed up his sort of career: ". . . honesty doesn't matter; efficiency doesn't matter; progressive vision doesn't matter. What matters is the chance for a better job, a better price for wheat, better business conditions." As Richard Croker, one of Plunkitt's political bosses, once replied when asked his opinion of free silver (an emotive issue in the 1890s): "I'm in favor of all kinds of money—the more the better."

One of the effects of massive emigration to the U.S.A. had been that the aristocrats who had run the cities were outnumbered. The immigrants came so quickly and in such large numbers, many of them speaking no English and without any social services to look after them, that they were a sea of voters to be won, and high-flown political theory went out the window. If you wanted a ped-dler's permit or a liquor license, you went to your neighborhood political boss; if you were cold you got a bucket of coal; if you were hungry, a bag of groceries; if your child was in trouble, you might get him out of it. The neighborhood boss, or ward-heeler, got out the vote on election day, and the winners of the election made millions in kickbacks and had thousands of jobs to pass out to their loyal servants.

It is a mystery to historians why the U.S.A. never developed a successful progressive political party: the country should have been dominated by working people, yet the labor unions had no legal right to organize until the 1930s and there was no meaning-ful Civil Rights Act until 1964. The answer is that the political machines had no vision at all. Croker also said, "There is no deny-ing the service which Tammany has rendered to the Republic. There is no such organization for taking hold of the untrained, friendless man and converting him into a citizen. Who else would do it if we did not?" But the real purpose of the game was getting into power and staying there, by any means necessary. (When one political boss did not join in the singing of the national anthem, an aide explained, "Maybe he doesn't want to commit himself.") The party machine was a boat on the ocean, somebody explained, and occasional reform movements were waves to be ridden. Men like Plunkitt were genuinely puzzled by periodic complaints of malfeasance: what was the point of political activity if not to bet-ter oneself?

Here is journalist and novelist William Kennedy on the subject of Albany, New York:

When I grew up, there was no sense of morality in regard to poli-tics. If you were Irish, you were obviously a Democrat. If you were a Democrat, you were probably a Catholic.... No matter what it was in town, wherever you could make an illegal dollar, that's where the Irish were, that's where the politics were, that's where the church was, that's where the morality was...the goodness walked hand-in-hand with the evil. But it wasn't *viewed* as evil. It was viewed as a way to get on in the world. Objective morality didn't interest Albany. The Irish didn't care about it. They understood that *they* had been deprived and now they were not. Now they were able to get jobs. In the previous era, when the Irish were not in power, they had *not* been able to get jobs. Their families were starving, and starvation for them was immorality.

All this was true in Hoboken. American democracy was a matter of mutual back-scratching, and Dolly learned early the value of political influence. Several members of the family had brushes with the law, including Dolly herself, but the most serious case was that of her youngest brother, Babe (significantly, perhaps, the only one to have been born in the U.S.A.). In 1921 Babe was convicted of driving the getaway car during a robbery in which a man was killed. Dolly did the best she could, allegedly borrowing a baby (Frank was five years old), pretending to be her brother's wife and shedding copious tears in the courtroom, but to no avail: Babe went to the slammer. That must have been terribly frustrating, but Dolly was already becoming a political activist, and before long everybody knew who Dolly Sinatra was.

One of her favorite stories was about accompanying an immigrant fruit vendor to court to help him get his citizenship papers. When the judge asked him how many stars there were in the American flag, he replied, "How many bananas inna bunch?... Say, Your Honor, you stick-a you business, I stick-a mine." But Dolly was there to mollify the judge, the fruit-seller became a citizen, and the party machine got another vote. She became the leader of the Third Ward in Hoboken's Ninth District, probably the first Italian immigrant to hold such a post in a town then still dominated by the Irish, and maybe the first woman as well.

Dolly went out every Saturday night to political parties; in fact, she came and went as she pleased, often taking her black midwife's bag with her as though she was going to work, and Marty never complained. She sang the songs, drank the beer and danced on the tables, making friends of some and intimidating others. Plenty of people had reason to be grateful to her, while on the other hand, as a former mayor of Hoboken said many years later, "The mouth on that woman would make a longshoreman blush...she'd curse your mother to hell without even blinking." The politicians accepted her as an equal because she left them no choice, and because she delivered the votes.

After thirty pro fights, Marty stopped boxing when he broke his wrists; he then lost a job on the docks because of his asthma, and Dolly cashed a political chit: she banged on the appropriate door and demanded a job as a fireman for her husband. Marty was duly appointed to the fire service in 1927, eventually rising to the rank of captain without ever taking a written exam. Although the National Prohibition Act had been passed in 1920, the local authority turned a blind eye to saloons, and Dolly opened a tavern called Marty O'Brien's. She had Cousin Vincent's paychecks coming in, she got free groceries from Marty's mother, and she didn't pay her bills if she could avoid it; now the family began moving up, first in 1927 to a three-bedroom apartment on Hoboken's Park Avenue, only ten blocks from Monroe Street but well out of Little Italy. Then, in 1932, Dolly had saved enough money for a down payment on a four-story house on Garden Street, with flats to rent out to tenants, thus realizing two American working-class dreams at once: not only home ownership, but income property, so that somebody else's rent made the mortgage payments. Furthermore, Garden Street was in an Irish neighborhood: Dolly had managed to move away from the Italians altogether, the better to practice her political wiles.

They moved to their new address in time for teenaged Frank to throw a New Year's Eve party, and all his friends could see that the Sinatras were doing well. They now had central heating, and not only an indoor toilet of their own, but a bathtub. The apartment had a baby grand piano, and the standard of decorating included plastic flowers. A friend of the family many years later described it all as "Guinea furniture," using a now-obsolescent epithet for southern Europeans, but she also remembered being very impressed at the time.

Accomplishing all this at the bottom of the Great Depression, as a provider Dolly could not be beat; but as a mother she may have left something to be desired. Frank Sinatra was just an

Italian-American kid, and if he hadn't decided to be a singer we might never have heard of him; but he knew from a very early age that he was different. His mother was loud, pushy, foul-mouthed and vulgar; the testimony of friends and neighbors many years later was that Frankie was embarrassed by his mother's antics, and also very conscious of the way she walked all over Marty. In other Italian families the father was at least allowed the illusion of being boss. His friends had up to a dozen brothers and sisters, while Frankie was an only child, which meant that his mother could afford to spoil him. The boy had eight aunts and uncles, two on his father's side and six on his mother's, and four living grandparents, all within walking distance; later there were nearly a dozen cousins, but as the oldest, Frankie was cock of the walk. Yet he would stand in his grandmother's doorway and stare into space, as though he were the last boy on earth. For all Dolly's garrulousness, she managed to raise a lonely child. (Many years later, when his daughter Nancy presented him with his first grandchild, Frank Sinatra's first concern was that she should have another one, saying, "It was very lonely for me.")

Dolly was almost never at home, and when she was she sent all the wrong signals. She had no taste, no judgement. She tried in vain to prevent Frankie from imitating her foul mouth, on one occasion washing his mouth out with soap, but children learn by example, not by being lectured. She was a snob, but had no taste, impressed only by political power; she had no respect for anyone who was not useful to her. This was not a good example for someone who was going to be in the public eye. Frankie loved his mother, and she no doubt loved him above all things, but many years later, when he was one of the most famous men in the world, he told actress Shirley MacLaine that he feared and admired Dolly at the same time: "She scared the shit outta me."

He had plenty of friends in the neighborhood, but Dolly inadvertently spoiled that too. Dolly bought her friends with political favors, and she taught Frankie to buy his friends too: the only thing that was important was power. The other children regarded the Sinatras as rich, because Dolly kept Frankie supplied with enough pocket money to buy treats for them. He was the best-dressed kid on the block, having so many pairs of trousers that his nickname was "Slacksie O'Brien"; he had his own charge account, and on some occasions he even bought clothes for others. Frankie naturally took advantage of his situation, yet he made no relationships which lasted beyond his teenage years. Much would be written in years to come about the Italian side of Frank Sinatra's personality, the need to surround himself with cronies and demanding absolute loyalty, like the *padrone* or clan chieftain, but this has nothing to do with nationality. Italians as a rule are anything but lonely, but Frankie never learned how to make friends the hard way; instead Dolly taught him how to cope with loneliness. She herself, for all her compulsive activity, may have been fundamentally lonely too.

Frankie was a mischievous boy, and already inclined to arrogance, but he was also a skinny little guy; if he got in trouble in the street, somebody else had to defend him. He was lazy and did not do well in school, unable to apply himself to anything that didn't interest him: he attended high school for just forty-seven days, and his schooling was effectively over at age fifteen. Dolly had hoped he would go to college and perhaps become an engineer, but there was no chance of that. She got him a job bundling newspapers at the *Jersey Observer*, where his godfather, Frank Garrick, was circulation manager; and when a sportswriter was killed in a car crash a few weeks later, Dolly told him to see Garrick about a promotion to the sports desk. Young Frankie went to the editorial room, but Garrick wasn't there, so he sat down at the dead boy's desk and made himself at home, saying that Garrick had sent him. The others resented this, and Garrick was instructed to fire him. He tried to explain to Frankie that he had overplayed his hand, but nobody was going to tell Dolly's son that he had screwed up: Frankie loosed a torrent of obscene insults at his godfather and stormed out of the room. Dolly had taught her son to expect to be able to manipulate people, but she couldn't teach him any judgement because she had none. None of the Sinatras spoke to Garrick again for over fifty years.

Frankie was definitely interested in girls; he had a car as well as his mother's money in his pocket, and he showered the girls with presents, but they didn't take him too seriously, because he didn't look like he was going to amount to much. Dolly herself was afraid he was going to turn out to be a bum. But there was one thing of value that she had taught him: If there was something he wanted badly enough, he could have it if he refused to let anything stand in his way. Maybe that is the only lesson an American can learn, or needs to learn; and before long Frankie had discovered what he wanted. He wanted to be a singer.

Chapter Two

The Kid Sings

Today's video generation will find it hard to imagine how important radio was without pictures, but the Sinatras' radio occupied pride of place on top of the baby grand piano. When Frankie was born in 1915, radio was still dominated by hobbyists, who were better operators and used more up-to-date equipment than the U.S. Navy; but during the First World War Congress decided that regulation was necessary, and by the end of the war the Navy controlled nearly all broadcasting.

The cable companies had long been seen as private monopolies, charging far too much for their Morse code services, but when the broadcasting of speech was becoming common, the U.S.A. was never going to set up independent public broadcasting, like Britain's BBC: that would have smacked of socialism. So patents were simply appropriated (such as those of Marconi, the virtual inventor of broadcasting, who was only a foreigner after all) and handed over to big business: to General Electric, RCA and the United Fruit Company, which already operated the world's largest ship-to-shore network. The first nationwide broadcast was accomplished when Frank Sinatra was a few months old; when he was not quite five, the national election returns were broadcast for the first time, and the following year, in 1921, bandleader Vincent

Lopez was the first to broadcast live. (It was soon discovered that record sales went up in cities where the recording artist was heard on the radio.)

Broadcasting itself did not turn a profit for the first few years; nearly half the stations in the country were owned by radio and electrical manufacturers. But also in 1921, the first commercial radio advertising was broadcast: a station owned by AT&T charged $50 for a ten-minute spiel for apartments being built in Queens. Russian-born David Sarnoff had worked in Marconi's U.S. office at age fourteen; at twenty-one in 1912, he became nationally famous as a wireless operator, staying awake for three days to report the sinking of the *Titanic*. Later he proposed the radio music box, with amplifying tubes and a telephone loud-speaker; in 1916 the world was at war and the idea was shelved, but Sarnoff knew that advertising would eventually pay the bills. In 1926 he was there when the federal government allowed the establishment of the National Broadcasting Company, with RCA owning half of it and GE and Westinghouse the rest. Another fledgling radio network had been owned briefly by Columbia Records, which sold it because it did not make money, but the Columbia Broadcasting System later turned a profit after all. Sarnoff's equal at CBS was Bill Paley, whose family business was cigars; he discovered broadcasting while looking for a way to sell stogies. Between them, Sarnoff and Paley invented much of the twentieth century.

It was no accident that NBC and CBS established headquarters near Tin Pan Alley in New York, where the nation's songs were published. The amateurs in broadcasting's earliest days had set the tone: radio was to be fun, helping to knit the country together by means of popular culture, as vaudeville, movies and baseball were already doing. But audience power was a myth. At first it had been assumed that broadcasting would set the people truly free, because anybody could do it; but nowhere in the press was the question ever addressed of the marriage between the airwaves and commercial interests. The audience with the most power would be the one that bought the most goods.

When Frank Sinatra was nine years old, broadcasting was already one of the most important and profitable industries in the country; and when he was a teenager, during the Depression, it became even more important, because it was "free" entertainment (if you could afford a radio). And similarly, if it is hard to recapture the importance of radio in the 1930s, it is also hard to imagine the phenomenal importance of Bing Crosby.

There were other stars: a light-opera tenor called Vernon Dahlart switched to country music and had a multimillion seller in 1925 with "The Prisoner's Song" (which he recorded for at least twelve labels); Gene Austin had another monster with "My Blue Heaven" in 1927. Bandleaders were also big, and Paul Whiteman was the biggest. Crosby started with Whiteman, singing in a trio called the Rhythm Boys, and went solo to become the biggest recording artist of the first half of the century by a very wide margin. He not only sold 300 million records, most of them at a time when the industry was much smaller than it is now, but he made over fifty movies, and on the radio he was inescapable.

Broadcasting was less formal then, and nearly all of it was live. On one occasion in the early days, broadcasting with Gus Arnheim's band from a nightclub in Los Angeles, Crosby would be playing cards with his cronies with the radio on, dashing upstairs on his cue to sing his song; at the end of one tune he said to the radio audience, "Deal me in, boys; I'll be right down." But Crosby was so popular that his records were broadcast long before the disk jockey was invented; radio stations programmed their own Crosby shows with records, some of them several times a day. During the Depression the record industry almost disappeared completely, but Crosby was a phenomenon in every way: in 1933, according to one reckoning, he had twenty hit records, at the very bottom of the Depression.

Crosby was one of the first to understand how to use a microphone. Broadcasting (and electrical recording) transformed pop singing, because it was no longer necessary to have the lungs of an opera singer: one could sing intimately, as if to each individual listener. Crosby made it sound easy, but the use of the microphone isn't as simple as it looks. Vocalists and radio announcers had to know how to avoid exploding consonants, excessive sibilants and the like; and a good singer had to use the microphone in interpreting a song, sometimes leaning in and singing softly for more intimacy, sometimes rearing back to pour on the passion. Words and phrases had to be tailored to the mike, and each song had its different requirements. Crosby was a master, and Sinatra became an even greater one. But not right away.

Frank probably listened to the radio the way kids today watch TV, and one of the people who had looked after Frank while Dolly was dipping chocolates and running the neighborhood was a babysitter, Rose Carrier, who took him to the movies. "He loved it," Rose said many years later, "not that he had any choice." (During hot weather the side doors of the cinema were open, and Rose and Frankie would sneak in, spending the money Dolly had given them on popcorn instead of admission, and incidentally teaching Frankie another American lesson: Rules are made to be broken.) Bing Crosby was not only ubiquitous on the radio, but appeared in as many as three films a year beginning in 1933. Crosby had been a heavy drinker and a party animal, and remained a womanizer most of his life, but after he hit the big time he looked after his career with some seriousness, and the image that emerged was that of an ordinary fellow who charmed everybody and always got the girl. Young Frank became a big fan. He took one of his girlfriends to a theater to see Bing in person, and she never forgot that he came away enchanted, convinced that he could and would be another Crosby. (Guitarists Al Viola, from Brooklyn, and Tony Mottola, from New Jersey, both saw Crosby, probably on the same tour; they were mesmerized by Eddie Lang, Crosby's guitarist, and both later worked with Frank.)

Experiencing showbiz as a fan and imagining being a star was natural enough, but Crosby's stardom had a special appeal to Frank. His mother had convinced him that he could do no wrong, but pleasing an audience looked safer and easier than personal relationships; the fans, too, could give their affection without much risk. Though it would bring problems of its own, fame like Crosby's would be a kind of cure for loneliness, or at least a palliative; but success depended on talent, and there was no evidence that Frank Sinatra had any talent at all. He would have to work very hard for the first time in his life to discover that talent and then to polish it. To be fair, too, whether he or anyone else understood it or not, he must have had an innate feeling for music, an

---

understanding of what it is and how it works, the way a sculptor has an understanding of the material he shapes. In the end Frank's need to communicate, an arrogance with vulnerability at the center of it, would make him the biggest star of all.

He had a picture of Crosby on the wall in his bedroom; according to one story, when Dolly realized that he was fantasizing about being a singer, she tore down the picture. Another story is that she threw a shoe at him and called him a bum; many years later he said, "There's always somebody to spit on your dreams." Neither of them could have imagined how hard the road would be until the world took notice of Frank Sinatra, but Dolly's worldliness was certainly realistic; how many kids wanted to be stars on the radio and in Hollywood, and how many succeeded? Besides, Frank had never shown any ability to stick to anything. But he began singing in public, and almost immediately he began showing signs that he was ahead of his time: again and again, he not only knew what he wanted to do but how to go about it.

Any ordinary kid wanting to be Crosby might have gone straight to Hollywood, or trudged around to booking agencies making a pest of himself. (Nowadays they make demo tapes and send them to record companies.) In 1933 or 1934 the Depression was still on and the Big Band Era hadn't really begun; dance bands were everywhere, but the bands themselves were not the stars, not yet. Frank had a superficial confidence in himself, a shield between himself and failure; he was a sharp dresser and did not look like a high-school dropout, and he knew how to turn on the charm. He understood the importance of radio exposure, and would sing over the air for nothing: local stations were willing to use cheap local talent because some of their advertising was for local businesses, after all. The networks had what were called sustaining programs for their affiliate (local) stations, who could take them or leave them: sustaining programs had no sponsors, hence low budgets. Guitarist Mottola remembered working with Frank at Newark's WAAT when they were both still kids. Frank already liked hanging around with musicians, but he couldn't afford to hire a band or even an accompanist, so he made himself useful, getting musicians together for live gigs on condition that they would let him sing, at school dances, weddings, anywhere he could gain experience.

For decades Catholic high schools in the U.S.A. have had their own dances on Friday nights, places for kids to flirt and socialize without getting into trouble. Meanwhile, however, at her Garden Street address Dolly had performed an abortion on a girl who subsequently had to be rushed to hospital; Dolly was put on probation for five years in the mid-1930s, and Our Lady of Grace turned down Frank and his musician friends because of his mother's reputation. It was not the first time he'd been embarrassed by Dolly, but it was the first time it had interfered with his chosen career. He kept his temper, but he went ominously silent and suffered from headaches, according to his girlfriend at the time. Possibly in order to make amends, Dolly bought him a public-address system, a microphone, amplifier and speaker, and gave him money to buy stock arrangements—sheet music—so that the bands could play the songs of the day. All this helped to ingratiate him with the musicians, and apparently he needed the help. "While I wasn't the best singer in the world," he said many years later, "they weren't the best bands in the country either." He also played the ukelele, which is probably best forgotten; he got thrown out of some places, and one girl refused to let him sing at her wedding. He'd sing on the local radio for nothing, and one friend who heard him on WAAT advised him to quit. But Dolly was not capable of being embarrassed, and maybe she began to understand how determined he was; when Frank was nineteen years old and doing nothing but singing anyway, she got him a gig at the local Union Club, singing five nights a week for a month or two, and he actually got paid. After that he had a kind of reputation, and could pester the local social clubs for work.

One of the local bandleaders, Harold Arden, had a steady gig at the Rustic Cabin, in nearby Englewood Cliffs; a vocal trio called the Three Flashes occasionally sang there with the band. James "Skelly" Petrozelli, Pat Principe (Patty Prince) and Fred Tamburro, the effective leader, would let Frank drive them to work in his car. Then the band and the trio were offered a chance to make some film shorts for Edward "Major" Bowes, a producer whose *Major Bowes' Amateur Hour* was a successful radio showcase. In those days a movie house showed musical and comedy shorts and newsreels as well as feature films, and some of the shorts were effectively advertising for radio programs; Frank begged to be allowed to take part, but Arden didn't like his singing and the trio didn't want him either. So Dolly went to see Tamburro, who lived in Hoboken's Little Italy, where she was the boss, and the result of her influence was that the trio cut Frank in on the filming. The short films were called *The Night Club* and *The Minstrel*, and Frank didn't sing but played a waiter, in blackface, which is an indication of where Major Bowes was at: blackface as a vaudeville tradition left over from minstrelsy was already corny in 1935.

The films were shown at Radio City Music Hall in October, but before that Bowes decided to audition the boys for his radio program, and thanks to Dolly's continuing pressure the Three Flashes became the Hoboken Four. They sang the Mills Brothers' version of "Shine," a blackface number, passed the audition and sang on Bowes's radio show in September from the stage of the Capitol Theater in New York. They won the amateur contest, according to the applause meter; but with the films about to come out, it was no doubt convenient for Major Bowes to have his screen stars win the radio contest.

They were also good enough for Bowes to sign them up for a tour. This was the tail end of the vaudeville era, and Bowes's touring company was a low-budget ancestor of the Ed Sullivan TV show of two decades later: With sixteen other acts ranging from bell-ringers to tap-dancers, for $50 a week plus meals the boys toured across North America to the West Coast and back, singing in theaters and grocery stores (the sponsor was a coffee company). Frank must have improved after a year or two of singing everywhere he could, for he replaced Tamburro as the lead singer in the group (though Tamby was still the nominal boss). The management tried to keep an eye on them, but all four would sneak out at night, breaking all the rules; and Frank had more luck than the others with the girls, which made them jealous. His voice was still too high and he certainly hadn't found a style of his own at the age of nineteen, but the voice was smooth, the vulnerability was there, and the effect on the women in the audience was already noticeable; all the boys were asked for their autographs, but Frank got more attention from the women, and would often disappear with one or another of them, a perquisite of entertainers since the first caveman beat on a log.

In fact, Frank had a knack for making himself the center of attention: he became the star of the whole troupe, the other boys said nearly fifty years later; but there would always be a difference between the larger group (the audience) and the immediate entourage. Frank may have been able to become the star of Major Bowes's number-five touring unit, but the other three members of the Hoboken Four were closer intimates, and they were not impressed. At least two of them used him as a punching bag. At a lunch counter, Patty Prince said many years later, Frank leaned over and said, "Why don't you beat me too, and make it unanimous?" Prince felt sorry for him, but one rather suspects that when it came to getting along with his peers Frank Sinatra had some way to go.

The tour with Major Bowes soon became tedious. Before the end of the year the Hoboken Four became the Hoboken Trio when Frank left, going back to the dreary round of singing anywhere he could. Dolly had seen to it that his time on the road with Major Bowes had been well reported in the local papers, so for over two more years he sang up and down the river, at weddings, political rallies, the Elks Club, the local radio stations (for free), anywhere they'd let him in.

He was learning the ropes. He pestered musicians, bandleaders and clubowners, as well as song publishers for the latest tunes and arrangements, and whereas earlier he'd been described as "pushy, like his mother," now somebody described him as "pushy, but polite." He was teaching himself more about how to charm people, something he never learned from Dolly; but the distance across the river to Manhattan must have seemed like a million miles. Finally, in 1938, there was an opening for a singing waiter and emcee at the Rustic Cabin, for which Frank managed to obtain an audition. By this time the Swing Era was well under way, bandleaders were among the biggest names in show business, and Frank knew that he had to get himself heard by those kinds of people. The Rustic Cabin had a radio wire direct to WNEW in New York City, an important station that broadcast live dance music on Saturday night; but the Cabin's bandleader, according to one story, was still Harold Arden, who still didn't think much of Frank's singing.

Dolly said in an interview some years later that when she heard that Frank's audition had been unsuccessful, she thought that was just fine, because she didn't want him singing in a nightclub anyway. If this story is true, it reveals an astonishing degree of selfish ignorance: the boy was a young man of twenty-two in 1938 and had already been a professional singer for several years; what did she think he was going to do if he didn't continue following the path onward and upward? This is an example of the mentality of the ward-heeler: for Frank to have been a local celebrity would have been enough for Dolly. In the event, however, he was so upset that she realized how much his singing meant to him, or so she said later. She called the mayor of North Bergen, Harry Steeper, who was also president of the New Jersey musicians' union; Frank passed a second audition and became a singing waiter for $15 a week.

In 1935, when Frank drove the Three Flashes to a film studio in the Bronx ("Hollywood on the Hudson") to make their films for Major Bowes, they drove across the George Washington Bridge, which then hadn't been open very long. The Rustic Cabin was a roadhouse near the New Jersey end of the bridge, the kind of place where people traveling to or from Manhattan might stop for a drink or a meal, and a good location for anyone hoping to break into the music business. Frank's confidence was now higher than ever. He had always told all his friends and any musicians who would listen that he was going to make it big, though all the breaks he had received up to that point were courtesy of his bossy mother. His friends humored him: "'Yeah, sure, Frankie. Sure you are,' we'd say. No one thought he'd ever make it, except for him, that is." Musicians still thought he wasn't very good: "We ridiculed him because he just wasn't that good. Even though he was singing at the Rustic Club, he didn't seem to have any talent. No style whatsoever." His voice was described as "high" and "tight." But it was probably also during 1938 that Frank began to take a few singing lessons, realizing like a lot of ambitious musicians before him that he had taught himself as much as he could and it was time he got some professional help. He went to see an

Australian-born ex–opera singer, John Quinlan, who lived in New York, and took lessons from him, apparently for several years.

Frank Sinatra is said to be by nature a generous man, but he is never sure how much credit to give, and finds it difficult to express gratitude. His mother, being essentially a small-time gangster who never did anything for anybody unless it was going to bring a pay-off, taught young Frankie to impress his friends with flash, but that didn't work, leaving him confused; as an adult, he could be brutally honest with himself, but he was afraid of being rejected, just as he was afraid of his own mother. So even if his heart was in the right place, in later years he would try to hide his generosity, because he knew that people would mistake his motives for Dolly's. And eventually these personal problems and hangups (of which we all have our share) were in addition to the problems that come with being rich and famous. So he once said, "I never had a vocal lesson—a real one—except to work with a coach a few times . . . . " But on another occasion he said, "If it hadn't been for [Quinlan's] coaching when my voice was about gone, I'd have had no career." Yet after poor health prevented Quinlan from accompanying Sinatra to the West Coast during his first rise to fame, he said, "I guess Frank didn't understand. He hasn't spoken to me since." It is as though Sinatra's self-confidence, having accomplished a great deal, also has to take all the credit, which is why the absolute loyalty he has always demanded of his associates takes such a fundamental, almost medieval character—if you are Sinatra's friend or employee, you are not allowed any other life, and if you forget that he doesn't like ketchup on his hamburger he'll throw it at you. All this is so obviously the legacy of the lonely child that one is embarrassed to point it out.

Yet Frank Sinatra would eventually wrest control of his life from his mother, in spite of everything. He had been singing long enough for his native intelligence to begin to take over. If he was singing "high" and "tight" when he began working every night at the Rustic Club, it is no wonder that before long his voice was almost gone. The first thing he would have learned from Quinlan was how to project his voice without working so hard. Much later, in the 1960s, Sinatra claimed to have adopted a *bel canto* style, which must have confused many listeners: *bel canto* means merely "beautiful singing"; originally it was the justification for the invention of opera itself, a fusion of music and drama at the end of the sixteenth century which was supposed to emulate the drama of the classical world. But the phrase later came to refer specifically to an eighteenth-century emphasis on beauty of sound and brilliant performance, which in practice often became precious at the expense of dramatic values. Sinatra meant it in the simple Italian sense of lyrical beauty, a combination of words and music.

Quinlan undoubtedly helped him to sing from the front of his voice equipment, that is, from his mouth, rather than from the back of his throat or even further down towards his diaphragm. Any regular visitor to Italy knows that Italian speech makes great use of the tongue and the lips to shape the words, which is why the Italian language sounds so expressive, why it is ideal for singing and why so many Italians have become good singers: they are already halfway to singing when they learn to speak. This is also the reason why English-speaking people (especially Americans) have to work so hard on the accent when they study another language; to an Italian, there is nothing more ridiculous than hearing that language spoken with what amounts to a "Noo Joisey" accent. Hence when Frank began taking singing lessons his speech also began to change: Quinlan was helping him with diction, the importance of which he was already learning. It was during this period that he was also learning how to use the microphone: as he put it many years later, the real instrument was not the voice, but the mike. It could hear your voice better than you could hear it yourself, and you had to learn to play it like a sax.

Frank was small but wiry, and always physically fit. He is said to have played basketball, run on a track and swum underwater, using the facilities of the technical school where Dolly had hoped he'd study; the object was not just to keep fit, but also to build up his wind and the ability to hold long breaths. Much later, in a 1955 interview, Sinatra confessed that "I believed, because of [Crosby's] leisurely manner of working, that if he could do it I could do it. The funny switch is that I've never been able to do it." Crosby's deceptively relaxed manner had to be worked at and was more difficult than it looked, while Sinatra was too uptight to be relaxed. But he was destined to have more depth of style than

Crosby anyway. At the Rustic Cabin he was well along in developing the means by which he would become a different kind of singer.

He still wasn't making much money; in fact Dolly complained that she had to give him money so that he could treat his friends when they came to see him at the roadhouse: the job was a net loss to the family's accounts. But by the end of 1938 Frank Sinatra was getting more work and becoming better known; he was not only broadcasting with the band from the Rustic Cabin courtesy of the wire to WNEW, but singing several times a week on fifteen-minute spots from WNEW's studios in New York, and once a week on another station in Newark, where the band included a string section. And his personal life was also becoming complicated.

Among the girlfriends from Frank's teenage days was Marion Brush Schreiber, who remained his friend for years although their romance never got off the ground. She lived in the Garden Street neighborhood; she knew about Dolly's sideline in abortions, but in that self-possessed way some teenagers have, she was not shockable. She was aware of Frank's admiration of Bing Crosby, she helped him and his musician friends get work in the early days, and she was there when Frank got married. He had been acquainted with Nancy Barbato since the summer of 1935; he met her in Long Branch, New Jersey, where she lived across the street from one of Frank's aunts. At the end of the summer, before getting involved with Major Bowes, Frank brought Nancy to Hoboken and introduced her to Marion, who recalled that Dolly approved of Nancy at first, because Nancy's father was a plasterer who could afford to live in a single-family dwelling with a front porch. Nancy's sisters were all married to professionals, such as accountants and lawyers, Marion said, and Dolly also liked that. But several years later, Frank liked women and they liked him, and his job at the Rustic Cabin offered plenty of chances to get into trouble.

At the end of 1938, having courted Nancy for over three years, Frank was also having an affair with a woman who was separated from her husband; Toni Francke became pregnant, and soon had a miscarriage, but, furious at the way she had been treated by Frank and Dolly (who of course disapproved of her), in November and again in December she had Frank arrested on morals charges. She was persuaded to drop the charges, but that was enough for Dolly: she had always tried to control her son's personal life, and of course to that extent he was not learning to control it himself; it was a wonder that he had been allowed to go on tour with Major Bowes, which took him out of his mother's sight. Dolly decided it was time for Frank to get married, foolishly thinking that that would keep him out of trouble. By this time Nancy had been in love with Frank for years.

On February 3, 1939, Frank Sinatra made his first record, a demo, with the Frank Manne Orchestra, the song being "Our Love," using the big tune from Tchaikovsky's *Romeo and Juliet* overture. It is not a bad record, as far as one can hear through the muddy sound; ripping off classical tunes was common and not entirely a bad idea, and Frank's treatment is probably a light-year or so ahead of what most pop singers were doing at the time: he sings the song as though he cares about it. Everything about the record, however, is mysterious: nobody knows who Frank Manne was, and the arrangement is well over four minutes long, far too long for a ten-inch 78 and impractical for a demo. One suspects that the recording session was some sort of wedding present; perhaps Frank had said to his mother that if she wanted him to get married so badly, she could make another contribution to his career by paying for a demo record. At any rate, the next day, on February 4, Frank and Nancy were married. The reception was at Nancy's house, and there were very few people from Hoboken there, but his faithful friend Marion was one of them. When she said goodbye, she wished Frank all the luck and happiness in the world, she said, and he kissed her. "I'll never forget him that day. He looked like the saddest man I'd ever seen." At the end of the month, Dolly got arrested again for another abortion; in March the new band of trumpeter Harry James made its debut in Philadelphia, and three months later James came to the Rustic Cabin looking for a singer.

The rest is history.

Chapter Three

The Band Singer

As Mr. and Mrs. Frank Sinatra settled into a three-room flat in Jersey City, Frank's pay at the roadhouse had been raised and Nancy worked as a secretary, so their combined monthly income was about $200. This was not bad for the time; the nation had not recovered from the Depression and there were nearly ten million people unemployed. Frank spent a lot of money on clothes, but Nancy was a good housekeeper, and she knew that Frank had to look sharp. He still hadn't made the big time, and his principal objection to marriage had been that having somebody around his neck might impede his rise to stardom; Nancy had promised not to get in the way, and did everything she could to encourage him and keep his spirits up.

Meanwhile the music business had changed considerably since Frank Sinatra had started singing. Ballroom dancing had been nationally popular since before he was born, and when Paul Whiteman had hired vocalist Morton Downey way back in 1919, everybody thought he was crazy: what did a bandleader need with a singer? But from 1935, the year that Frank toured with Major Bowes, the jazz-oriented dance band was at the center of American music. The Swing Era, or Big Band Era, had got under way with the sudden huge success of Benny Goodman, who was billed as the King of Swing. Bing Crosby was still the biggest name in show business, but he was virtually the only solo singer: the way to fame as a vocalist was to sing with one of the swing bands, and new ones were forming all the time.

The band at the Rustic Cabin was being led by a trombonist called Bill Henri in mid-1939, according to Burt Hall (then known as Harry Zinquist), who played sax in the band. He remembered hanging around with other musicians in a small club in Bayonne a few years earlier, using the rehearsal room; Sinatra would show up to listen and sing a couple of songs. As John Rockwell has pointed out, the club scene in the 1930s was not much different "to that faced by Bruce Springsteen in the sixties and Jersey rock bar-bands to this day: fairly active, but rarely leading anywhere beyond itself—the distance across the Hudson sometimes seemed infinite." The young men in the band at the Rustic Cabin proba-bly all hoped to go on to bigger things; on their nights off they would go visit other, similar bands where their friends were play-ing: in those days quite a few hotels and restaurants had live music for dancing. But the band at the Rustic Cabin had song-pluggers bringing them tunes and probably even free arrangements, because they broadcast from eleven-thirty to midnight on WNEW's *Dance Parade* program.

By now Sinatra was better known, and his singing was reach-ing a certain professional plateau: if he wasn't the singer he would become, musicians could hear what he was trying to do. It was only a matter of time before somebody hired him away from the New Jersey roadhouse. There was a rumor that trombonist Jack Miles wanted to leave Guy Lombardo and start his own band, and was interested in Sinatra. Tommy Dorsey, one of the most suc-cessful of all bandleaders, was setting up as a contractor, running other bands as well as his own; he was behind the Bob Chester band, which was intended to compete with Glenn Miller: Sinatra actually rehearsed with the Chester band and may have made demo records with it which were subsequently lost.

Among the people who used the George Washington Bridge on their way in and out of New York were bandleader Red Norvo and his wife, singer Mildred Bailey, who were also known as "Mr. and Mrs. Swing." Mildred's brother, singer and songwriter Al Rinker, had been an original member with Crosby of the Rhythm Boys, and it was on their way home from a visit to Rinker one Sunday evening that they stopped at the Rustic Cabin. Mildred was a considerable talent scout: When she first heard Billie Holiday, she said, "That's gal's got it!" And when she heard Frank Sinatra, she told her husband, "That kid can sing!" Norvo later said, "There were so many great songs coming out at that time and we needed a male singer to help Mildred out." They called him in July 1939, but they were too late. Harry James had beat them to it.

A few months younger than Sinatra, Harry James had begun playing trumpet professionally at the age of nine, in a circus band led by his father. As a teenager he joined Ben Pollack, a bandleader who had hired Jack Teagarden, Glenn Miller, Benny Goodman and many others. In March 1937 James joined Goodman, and became one of the stars of that band. By January 1939, he told George T. Simon, he could not play his solo on Goodman's "Sing, Sing, Sing" anymore; the arrangement made him a nervous wreck. He left to form his own band with Goodman's blessing and his backing. "At least with my own band, I could play the tunes that *I* wanted to play." Eventually he became one of the most successful leaders of the 1940s, but success was not automatic. He had made a few records under his own name, but although lots of jazz fans could name the soloists in a band like Goodman's, Harry James had no recognition factor as a bandleader, and his group would have to find its own identity and its own audience. So the new Harry James band was struggling in 1939, but the world was younger then: it didn't cost so much just to live in those days, and the band was getting arrangements from Andy Gibson, a good writer; it had started to record for Brunswick in February, the future looked bright enough, and the band needed a boy singer.

In June 1939 James's wife was Louise Tobin, a good singer who for most of that year worked for Goodman, who could pay her a lot more than her husband could. In their hotel room in New York, Louise remembered many years later, she was packing to leave for a gig the next morning when she heard the band playing over the radio from the Rustic Cabin, and woke up Harry because she thought the singer, whoever he was, was pretty good. However it happened, Harry was impressed, but hadn't caught the singer's name, so the next night after his own last set he drove across the George Washington Bridge to visit the roadhouse.

Some said that by June 1939 the kid from Hoboken had long since graduated from waiting on tables; James joked that when he inquired about the singer somebody told him, "We don't have a singer, but we have an emcee who sings a little." In any case, as we know with our hindsight, Sinatra was not going to be stuck in the roadhouse much longer, but he didn't know that then. Jack Miles hadn't left Lombardo after all, Bob Chester had decided to save money by having a saxophone player double as a vocalist (a mistake that many bandleaders made), and Red Norvo hadn't called yet. Sinatra was so anxious to leave his roadhouse days behind him, he said later, that he grabbed James by the arm and wasn't going to let him leave. James offered him $75 a week, and Frank Sinatra opened with the Harry James band the same month, first at the Hippodrome Theater in Baltimore, and then at the Paramount in New York. At first Harry thought Frank should change his name: he had once billed himself briefly as Frankie Trent, playing somewhere in New Jersey (Trenton, no doubt), and Dolly had blown her stack; that was one thing she was right about. He told Harry that he had a cousin called Ray Sinatra who was a successful musician, and the name would be good enough for Frank too.

Harry James and Frank Sinatra became and remained friends for the rest of their lives. They were both young and ambitious, they were both skinny (somebody said that together they looked like a pair of scissors) and they were both very confident. Louise said that Harry, like Frank, never doubted that he would be successful. But Harry James was the more experienced musician by a wide margin, and it was now that Sinatra began to learn the lessons that would make him the greatest of all the singers in the era to come. During the Swing Era the bands were divided into "hot" bands like Goodman's, very much jazz-oriented, and "sweet" bands like Lombardo's, with little or no apparent jazz content; but by 1939 some of the bands were touching both bases in order to please the largest number of customers. And nobody knew better than Harry James both how to play jazz—trumpet players in Texas, where he grew up, were said to tremble at the sound of his name—and that there was nothing wrong with sentimentality, if it was honestly felt.

Furthermore, James knew what Sinatra was trying to do, and encouraged him. Another thing that was changing in the late 1930s was the role of the vocalist, who had been an extra added attraction, singing a chorus and then sitting down and smiling while the band played on; but on Frank's demo record in early 1939 the arrangement of "Our Love" allowed him to sing the song all the way through, and then gave him another half-chorus at the end, as though to remind us whose record it was. That arrangement was unusually long, but more remarkably, Frank's first recording with Harry James, "From the Bottom of My Heart," does the same thing. Between July and November Frank recorded ten arrangements with the James band, and nearly all of them sound like they were designed to feature the vocalist.

When Harry James finally found his own formula, his own combination of his horn, the band's vocalists and the right mixture of jazz and warm ballads, his first big hit was "I Don't Want to Walk Without You" in early 1942, which he recorded because he loved the way Judy Garland sang it. But the singer on Harry's record was Helen Forrest, widely regarded as one of the best band singers of the era. She had been discovered by Artie Shaw, and in the Shaw band had the advantage of working alongside Billie Holiday for a few months; she'd also worked for Benny Goodman. James was still struggling and couldn't really afford Forrest in 1942, but he wanted a girl singer, and the guys in the band voted her in. She told George T. Simon,

> I'll always remain grateful to Artie and Benny. But they had been featuring me more like they did a member of the band, almost like another instrumental soloist. Harry, though, gave me just the right sort of arrangement and setting that fit a singer. It wasn't just a matter of my getting up, singing a chorus, and sitting down again.

Talking to Sheila Tracy, Forrest was more specific:

> Harry James was wonderful. When I joined him I said, "There's only one condition: I don't care how much you pay me, I don't care about arrangements. The one thing I want is to start a chorus and

finish it. I want to do verses, so don't put me up for a chorus in the middle of an instrumental." He said, "You got it," and that was it.

Some of the bandleaders understood almost as soon as the Swing Era began that jazz-influenced music had never been at the center of American pop before, and that the fans not only liked the jazz, they also liked to dance and they liked the vocalists. The seeds of the following era, the era of the pop singer, were already germinating; hadn't the Casa Loma Band, keeping the flame of jazz alive on college campuses since the beginning, also had hits with smooth vocals by Kenny Sargent as early as 1933 ("Under a Blanket of Blue," "It's the Talk of the Town")? Another of Harry James's big numbers, in 1945, was "I'm Beginning to See the Light," a Duke Ellington tune with words by Don George, with yet another singer, Kitty Kallen. In 1971 James said, "When Frank joined the band, he was always thinking of the lyrics. The melody was secondary. If it was a delicate or a pretty word, he would try to phrase it with a prettier, softer type of voice. The feeling he has for words is just beautiful." So James encouraged him. James never got enough credit for knowing how to choose singers and what to do with them; he built his band around his vocalists and his own horn, and his list of over seventy hit records in fifteen years is evidence that he knew what he was doing. And he started doing it in 1939, with Frank Sinatra.

A fledgling bandleader, however, did not get the pick of all the songs that were being published. Of the ten tunes James and Sinatra recorded together, "Ciribiribin" was a vocal version of James's signature tune, written in Italy in 1898, and "My Buddy" was a seventeen-year-old song by Gus Kahn and Walter Donaldson, while the other eight were new pop tunes of the time. "From the Bottom of My Heart" and "Here Comes the Night" are such obvious titles that they've been used more than once; "On a Little Street in Singapore" is an example of what has been called the "unlucky mulatto" genre, along with "Poor Butterfly" and other songs about a certain kind of doomed love. Three of the songs were written or co-written by Jack Lawrence, a skilled Tin Pan Alley hack who did a number of memorable things: his "If I Didn't Care" was a huge hit by the Ink Spots in 1939, and remained their most famous number; ten years later Lawrence wrote "Linda" for his lawyer's baby daughter, another big hit, by Ray Noble's band with Buddy Clark singing. (Linda Eastman grew up to marry Paul McCartney, and now promotes vegetarian dog food, among other things.) Lawrence was a dab hand at writing words for instrumentals and foreign songs in an era that is gone forever: the words didn't have to be very good, but enabled publishers to sell more copies of the tune, and Dinah Shore to have one of several hits with "Delicado" in 1952, for example. He wrote English words about gondoliers for "Ciribiribin". He co-wrote "All or Nothing at All" with Arthur Altman (the middle eight sounds like it was borrowed from Cole Porter's "Begin the Beguine").

But Sinatra sounds marvelous. On "From the Bottom of My Heart" and "Melancholy Mood" his phrasing is immediately unique: he is indubitably singing, not chanting or talking the words, yet the rhythm of the words is easy and conversational; my guess is that he had already learned more from listening to jazz-oriented music than Crosby ever did. (On "Melancholy Mood" James plays a fine muted, growling trumpet in the style of Duke Ellington's Cootie Williams.) A couple of the tunes have a mushy beat, suitable only for romantic dancing; "My Buddy" is pleasantly lighthearted; "All or Nothing at All" ends on a bravura high note, which is a little corny, but my favorite of the lot is "It's Funny to Everyone But Me," which is heartfelt love-lorn: completely believable and looking forward to some of Sinatra's best records of the next decade, while the band humming along and interjecting comments ("It's the talk of the town!") adds to the charm.

None of the records were hits when they were new. I don't know what the original 78s sounded like; in reissues they usually sounded like they were recorded in a gloomy echo chamber, but Columbia finally made very good transfers for CD in 1995, revealing that they were very good recordings after all. But "All or Nothing at All," for example, did not get its first release until 1940, when there was an ASCAP strike against the broadcasters: Lawrence's songs, and for that matter virtually all the tunes Harry James was playing, would have been published through the

American Society of Composers, Authors and Publishers, and thus would not have been played on the radio during the strike. Maybe the reason not many people bought the record is because not many people heard the song.

Meanwhile, before any of the studio recordings were made there were broadcasts from the Roseland Ballroom, some of which were recorded off the air. Pee Wee Monte had been a road manager for Benny Goodman's band, and came along to work for Harry James when James left Goodman; Pee Wee and various members of his family worked for James until James died in 1983 (and nobody ever had a contract: that's the kind of loyalty that James inspired). The Montes recorded about 1,200 tunes off the air on transcription disks over the years, and seven of these airchecks with Sinatra have transferred nicely to CD (on Columbia, but also on a three-CD set on the Hindsight label, celebrating a decade of Harry James's career and featuring eight vocalists). That first band plays very well, and young Frank Sinatra sounds good on several numbers recorded in July and August. The first Sinatra vocal is "Star Dust": the band had been playing the tune as an instrumental before Frank joined, and probably they just tacked the vocal on to the front of the arrangement, making it nearly four minutes long. Sinatra sounds like he's enjoying himself singing in a famous ballroom instead of a New Jersey roadhouse; the word "inspiration" becomes "inspeeration," which is probably a jokey reference to the way some other vocalists pronounced it. (The rest of the James arrangement of "Star Dust" includes some tricky writing for the reed section, and sounds as though it might have been inspired by Coleman Hawkins's classic "Body and Soul" of the same period.)

Other tunes Sinatra was singing with James included "If I Didn't Care" (one wonders if Jack Lawrence didn't own a piece of the band), "My Love for You" (with an impressively accurate falsetto on the word "you" at the very end), "Moon Love," adapted from Tchaikovsky's Fifth Symphony, and "The Lamp Is Low," from Ravel's *Pavane pour une infante défunte*. The last is really fun: He does fine with Ravel's lovely tune, but the song's introduction is definitely not Ravel: it is hackwork by Mitchell Parish (who also wrote the words for "Star Dust") and his co-writers,

Sinatra is accompanied here by a piano that sounds like it's out of tune, and it is all so dumb that on the word "my" in the phrase "Let my heart softly tell you" he sounds as though he can hardly keep from laughing.

Frank Sinatra's first praise in the press came about when the band's manager, Jerry Barrett, asked George T. Simon to give the kid a good write-up. Simon liked the band anyway, so he wrote in *Metronome* magazine about Sinatra's "very pleasing vocals" and his "easy phrasing." But not long after that, *Billboard* criticized him, saying that "he touches the songs with a little too much pash," the traditionally corny *Billboard* prose matching the traditional way in which showbiz publications never quite know what is going on, and Sinatra was furious. On another occasion, when somebody asked Harry James about his kid singer, Harry supposedly said, "Not so loud! The kid's name is Sinatra...No one ever heard of him, he's never had a hit record, he looks like a wet rag, but he says he's the greatest. If he hears you compliment him, he'll demand a raise tonight." This is a famous story and a good one, but it was probably a sendup: Harry James was just as young, ambitious and confident as the kid from Hoboken, he also looked like a wet rag, and Sinatra knew there wasn't any money for a raise anyway.

Although Sinatra's voice was still on the light side, he sang the words as though they meant something, which was new and modern. The way Bing Crosby delivered a lyric, we were convinced that we could sing as well as that; Bing was a regular fellow who wanted to be a boyfriend, but if the girl didn't invite him in it wouldn't quite be the end of the world. To Frank Sinatra, however, the invitation was very important: he wanted to be a lover, not a boyfriend. The passion that came through in his singing was understated; you couldn't put your finger on it, but it was the passion in his life transmuted into music. He had married his teenage sweetheart, perhaps against his better judgement; he feared and probably disapproved of his mother if he could have admitted it, while he wanted to admire his father but could not; he himself was badly educated, and his confidence had the kind of brashness that was protecting something. His passions had a lot of constraints on them, but there was another kind of confidence that was genuine: he had the understanding of an artist which allowed him to transmute his frustrations into his work, so that, like Billie Holiday, he could make a song seem to be a better song than it was.

But Frank Sinatra wasn't hitting the big time fast enough. The critics liked the James band, but it didn't set the world on fire at the Paramount in June, or at the Roseland in July; its famous gig was at the Steel Pier in Atlantic City in August, and it also played Roseland again and the 1939 World's Fair. At least the band could eat Nancy's cooking if they didn't have any money. Then they headed west on tour, and Nancy came along. In Chicago and Denver business was lukewarm, and everybody was looking forward to the Palomar in Los Angeles, where Benny Goodman himself had suddenly hit four years earlier, but the Palomar burned down on October 4. (Charlie Barnet's band lost all its arrangements and instruments in the fire, but Barnet typically said, "Hell, it's better than having bombs dropping on your head." Poland was being invaded at the time.) The James band got an emergency booking in a restaurant in Beverly Hills, and it was a disaster: it was the wrong kind of place, too small for a big band, and the management hated them. James had discovered a girl singer from Georgia, Yvonne Marie Jamais, and renamed her Connie Haines; it was contemporary wisdom that the girl singer was more important to the band's success than the boy, but when business was so bad that he couldn't keep both of them, James let Haines go rather than Sinatra. Nancy remembered years later that she once cooked a meal for four people with a dollar: spinach, hamburger and mashed potatoes. Then the band headed back east.

In Chicago there was an annual Christmas benefit for the musicians' union at the Hotel Sherman, and the local union boss was James Caesar Petrillo, soon to be elected national leader of the American Federation of Musicians: any bands in the area had to make their appearance at Petrillo's benefit. Among the other bandleaders taking part was Tommy Dorsey, whose boy singer, the likeable Jack Leonard, quit while they were in Chicago. Dorsey had long been aware of Frank Sinatra. In fact Sinatra had once had a chance to sing for Dorsey, but dried up: he opened his mouth and nothing came out. But in Chicago Dorsey offered Frank $125 a week. Stardom was just a matter of months away for both The Voice and The Horn, but The Voice's wife was pregnant, and The

Horn (Harry James) could hardly afford the $75 a week Frank was getting. The James band was about to be demoted from the full-price Columbia to the budget Varsity label during 1940, while Tommy Dorsey was one of the biggest names in show business.

The Dorsey brothers, trombonist Tommy and alto saxist Jimmy, had co-led the Dorsey Brothers Orchestra from 1928 until 1935, when they could not get along any longer. They were each success-ful separately, but by the end of 1939 Tommy had had three times as many hits as Jimmy. The American record business of the late 1930s was tiny compared to later decades; it had not yet recovered from competition with radio in the 1920s and the Great Depression in the 1930s. There was not much money in records, and there were only three major labels, selling most of their output to the jukebox industry. In these circumstances, ninety Dorsey hits in four years is very impressive indeed. The sales of the Frank Sinatra–Harry James record of "All or Nothing at All" in 1940 were low, but may have been enough for a record to break even in those days; Tommy Dorsey's prolifically recorded band, on the other hand, was so pop-ular that virtually all its records did that well, and some of them were among the biggest hits of the era. Sinatra knew that with Dorsey's band he would get more attention from the record labels, from the critics, from the fans—from everybody.

The difficulty was leaving James. Sinatra said later that opening a vein would have been easier. Harry and Frank had struggled together and supported each other for six months; they believed not only in themselves, but in each other, while Frank had learned a lot from Harry. Furthermore, Frank's contract with James had several months to run. But the break had to be made. Frank went to Harry's hotel room and paced up and down until Harry finally asked him what was up. When Harry found out what was at stake, the story goes, he called for Frank's contract and tore it into small pieces; and when he parted with the James band, Sinatra said many years later, tears came to his eyes, and as the bus pulled away without him, he had to suppress the urge to run after it. For the rest of James's life, Sinatra called him "Boss," and joked about coming back to fulfill the rest of his contract.

Sinatra recommended young Dick Haymes to replace him in the James band, and helped to break him in; the sudden change in the

Monte-James broadcast recordings from Sinatra to Haymes is instructive. Haymes was a good singer, and would also be very successful in the 1940s, but in the early years Haymes sings absolutely straight compared to Sinatra, as though he is still afraid to express himself: Sinatra was less than a year older than Haymes, but already a considerable stylist as pop singers went in 1939. Yet when Sinatra made his debut with the Dorsey band (accounts differ: January 1940? Minneapolis? Rockford, Illinois?) he was just twenty-four years old, and he encountered the most important teacher he ever had.

While Harry James was relatively easy to get along with, Tommy Dorsey was a volatile boss and a tough businessman. Every successful bandleader was plagued by song-pluggers and publishers anxious to make deals, but Dorsey knew his music backwards and forwards. When he split up with his brother Jimmy and began recording for Victor in September 1935, he had taken over the Joe Haymes band, and the new ensemble had to do some shaking down before it acquired the Dorsey stamp; one of the first hits the new band had was "Take Me Back to My Boots and Saddle," a song which had been introduced by Gene Autry that year (the "singing cowboy" was then a new sensation). Arranger Paul Weston had stayed with Tommy when the Dorsey brothers split, and left him just before Sinatra arrived; he tells a story about Dorsey and a song-plugger:

> Jonie Taps was with Shapiro Bernstein, and they published dreck, you know, like "Take Me Back to My Boots and Saddle" and "I'm Headin' for the Last Roundup" and stuff like that, which Tommy—he refused to play most of 'em, but once in a while he'd play one for Jonie. Now, Jonie would come in to the Astor Hotel, and walk down to his table, and order dinner. . . and as he would *appear*, even if Tommy was in the middle of a ballad, Tommy'd put the horn down and go "worf! worf! worf!" at him. For publishing dogs. And the people in the Astor Hotel, they thought, "What *is* this? Tommy's stopped *playing*. . .! And now he's *barking* at this little *man*!"

In George T. Simon's book *The Big Bands* there is a marvelous photograph taken in 1939 of Tommy Dorsey surrounded by music publishers and songwriters, from Johnny Green (author of "Body and Soul") and Jack Mills (who manipulated Duke Ellington for many years) to Jonie Taps and a dozen others. The photo is a sendup: everybody is grinning like hyenas at a kill except Dorsey, who has his head in his hands; but few people ever got the best of Dorsey. He would sometimes lose his temper and fire his whole band, only to hire them back the next day. When bassist Sid Weiss worked up the courage to ask Dorsey for a raise one evening, Dorsey chased him around the ballroom on the Astor Roof in New York, threatening to kill him. Dorsey didn't mind firing people, but he didn't like them to quit: when the Swing Era was over, in the early 1950s, Dorsey was still getting the best dance-band gigs in the country, and another bassist, Billy Cronk, tried to leave:

> I quit the band once and he got so mad at me he chased me three blocks, grabbed me and put me up against a wall (he was much bigger than me) and said, "Nobody quits the band, I fire them." So I took back my notice and he threatened to fire me! "We're not married—you can get lost any time you want!" said Tommy. So, of course, I stayed.

Trombonist and arranger Billy VerPlanck joined in 1956, when the end was near; Dorsey was still giving the music business everything he had, and expected the same of everybody else:

> When I joined the band he said, "All I want is 110 percent." I said, "Jesus, Tommy, there's only 100 percent in a man. Where's the other 10 percent?" "I don't know, baby, but if you don't give it to me you're fired!" This guy put the fear of God into you.

It was during a gig at the Palmer House, apparently in December 1939, that vocalist Jack Leonard quit. He'd been with Dorsey four years, longer than most people lasted; Dorsey called a rehearsal after a performance when nobody had had anything to eat all day, and blew his top because a trumpeter friend of Leonard's sneaked out to get a sandwich. Leonard could take no more, but Dorsey already had his eye on "that skinny kid with James."

Dorsey had no intention of sitting on his enormous success in

1935–39. The competition was hotting up at the peak of the Swing Era: Dorsey probably admired Harry James's musicianship, and Harry's wasn't the only new band entering the lists. By the end of 1939, Glenn Miller's was a huge success, having hit even bigger than Benny Goodman had in 1935 when he started the whole thing. And bands like James's and Miller's were treading on Dorsey's turf: Miller in particular was incredibly good at playing sentimental smoochers for slow-dancers on the one hand, and uptempo arrangements to keep the jazz fans happy on the other, so that he won honors in both the sweet and jazz categories. Dorsey was updating and modernizing his image, and Frank Sinatra was not the only new face in the band in 1940.

Dorsey had hired a group called the Pied Pipers to sing on his radio show for several weeks in 1939; they were an octet, seven guys plus Jo Stafford, and they sounded like a whole band. A little later, when they weren't getting much work, Stafford got a phone call from Dorsey: he wanted to hire the Pipers as part of the band, but not all of them; he only wanted a quartet. "Funny you should ask," she said. "Some of the guys have dropped out." So four Pipers joined Dorsey, two weeks before Sinatra did, and became an integral part of the new Dorsey sound. Their kind of cool "modern" close-harmony singing was soon taken for granted by the fans during the Swing Era, but it is very impressive technically, and well beyond most of today's vocalists, who all want to be soloists. The other members of the original quartet lineup were Chuck Lowry, John Huddleston and Clark Yocum, who also played some rhythm guitar in the band; Stafford herself sang so in tune that she may as well have had perfect pitch, and later became one of the finest pop singers of a new era.

The first time Sinatra rehearsed with the band she noticed how skinny he was, but as soon as he opened his mouth she knew that he was special: The band had just finished the gig at the Palmer House and went to Minneapolis on the train; the Pipers already knew their routine, but Sinatra had to rehearse.

The first time I ever saw him, or heard him, was that night when Tommy introduced him as the new vocalist, and he walked on to do his stint. About eight bars into the song I thought, "Boy, this is something else."... Most boy singers in those days sounded like Bing Crosby. Crosby was the big thing. But this kid didn't sound like Crosby. He didn't sound like anybody I'd ever heard before. And he was sensational.

The public agreed. In May 1940 when Sinatra appeared at the Astor Hotel in New York with Dorsey for the first time, he stopped the show, which rarely if ever happened to a band singer, and the crowd wanted encores. But there weren't enough Sinatra features in the band's book yet, so Sinatra and pianist Joey Bushkin had to improvise a duet spot.

Another asset added to the band in Chicago was the new drummer. Buddy Rich was a seasoned pro, a prodigy who had been playing in vaudeville since the age of four as Baby Traps, the Drum Wonder, and had been playing first-class jazz from a very early age. Trumpeter Bunny Berigan had played on some of the biggest hits of the era, first with Goodman and then with Dorsey; when Berigan formed his own band he was one of the first to hire Rich. Artie Shaw, like Goodman, had been one of the most successful freelance clarinetists in popular music, and formed his own band in early 1938; Rich soon joined Shaw, his technique, energy and sheer power helping to kick that band from nowhere to $25,000 a week by the end of the year. Then in November 1939, Shaw, who hated the music business, walked away, leaving the band high and dry while he took a vacation in Mexico. Bassist Sid Weiss, powerful trumpeter Chuck Peterson and Buddy Rich all joined Tommy Dorsey.

But Buddy Rich was fussy about his music and was not so easy to hire. Rich's sister Marge was a dancer, touring in an act with her husband, and they were staying in the same hotel:

We all left the hotel at the same time. He went to hear Dorsey; we went to do our show. [Later] we started to walk down Dearborn Street, and we bumped into Brother.

"Where are you going?" we asked him.

"Dorsey's not playing my kind of music. I'm going back to New York."

Rich wanted to play jazz, and Dorsey's music sounded stodgy

to him, but Dorsey had one more ace up his sleeve, perhaps the most important of all: he had hired a new arranger. Sy Oliver had been writing for the Jimmie Lunceford band for many years, and had set the character of one of the most successful of all the black bands. Jazz (and therefore dance music) was being smoothed out from a two-beat to a four-beat music: Each bar has four beats in it, but the legacy of New Orleans jazz (or marching-band music) was a strong accent on 2 and 4, while "modern jazz" and "bebop" were just around the corner, and rhythm sections were moving towards four equal accents in a bar: indeed, the whole rhythmic nature of popular music would change. (In fact, it split. Rhythm and blues and then rock 'n' roll would preserve two-beat by putting even more weight on 2 and 4: a backbeat.)

But Sy Oliver had the knack of writing a two-beat style with an irresistible lilt which was perfect for the transition period of the 1930s and 1940s, because it neither intimidated dancers nor offended jazz fans. A good arranger was also effectively a composer, and Oliver had the technical skill to take a dopey tune like "Organ Grinder's Swing" and turn it into one of Lunceford's biggest hits. Lunceford's was a superb show band, which could do anything any other band could do, but it was a black band, and the cruel fact was that Dorsey could afford to offer Oliver several times what Lunceford was paying him.

Rich certainly knew who Sy Oliver was, and before he left town the next day Dorsey talked him into coming to an afternoon rehearsal to hear a couple of new charts by Oliver. He liked what he heard, Dorsey promised to have some drum features written for him, and Rich joined the Dorsey band on the spot. But if Dorsey would be hard to get along with he also knew what he was letting himself in for. In 1987, interviewed by Mel Tormé for his entertaining book about Buddy Rich, Sinatra recalled being introduced to Rich: Dorsey said, "I want you to meet another pain in the ass."

> That's what we were in the band. Between Buddy complaining that the tempos were not quite proper and my saying there weren't enough ballads in the library, we drove the old man crazy. But with all of that, he loved both of us. We really were the pets of the band.

And they were: they got away with murder. They were both young, ambitious, extremely talented and attractive to the opposite sex; they were both arrogant, and lacked the instinctive class of a Harry James. At first they got along like lovers. When Sinatra got on the bus to travel with Dorsey to a one-night stand, the seat next to Rich was empty, so he sat there; and the seat you chose on the band bus was your seat forever. Later Sinatra asked somebody, "How come that seat was empty?" and somebody said, "Because he's a pain in the ass. Nobody wants to sit with him!" But Rich had already said to Sinatra, "I like the way you sing." So they told each other their life stories, and they shared a room on the road. Many years later Rich said that what started the trouble was Sinatra clipping his toenails in bed; what Sinatra remembered was reading in bed, the lamp keeping Rich awake. The truth was that Rich's jazz drums and Sinatra's ballad singing were supremely compatible, but only when Dorsey was laying down the law: at any other time they each wanted to be the star of the band. The fans loved both of them. "Hawaiian War Chant" had been a popular Dorsey number since 1936, but Rich on his tom-toms and Ziggy Elman on trumpet made it a new showpiece, while one of Oliver's arrangements for Rich was "Quiet Please" as early as July 1940, and Rich was invited to shine on any number of uptempo items. But it drove him crazy when Sinatra got his name on a poster, and Rich would drive Sinatra crazy by eschewing subtlety and playing *boom-chick, boom-chick* behind his vocals, or by pushing the tempo. It came to a head in August 1940, backstage in New York's Astor Hotel. Jo Stafford told the famous story:

> They were yelling at each other, about what I don't know. I wasn't even listening. Suddenly, out of the side of my eye, I saw Frank pick up one of those pitchers [of ice water] and hurl it at Buddy. It crashed into the wall right over my head. For years after that, when we played the Astor, one of the Pipers, Chuck Lowry, used to write little things around the pieces of glass embedded in the wall.

Then they were going at it with fists and had to be pulled apart, and Dorsey sent Sinatra home, saying, "I can live without a singer tonight, but I need a drummer." Sinatra had lost face by being sent home; he got even in a way that illustrated the depth and danger in his personality. A few nights later, on his way to work, Rich was jumped and beaten up by two hoodlums, so that that night he sat behind the drums with bruises on him; the incident was written up in *down beat* magazine in December 1941. Rich thought he knew what had happened, and eighteen months later, when Sinatra was leaving Dorsey, he called Sinatra on it. Rich told Mel Tormé that Sinatra admitted to him that he had hired a couple of pals from Hoboken to beat him up.

Rich and Sinatra recognized and respected each other's talent; it was just that they were both spoiled brats and borderline hoodlums. Rich's parents had been making a living in vaudeville when his talent had suddenly overwhelmed the act: as a small (probably hyperactive) child he dominated their lives and came between his mother and father. Jo Stafford knew him well in those years, yet she knew she did not know him at all:

Buddy liked me. We never had any problems, but there wasn't an obvious humanness, a closeness. We talked to each other along the way, of course, and I could talk a lot about him—except for really knowing him, the person.... Only way I can explain it—when he played a long solo—he played the melody. I knew where he was every minute. But he was remote.

Constantly on the verge of behaving like monsters, compulsive, sometimes cruel practical jokers, few could get close to the two men, few could know them; the vulnerability came out only in the music. Rich and Sinatra were too much alike.

The band was full of strong personalities. Connie Haines had worked freelance for a while after leaving Harry James, and then joined the Dorsey band in April 1940, not long after Sinatra; she had a little-girl voice that was an acquired taste, but she was a popular entertainer with a lot of presence onstage, and Frank resented her. She said many years later that Sinatra, the northern urbanite, thought he was superior to her, a southerner from Savannah. When they sang duets, if Frank was giving her a hard time, she could upstage him: she would make eyes at a guy in the audience, or step away from the mike between choruses and dance a little. Frank would say, "Do your thing, cornball." Finally Frank demanded that Tommy fire her, but Dorsey fired Frank instead. For two weeks the band worked with Milburn Stone (who later played Doc on TV's *Gunsmoke*) until Frank apologized.

Trumpeter Bunny Berigan had failed as a bandleader because he was a poor businessman, and his band recorded too many second-rate pop songs; he rejoined Dorsey, his old boss. Berigan was a serious alcoholic who would soon be unable to play his own most famous solos, and he died in June 1942, less than thirty-four years old. But in early 1940 he was still playing well, and Dorsey loved him, keeping his chair open just as Paul Whiteman had done a decade earlier for Bix Beiderbecke. Other Dorsey sidemen were also among the best in the business: it was with Dorsey that Sinatra met tenor saxist Heinie Beau, for example, who would work with him many times. Nobody was more arrogant than Sinatra, but it is also true that nobody was more willing to learn from people who knew more than he did. And it was Tommy Dorsey himself who was the greatest teacher. Like all the best bandleaders, he was a great talent scout, and he knew that Sinatra was becoming a very fine singer. He could hear that one of the things that set Frank apart was his phrasing, and as an ace horn player he knew that the ability to phrase as one pleased was about legato: the ability to make phrases as long as one wished.

The most talented people, no matter how arrogant they are, are nearly always willing to acknowledge talent in others. Buddy Rich admired Don Lamond and Dave Tough among white drummers, and Chick Webb, Jo Jones, and Sid Catlett among the blacks. Sinatra has been generous with his praise over the years for Tony Bennett, Vic Damone, Billie Holiday, and other singers. As for Dorsey, in 1936 RCA Victor had sold a few 78s by releasing back-to-back recordings of Hoagy Carmichael's "Star Dust" by Goodman and Dorsey. (Kids loved the song, one of the most popular ever written; if they didn't know the name of it, they'd come up to the bandstand and request "Sometimes I Wonder" from the lyrics by Mitchell Parish.) In 1941 Artie Shaw had come back from temporary retirement, formed a new band and went back to the top of the charts with "Frenesi," a tune he'd discovered in Mexico; then RCA A&R man Harry Myerson wanted to repeat the "Star Dust" gimmick, this time with back-to-back versions by Shaw and Dorsey. Dorsey made a fine new recording with a Sinatra vocal, but meanwhile he had heard Shaw's instrumental version, with a superb trombone solo by Jack Jenney, and refused to go on the back of it. Both records were top-ten hits in the then-new *Billboard* chart, but fifteen years later, in 1956, just as rock 'n' roll was sweeping it all away, Shaw's classic version was voted their all-time favorite record by America's disk jockeys. Dorsey knew a great record when he heard it, even if it was somebody else's.

Dorsey also played trumpet, and some say he played better jazz on that instrument; but as a jazz trombonist Dorsey (like Glenn Miller) knew that he was hopelessly outclassed by Jack Teagarden, whose Texas style was the ultimate in making the difficult sound easy. At an all-star recording session in early 1939, a record producer wanted Dorsey to play the blues (on an arrangement called "The Blues") but Dorsey flatly refused, saying, "You've got Jack here." The classic, gorgeous solution was to introduce the arrangement with Dorsey playing twelve bars of legato melody while Teagarden improvised an obbligato around it. For no one could play a prettier, smoother legato than Tommy Dorsey.

Sy Oliver also gave Sinatra pointers, teaching him to allow the beat to carry him along rather than pushing it, as many young singers try to do. Sinatra was also a Billie Holiday fan, photographed at ringside listening to her in clubs. ("Bending those notes," she said later. "That's all I helped Frankie with.") It may have been Holiday who first took Sinatra to hear Mabel Mercer. Tony Bennett said that both he and Sinatra were listening to Mercer in the 1940s, and Sinatra later (at different times) gave equal credit to Holiday and Mercer as influences. Mercer's phrasing was like the punctuation in a poem, yet the result was musical dignity, not just literalness. And Sinatra also heard the long lines he wanted to sing in the violin playing of Jascha Heifitz. But for a singer the horn player's legato was more to the point, and Tommy Dorsey was the biggest influence of all.

The technique called circular breathing that some horn players use has to do with closing the epiglottis (the passage to the lungs) and playing the horn using the air in your cheeks while you are drawing air into your lungs through your nose. (I have heard Chico Freeman play exquisitely long lines on a big wooden bass clarinet at Ronnie Scott's in London, appearing not to breathe for what seemed like minutes at a time.) Some writers have assumed that this is what Dorsey did, and that this is what Sinatra learned from him, which is absurd: the sound of singing is the sound of air passing the vocal cords, which are in the larynx, well below the epiglottis; it is impossible to sing and inhale at the same time. In any case, circular breathing was not Dorsey's secret. Sinatra sat on the bandstand and watched Dorsey, trying to figure out when he breathed, and apparently Dorsey could feel the kid's eyes on the back of his jacket: Finally he turned around one night and said, "Haven't you seen it yet?" Then he shared his secret, and Sinatra explained it years later: with the trombone mouthpiece to his lips Dorsey would inhale between phrases through a tiny airhole in one corner of his mouth (Sinatra called it a "pinhole"). The breaths were so small and short that the listener did not perceive them. This kind of skill takes so much practice, such dedication to craft, that only musicians and athletes can understand it: the rest of us, by comparison, spend our lives bumping into things. And this was one of the most important stages of the development of Frank Sinatra's artistry.

Billy May was keeping an eye on all this. A trumpet player and arranger who played with Charlie Barnet in 1939, May first met Sinatra on the West Coast around the time the Palomar Ballroom burned down, and later made albums with Sinatra in the 1960s and 1970s. Sinatra was so arrogant, May said, that he was regarded at first by the men in the James band and later in the Dorsey band as a wise guy, but the men soon came around, because Sinatra ultimately had the talent: like other wise guys in the history of music—Jelly Roll Morton comes to mind, as well as Rich— Sinatra could back up his mouth with his performance. Before long he had promoted himself to a sort of straw boss, leading the band at rehearsals when Dorsey was late; as a singer he was not playing in the band and could stand in front and beat time. When Dorsey turned up, muttering apologies, Sinatra would give his boss a dirty look. But it was the records that Frank Sinatra made with Tommy Dorsey in 1940–42 that virtually defined that era of pop music, and in retrospect were the beginning of a new era, that of the dominance of the pop singer.

Frank Sinatra recorded about ninety songs with Dorsey between February 1940 and July 1942. A bandleader as successful as Dorsey had his pick of what he wanted to record; first there were the publishers and the song-pluggers to contend with, and the record producers at Victor in those days were underpaid and not averse to pushing a song in exchange for a piece of it, but nobody told Dorsey, Shaw, Goodman or Duke Ellington what to do. Even so, some of the songs have been forgotten, but as I never tire of pointing out, they were all current pop songs, and nobody knew which ones were going to be hits, let alone which would become standards. The remarkable thing is the number of good songs there were.

In February and March 1940 Sinatra recorded thirteen tunes at six recording sessions: "The Sky Fell Down," "Moments in the Moonlight," "The Fable of the Rose" and several others aren't up to much; "Yours Is My Heart Alone" is by Franz Lehár, from a 1929 operetta, and sounds it; "Hear My Song Violetta" was a stiff German import; and the arrangement of "I'll Be Seeing You," surprisingly, is a bit too bombastic. But already on the first recording session, Sinatra's second side with Dorsey seems to mark something new. "Too Romantic" (by Johnny Burke and James Monaco) has a nice tune and clever words: "You know you're much too near and I'm too romantic / Wouldn't I be a sight on a bended knee!" sends up and celebrates the romantic conventions at once; but it is the way the tune and the words go together that make this sort of craftsmanship work, and Sinatra's sweetness also has a kind of deadpan insouciance. Dorsey was telling Sinatra to listen to Bing Crosby, and how important the words were, as though Sinatra hadn't been listening to Crosby for years; "Too Romantic" was introduced by Crosby himself in the film *Road to Singapore* in 1940: if Crosby hadn't noticed Sinatra until then, he must have known when he heard this track that the competition was getting serious. (Crosby later said, "Frank Sinatra is the kind of singer who comes along once in a lifetime—but why did it have to be *my* lifetime?")

From the second recording session, "Shake Down the Stars"

doesn't quite make it, but it is co-written by one Chester Babcock, who had renamed himself Jimmy Van Heusen, and who would become one of Sinatra's closest friends for many years; in fact, someone said, the only man Sinatra actually wanted to *be*. From the third session, "Say It" isn't quite first-rate (although it's by Frank Loesser and Jimmy McHugh), but it is interesting for the way Sinatra delivers the first two words; "Say it" has to be sung on one note as though it were one word, and there are few singers who could have pulled that off as well as he does. But the other song from that third session is another masterpiece: Burke and Van Heusen had got together and produced "Polka Dots and Moonbeams," one of the all-time great smoochie-cabaret songs, another combination of words and melody that works wonderfully well: "The music started and was I the perplexed one / I held my breath and said, May I have the next one..." It is a story song, almost harking back to the Tin Pan Alley of the turn of the century (which everyone still remembered in 1940), yet the way Sinatra both sings the song and tells the story, every pause, accent and phrase exactly right, is indubitably modern, while it is a story we have already heard many times, and can never tire of.

"Too Romantic" (with Johnny Mince's superb clarinet rising out of the ensemble) and "Polka Dots and Moonbeams" (with a fine tenor solo, probably by Babe Russin) were fairly slow. The arrangement of "Imagination" (another Burke–Van Heusen song) is a little too busy, although it remained associated with Sinatra. "East of the Sun" is a delight, by the Sentimentalists, a nonet from within the band: the tempo here is an amiable lope, and the cool group chants behind Sinatra ("...We'll build a dreamhouse [A righteous pad!] of love, dear [Where you can really lay it on me!] ... ") so that the hepcats in the audience could be sentimental without embarrassment. Meanwhile, on April 23, the band had unsuccessfully recorded one of the slowest hits of all time. One of Jack Leonard's two big mistakes, he said, was that he had not put up with Dorsey's temper just a little longer:

We played the Canadian National Exhibition and I was lying on my bed in the Royal York Hotel in Toronto. My roommate in those days was Carmen Mastren, the guitar player. The telephone rings, and there's this girl on the line who I think is a fan, and she says, "Hi, is Carmen there? I have a song for him." We had a lot of girls in those days, and I'm thinking, "Yeah, right, you have a song for Carmen." Well, it turns out that she gives Carmen the song, and it's a knockout.... We finally nail Tommy, sit him down and play him the song, and he says, "Jack, as soon as we get off the road, this song is for you." It was shortly after that, maybe two or three months, that we wind up in Chicago and I quit. Had I stayed, "I'll Never Smile Again" would have been mine, not Frank's.

"I'll Never Smile Again" had been written by pianist Ruth Lowe, a native of Toronto, who played on the radio in Canada and later in the American all-girl band of Ina Ray Hutton; she wrote it supposedly after the death of her husband, though that story seems to have been a piece of press-agentry. Another story was that it won a songwriting contest, but Lowe had nothing to do with Dorsey's contest, which was then broadcast each week, a gimmick to help him find songs to publish. "I'll Never Smile Again" had been played by Percy Faith on the radio in Canada and a demo made, but there is evidence that Dorsey wasn't all that enthusiastic about it (he allowed Glenn Miller to record it first). It was so slow and so simple, almost lugubrious, that Dorsey's arrangement didn't work, not even with the Pied Pipers backing Sinatra to make a lovely vocal mix. (There were too many ballads anyway to suit Buddy Rich, but he reserved a special depth of dislike for "I'll Never Smile Again.") A month later, though, on May 23, the band tried again, there was a celesta in the studio, and maybe it was on that second attempt that somebody had the bright idea of using pianist Joe Bushkin on the celesta, to introduce and decorate the arrangement. The result was a number-one hit in the U.S.A. for twelve weeks.

"I'll Never Smile Again" was number one when I was born, and my mother never forgot it. It was probably the record that made her a Sinatra fan; she didn't particularly want to be having a baby at the age of twenty-one, married barely a year, and was fed up with being pregnant by the time I appeared, so the record probably fitted her mood perfectly. "It was all you *heard*," she said of the song, and she meant on the radio. But that was during the

ASCAP strike, when most current American songs were not being heard on the radio: this is one reason why so many out-of-copyright classical tunes were being fitted with words and recorded by all the dance bands. But if "I'll Never Smile Again" was first published in Canada, it may have evaded the ban on ASCAP copyrights being played on the radio; or perhaps Dorsey published it himself in the U.S.A. through a BMI company, and maybe that's why he recorded it. However it was made, the record went a long way to make Sinatra nationally famous. In those days the vocalists often didn't even get their names on the record labels, but by now everybody knew what the kid from Hoboken sounded like, his name began to become common currency, and it is also clear in retrospect that he was reaching his first maturity as an artist.

Good as Harry James's first band was, Tommy Dorsey's was the best in the business when it came to presenting the ordinary pop songs of the era. Some of Glenn Miller's hits sound dreadfully lumpy today, and listening to a large number of the Dorsey-Sinatra tracks in chronological order is not something one would often do: who wants to hear "The Call of the Canyon" again? But on the bandstand Dorsey would have known how to call the tunes, varying the fare, and even in a straight Sinatra compilation it is remarkable what good popular music this was: there is no editing here, no electronic gimmicks; these people played these arrangements every night on the bandstand, so that playing them in the recording studios was a piece of cake. Those of us who were jazz fans, growing up in the 1940s and 1950s and pawing through stacks of old 78s, discovered Dorsey's hits of the 1930s: Irving Berlin's "Marie," with its straight, sweet, innocently swinging vocal by Jack Leonard, and the band chanting hip paraphrases behind him; "Song of India" from Rimsky-Korsakoff, "Boogie Woogie" from Pinetop Smith, "Hawaiian War Chant" from heaven-knows-where: all with famous hot solos by Bunny Berigan and Bud Freeman. But in the 1940s the nation and the record business were recovering at last from the Depression, and much of the music was for dancers, or for sweethearts holding hands (or wishing they had someone to hold hands with); and what keeps most of these sides from the early 1940s from palling is that the arrangements are clever, and the band is always swinging. It is very difficult to swing at the slowest tempi (Al Klink, Glenn Miller's tenor saxophonist, said years later, "We were too *scared* to swing"), but the pulse of the Dorsey band never plodded.

There was often a two-beat feeling on ballads, and on "Where Do You Keep Your Heart," for example, when Sinatra's vocal is over and the band is taking it out, Rich's emphasis on the back-beat reminds us that rock 'n' roll is just around the corner. (Rich would not like us making that connection, but it was his double bass-drum setup that helped Oliver's two-beat feeling to work so well; and the band was seeing to it that both romantics and dancers were served before the record was over: the song itself was one of the dumber ones.) "Whispering" (with the Pipers) revives a twenty-year-old song and gives it a fully modern (and very hip) four-beat treatment; then on "Trade Winds" we are firmly back in two-beat territory: this has romantically inane words, but both the arrangement and Sinatra's navigation of the unusual tune are noteworthy, and it is fully Sinatra's vehicle. He sings it right to the end so that there's nothing left to take out (it was a top-ten hit, and sent up in a Warner Brothers cartoon). "The One I Love (Belongs to Somebody Else)" is a Sy Oliver master-piece. Dorsey had recorded an older arrangement of the tune with Jack Leonard in 1938, but the 1940 version was a bigger hit, and remained associated with Sinatra; the band has a ball with Oliver's chart for fully two minutes before he gets a chance to sing it, backed by the Pipers.

Nearly all the tunes are introduced by Dorsey's unmistakable trombone, either open or muted; but the main thing is that the band's beat never failed to lilt. The quality of the arrangements and the playing of the band, especially the rhythm section, beat Glenn Miller for sweetness with integrity, even if half the songs are forgettable. There are ironies here: these are mostly sentimental and romantic ballads, yet wise-guy Buddy Rich as the backbone of the rhythm section deserves much of the credit (along with Weiss on bass), while Dorsey, billed as "The Sentimental Gentleman of Swing," was usually about as sentimental as Attila the Hun. It is hard to remember that before the Second World War even the most hard-boiled were still trying to believe in the possi-bility of living happily ever after. And who was more hard-boiled than Mr. Sinatra himself? "(I found your lips tonight but) Where Do You Keep Your Heart" indeed: he could sing a song like that and almost make us believe it over fifty years later, because *he* believed it. "I could make you care/ If only you'd let me/ I could make you care/ You'd never forget me": the very pretty arrangement does not even state the tune, it is left to Sinatra to come along with the unadorned melody, serving it up like a gem in a perfect setting; and as for the lyrics, how many yearning lovers have not wallowed in just such self-serving tautology? (And maybe they still do, only nowadays they're not supposed to admit it.) Sinatra was revealing something in his music that he could not reveal in any other way, and his audience was beginning to respond in a way that would soon make headlines and inaugurate a new era in popular music.

In November, while "I'll Never Smile Again" was still selling, the new recording of "Star Dust" completed the Dorsey-Sinatra recordings for 1940, the arrangement introduced by Bushkin on the celesta to remind the fans of one of their favorite records of the year; and if Shaw's version of "Star Dust" was still the deejays' favorite record fifteen years later, the version with Dorsey, Sinatra and the Pied Pipers was also in their top-thirty all-time favorites. (His pronunciation of "inspeeration" had mellowed somewhat.) The great records continued in the new year: on January 6, 1941, "Oh, Look at Me Now' was a duet with Connie Haines, backed by the Pied Pipers, and one of the biggest hits in the country for several weeks. (Haines sang better on the other side, because she was allowed to sing lower; it was another duet called "You Might Have Belonged to Another," a lesser song.) "You Lucky People You" and "It's Always You" are both by Burke and Van Heusen, the former nicely upbeat, and if they are not masterpieces they're not bad either; that team was almost incapable of writing a clinker. "I Tried" is so-so; "Dolores," co-written by Frank Loesser, was a huge hit, and it's hard to dislike, but all these years later the song and its treatment seem to touch too many bases: the melody memorable on purpose, the Pipers humming too much all the way through it.

At his third recording session of the new year came an unusual Dorsey record, featuring two of his vocalists in the way they deserved, and to heck with commercial considerations. Dorsey was too good a musician not to notice how good a singer Jo Stafford was; the reference books all say that her first solo was on another tune the following month, but on January 20, 1941 Dorsey made two twelve-inch sides featuring Jo on one side and Frank on the other, reaching back a decade for two fine songs. He recorded Jo on "For You," by Al Dubin and Joe Burke, a song already well known in a version by Kenny Sargent with the Casa Loma Band; and Sinatra on Vincent Youmans's "Without a Song." Oliver's arrangement, Dorsey's trombone and Sinatra's singing made a memorable record, nearly four and a half minutes long, at a medium tempo which, given one of Oliver's best two-beat treatments, is neither fast nor slow, but timeless. Dorsey just plays the melody in Oliver's setting, except for an occasional jazz accent, as though the spirit of hope behind the song is trying to burst out; then the vocal starts halfway through, introduced by a celesta. Sinatra sings lower than usual and does a fine job, when suddenly, twice, on the words "I'll never know," he tweaks the tune or bends a note, and puts the cap on the whole thing: it is a great and still-legendary piece of pop music. The record was not much of a hit at the time, because twelve-inch 78s did not sell well in the pop market; but in those days records stayed in print and could do well in the long run, because people liked them: the accountants at the record companies took orders instead of giving them.

And at the next recording session something even better happened. Four tunes were recorded, the two Sinatras both being hits. "Do I Worry?" is an okay ballad, but the record reminds us that it wasn't Sinatra singing "doo-be-doo-be-doo" in those days. The Pipers did all that doo-be-dooing and humming better than anybody else, but perhaps sometimes it was overdone. This had Jo's solo on the other side on a song called "Little Man With a Candy Cigar," and a vehicle for the Pipers called "Watcha Know, Joe?" was backed by a Sinatra solo on one of the best records he ever made, "Everything Happens to Me." Matt Dennis was nearly two years older than Sinatra, working for Dorsey and his publishing company; he had written the music for "Little Man," which remained obscure, but he also worked with lyricists such as Bob

Russell, Sammy Cahn, and his partner on "Everything," Tom Adair. As for Sinatra, he was an emotional mess. It was a twenty-five-year-old with a lot of unsatisfied longings who recorded "Everything Happens to Me," one of those perfect marriages of words, music, arrangement and singer.

His first child, his beloved daughter Nancy, had been born in June of the previous year (Dorsey was Little Nancy's godfather), and his marriage would last most of the decade, but he was never actually husband material. There were always plenty of women, but sex could satisfy his longings only temporarily. He was hitting the big time at last; in May 1941 *Billboard* named him top male band singer, and by the end of the year he had pushed Crosby out of the top spot in the *down beat* poll. But it was still somebody else's name on the record label: he had become the Dorsey band's biggest asset, and Dorsey was aware of it. There were whispers that Jimmy Dorsey's Bob Eberly (a much better singer than his brother, Glenn Miller's Ray Eberle) was thinking about going solo. There were still virtually no other solo singing stars, certainly none of Bing Crosby's stature, but there were scads of good young boy singers coming up: Eddy Howard would leave Dick Jurgens to lead his own band in 1940; Jack Leonard had gone solo (he turned down an offer from Glenn Miller, another mistake upon leaving Dorsey); Dick Haymes was clearly going to be good enough sooner or later, and Perry Como with Ted Weems had been tugging earlobes for several years. Crosby had been around for nearly a decade, his crown was going to be up for grabs, and Sinatra wanted to be one of the first contenders. He knew that Dorsey hated people to quit, so he began preparing his ground. He didn't know how he was going to get out of his contract, but it was customary to give two weeks' or a month's notice for an ordinary sideman. So in September 1941 he gave Dorsey a year's notice. Dorsey ignored him.

Sinatra already had an entourage: Nick Sevano was a pal from Hoboken who had started by helping Sinatra pick out his clothes; Hank Sanicola was a pianist-turned-bodyguard, and the one person who didn't take any nonsense from Sinatra (or anybody else). Both would be shed when the time came, but meanwhile they were the ones who made excuses to Nancy when her husband didn't come home. He couldn't get along with Buddy Rich or Connie Haines because he perceived them as lacking class, while he himself hardly knew which fork to use, and still had a deeply unfashionable New Jersey accent when he wasn't singing; but while his entourage thought he was crazy to want to go solo, for all his problems and shortcomings his absolute confidence in his talent swept everyone along. The fact was that the kid electrified audiences, and even Dorsey was astonished by it. Somebody described him as looking like a debauched faun, but girls were actually starting to swoon, and Dorsey was so amazed at first, standing on the bandstand with his horn, that he would almost forget to take his solo. The band was amused: as a prank they would take their horns out of their mouths and make an "Oooohhhh!" sound. "Remember," said Dorsey, "he was no matinee idol. He was a skinny kid with big ears. And yet what he did to women was something awful." But for all Sinatra's confidence and success, he still wanted to know: *When will it be my name on the record label?*

While I have been writing this, my wife came into the room and sat down while "Everything Happens to Me" was playing. When it was over, she sighed and said, "My father really loved that record." In April 1941, when it hit the U.S. top ten, her beloved father was an ordinary young fellow from Milwaukee, not quite twenty-five years old, tall, not bad looking, still single and attending business college. He loved baseball and big-band jazz, and he was probably wondering what would become of him. *There aren't that many jobs going, the world is plunging into war, and who wants to go to the movies with me?* And what he heard on the radio in 1941 was a mere four bars of intro—"Black cats creep across my path until I'm almost mad / I must have roused the Devil's wrath, 'cause all my luck is bad"—and then:

I make a date for golf, and you can bet your life it rains.
I try to give a party, but the guy upstairs complains.
I guess I'll go through life just catchin' colds and missing trains;
Ev'rything happens to me.

I never miss a thing, I've had the measles and the mumps.

And every time I play an ace my partner always trumps.
I guess I'm just a fool who never looks before he jumps;
Ev'rything happens to me.

> At first my heart thought you could break this jinx for me,
> That love would turn the trick to end despair.
> But now I just can't fool this head that thinks for me,
> So I've mortgaged all my castles in the air.

I've telegraphed and phoned, sent an airmail special too;
Your answer was good-bye, there was even postage due.
I fell in love just once and then it had to be with you.
Ev'rything happens to me.

I've never drawn a sweepstake or a bank night at a show,
I thought perhaps this time I'd won, but Lady Luck said no.
And though it break my heart, I'm not surprised to see you go:
Ev'rything happens to me.

The words, now, are sweetly anachronistic. Nobody telegraphs anymore. A "show" was a movie in the U.S., as in "Let's go to the show": during the Depression they gave away dishes at the movie theater, and on bank night a small amount of cash, anything to get people to come. But the craft is in the way the words fall. The arrangement is by Axel Stordahl, but with the Dorsey band's very best two-beat treatment. Sinatra is backed by a lovely woodwind choir, muted brass gently commenting at the end of each line; the two-beat lilt at the perfect slow tempo has three or four syllables jammed into the first half of each bar, but only one or two in the next: "make a date / golf," "bet your life / rains," "try to give / party," "guy upstairs /'plains;" thus the singer's resignation is reinforced by a sort of shuffle beat. This is a young man's song, full of yearning and loneliness, but with a touch of humor too: *Maybe things will get better.* And Sinatra's long lines come into play here: you don't notice where he breathes, and you don't care. Bing Crosby never made a record with which a twenty-five-year-old man, standing around on a street corner on a Saturday night with his hands in his pockets, could have identified this much: during

---

his free time Sinatra was a wise guy, but when he was singing a song like this the song became more important than he was, and the result was that he became the hero of his generation. He knew, he understood. He yearned.

It was now that the running and swimming Sinatra had done when he was younger began to pay off: he weighed only 130 pounds in those days and wanted to build himself up, but the lung power was more important than he could have imagined, for what he did with a song that made him different from his competitors depended on being able to sing eight bars or more without a break. You can't express the ideas in the lines if you have to break them into bits, turning them into a nursery rhyme; nor can you take proper advantage of word-groupings such as those described above if you have to interrupt to take breaths. Indeed, the whole Dorsey band played in this seamless way on every arrangement, which is what made it one of the best. Alto saxist Arthur "Skeets" Herfurt had left Dorsey before Sinatra joined the band, but would work with Sinatra in the future; he remembered that Dorsey would sometimes make the band play a whole page of an arrangement without drawing a breath, and named Dorsey as his teacher, as Sinatra did.

Dorsey also helped Sinatra to develop his knack for finding the right songs. There weren't any more by Burke and Van Heusen for a while (they were in demand elsewhere: Crosby soon hit with their Oscar-winning "Swinging on a Star"). But Dennis and Adair were employed by Dorsey, who was building up his publishing portfolio, and they didn't stop with "Everything Happens to Me"; they were on a roll. The very next Sinatra record was their "Let's Get Away from It All," a two-sided 78, the first side featuring Jo and the Pipers, the second adding Haines and Sinatra (and the song itself perhaps the first in a Sinatra genre: later he would travel with "South of the Border," "It Happened in Monterey," "Come Fly With Me"). They followed up with "Violets for Your Furs" (arranged by Heinie Beau) and "The Night We Called It a Day," four songs permanently in the Sinatra canon.

It is almost a relief to report that not all the songs recorded by Dorsey and Sinatra in 1941–42 were masterpieces; showbiz can't be all free beer and pretzels. For some reason Dorsey recorded "Free for All," also by Dennis and Adair, a strange bit of quasi-patriotic optimism with a march tempo sounding like it was intended for a war-bond rally, but several months before Pearl Harbor. Taking the cake, though, speaking of Hawaii, is "Neiani," copyrighted by Dorsey's two arrangers, Oliver and Axel Stordahl: it is the obligatory Hawaiian song. Ever since the 1920s there have been periodic Hawaiian fads in American popular culture; country music's steel guitar came from the Hawaiian fretless guitar, played in the lap. (I suppose "Hawaiian War Chant" has to be counted in this genre, being co-written by a Hawaiian prince, but Dorsey had turned it into instrumental big-band jazz.) "Neiani" was one of the goopier examples of Hawaiian kitsch, and another example of the "unlucky mulatto" genre ("I found her in Hawaii, my Neiani"; "I left her in Hawaii ... "). "Free for All" and "Neiani" are almost the only two of all these tunes for which alternative takes have survived; maybe they had to be attacked twice because nobody really liked them. Buddy Rich must have hated them.

A nice version of Irving Berlin's "Blue Skies" had a straight Sinatra vocal and the band being wise guys in the background; "You and I" and "Two in Love" were not bad songs, the former the theme song of a popular radio program, both written by Meredith Wilson, who went on sixteen years later to write the Broadway hit *Music Man*; and there were a few other fairly useless ballads ("I Think of You" had a nice arrangement; the tune was borrowed from Rachmaninoff and recycled a few years later as "Full Moon and Empty Arms"). But a marvelous new film song by Ralph Freed and Burton Lane, "How About You," rounded out 1941. The performance is curiously straight; it was a song for a more mature man, and Sinatra would make more of it in the future.

The new year of 1942 began with the next chapter in the struggle to make Sinatra as famous as he wanted to be: his own first recording session. The band had made a film in 1941, *Las Vegas Nights*, with one song by Sinatra, and went on to the more elaborate *Ship Ahoy!* in 1942, which was shot in color, had two songs by Sinatra and a famous, cleverly choreographed sequence with Buddy Rich and Eleanor Powell dancing together. Hollywood had a powerful effect on both Rich and Sinatra: Rich got a crush on Lana Turner that he didn't get over for years (she apparently ate several men for breakfast every day), while Sinatra realized that if he was going to be the biggest singing star in the world he may as well be a movie star too, and that he would much prefer living in California to New Jersey. He had never been faithful to Nancy, but during the making of the first film he fell for a blonde starlet called Alora Gooding and virtually lived with her, perhaps understanding for the first time that his marriage could not last. Meanwhile, he kept reminding Dorsey that he wanted to leave, and he was so nervous and worried about his career and about things in general that he actually consulted doctors: skinny ever since a childhood bout with appendicitis, now he was actually losing weight.

As powerful as Dorsey was in the music business, the audience reaction to Sinatra on the bandstand, on record, on the radio and in the film meant that the entertainment business was starting to wonder what the skinny kid might be worth by himself. Sinatra knew he could have a recording contract with a major label when the time came; Manie Sacks, a top executive at Columbia Records, had become a fan as well as a close friend. Meanwhile, after a lot of lobbying, Dorsey reluctantly agreed to allow Sinatra to make some solo records. Some say that Dorsey saw to it that Sinatra's first records under his own name came out on Bluebird, RCA's budget label, rather than full-price Victor, just to remind Sinatra who was boss, but that is probably nonsense; one of the biggest acts in the music business at the time was the Glenn Miller band, which had over a hundred hits in 1939–42 on Bluebird before switching to Victor. Miller's attitude was probably that the kids he was trying to reach would be able to buy more of his records at 35 cents each than at 75 cents; Sinatra's first solo efforts, too, would probably sell more copies on Bluebird.

At any rate, a recording session of January 1942, in Hollywood, used some of Dorsey's men, augmented with woodwinds, strings and even a harp, on four tunes arranged and conducted by Axel Stordahl, and a change in the direction of Sinatra's career was evident. Stordahl, two years older than Sinatra and a Dorsey arranger for six or seven years, relished arranging for a full orchestra rather than a dance band; both Stordahl and Sinatra worked hard and rehearsed like demons, and the records were very good of their kind. Indeed even the recording balance is impressive. What Stordahl produced is what has been called the "rustle of spring" school of accompanying singers. The tunes were "The Lamplighter's Serenade," "The Night We Called It a Day," "The Song Is You" and "Night and Day." "Lamplighter," co-written by Hoagy Carmichael, was being recorded by everybody, but it is hard now to hear why; the other three, by Dennis and Adair, Kern and Hammerstein, and Cole Porter respectively, were better songs and remained associated with Sinatra, but, as with "How About You" from the previous month, he would make more of them when he had more confidence, and when he could free himself from the cosseting of the arranger and the studio. Of the four sides, "Night and Day" was the biggest hit at the time; it was probably the equivalent of a top-twenty hit, but it is fun to speculate that certain music-business interests (such as Dorsey) were able to use their influence to keep it off the *Billboard* chart. Sinatra's head was big enough as it was, but he was as pleased as a child with his work.

He also knew what he was doing. However he may have behaved elsewhere, in the recording studio he was in complete control of himself and everything else, and he was also utterly fair and evenhanded with musicians, so long as they gave him the best they could. Harry Myerson was the RCA A&R man for the four sides of January 1942, and said later, "Popularity didn't really change Sinatra. On the first date he stood his ground and displayed no humility, phony or real." The music was the most important thing, the acting or interpretation went into the music, and no other exercise of personality was necessary, or even possible. For that matter, with Sinatra what you saw was what you got: as difficult as he could be, there was never really any "face" to him. If he was sore at you, you had no doubt about it; it was not going on behind your back, and the best thing you could do was stand up to him. And it was in the recording studio, from the earliest days, that the complete professionalism of which he was capable was manifest.

While everything Sy Oliver did had a jazz feeling, Axel Stordahl was not a jazzman at all, and on the four sides of January 1942 an important aspect of Sinatra's emerging style was kept tightly wrapped: namely the jazz content. Perhaps this is as good a place as any to deal with the question of whether or not Sinatra was a jazz singer. In my opinion, at his best he might have deserved to be called a jazz singer. What made "Everything Happens to Me" and quite a few others such great records is the feeling that he is making up the words as he goes along, that you don't know what he is going to say next; it seems that he is interpreting the song according to his own feelings and to the need of the moment, rather than singing it as written, which is one of the essences of jazz. Yet interpretation is not improvisation. His passion was of a different kind, and his control over himself as an artist was too absolute to allow him fully to be a jazz singer. It is a paradox in Sinatra, the man for whom "Anything Goes," that there was an element that could not let go; and the resulting tension is one of the things that made him a great interpreter. Finally, if there has to be a demarcation, we have to allow him a category of his own: the greatest of jazz-influenced pop singers. As Gene Lees put it, he made things difficult for other singers: after Sinatra, if you sounded like him you were imitating, but if you didn't, you sounded like you were doing it wrong.

The fact that throughout his subsequent career he probably sang a song the same way many, many times is not important; this had to be expected if a tune was to be performed hundreds or thousands of times. This is one of the things that Artie Shaw found maddening: he didn't *want* to play his hits over and over, while other leaders insisted that their men play the same solos on the bandstand that they played on the records; many of the fans, listening to the records over and over again, had memorized the solos and had no idea they were supposed to be improvised. Jazz, in Whitney Balliett's famous phrase, is the sound of surprise, but the improvised solo doesn't always work, and chance-taking is seen as antithetical to commercial success: the product has to be reliable. That is why the jazz element began to be superseded in the popular music of the 1940s, and it is also why fans of Sinatra and Ella Fitzgerald, many of them, don't want their favorites to be labeled "jazz" artists. During the 1940s the record industry was finally recovering from the Depression (the gold-record gimmick for a million-seller was invented in 1941), and jazz soon became a dirty word in the marketplace, which is partly why rock 'n' roll was later invented, in an attempt to restore at least an illusion of risk.

Meanwhile, in 1942 a great many of Sinatra's fans were putting on uniforms. The whole world was in a holding pattern until the outcome of the Second World War was decided, and nothing would ever be the same again. Sinatra recorded fifteen more tunes with Dorsey between February and July, and somehow one is not surprised that the earlier peaks were not matched. "Snootie Little Cutie" should have been fun, written by Bobby Troup, who was on Dorsey's staff that year (and who would later write "The Girl Can't Help It" for Little Richard). "Snootie" is a duet loaded with period slang: Connie Haines was the "dapper little flapper," Sinatra the "mellow little fellow," but they sound bored, and when he sings, "You're a vain little Jane, but you're sweet," you can almost hear his clenched teeth. "I'll Take Tallulah" is a production number from *Ship Ahoy!* which may have worked on-screen, but Dorsey's version on record was a dreadful, noisy thing, though something of a novelty hit at the time.

There are also some more or less dreary ballads, and then in May a disaster: Dorsey adds a string section to his band. Harry James, Artie Shaw and a few others had done it; Dorsey didn't want to be seen to be left behind, and he had Stordahl to write for the strings, and strings were often seen as lending class to the act, however inappropriate to this or that context. Most if not all of the 1942 Dorsey arrangements for Sinatra seem to be by Stordahl rather than Oliver, and Stordahl knew better than some what to do with strings, but now he was writing not to suit himself and Sinatra, but to suit Dorsey. A few of the songs—"It Started All Over Again," "There Are Such Things," "Be Careful It's My Heart"—aren't bad ones, but they turn to treacle. (Perhaps Dorsey's true attitude to strings was revealed a few years later, in 1946, when he asked Nelson Riddle not to give them so much music to play. "Frankly, they're only a tax dodge," he added.) And then, in August 1942, Frank Sinatra got his way and left the Dorsey band.

This immediately raised the problem of how he could afford to live like the star he was rapidly becoming. Sinatra always spent money like water anyway, and now he was effectively becoming self-employed and would have no regular income, at a time when he wanted to move to the West Coast and buy a house for his family. He wanted Stordahl to come with him as his music director, so he offered him several times as much as Dorsey had been paying him, which must have angered Dorsey still more. If he had a standard three-year contract with Dorsey, it only had a few more months to run, but he was in such a hurry that he signed with General Amusement Corporation (GAC), a booking agency, and for an advance of $17,000 from Dorsey signed an agreement with him that gave Dorsey a third of his gross earnings over $100 a week for ten years, as well as 10 percent to Dorsey's personal manager as a finder's fee for bringing Frank to Columbia Records. His last appearance with Dorsey was in September, and within a year he was refusing to honor the agreement.

It was with Dorsey's band, his arrangements and his booking agency that Sinatra had achieved national fame, but now of course he whined to the newspapers about the agreement he had been in a hurry to sign; Dorsey began to look like the bad guy. There had to be another settlement, and there has been gossip ever since that gangster pressure on Dorsey was involved. Dorsey's own booking agency, Music Corporation of America (MCA), wanted Sinatra, and some fans were picketing Dorsey's band, and Dorsey had to sue Sinatra to get some of the money he legally had coming. Another factor was that the American Federation of Radio Artists gave permission for bands like Dorsey's to do "remote" broadcasts from ballrooms without extra payment: remember that radio programs without sponsors were called sustaining programs, and AFRA's lawyer (also Sinatra's lawyer) was threatening to prevent Dorsey from doing "sustaining remotes," which were valuable publicity. A new settlement was in everybody's best interests. In August 1943, Dorsey accepted $60,000 from MCA, which came out of Sinatra's earnings, some of it an advance from MCA and some from Columbia, an advance on his record royalties. In addition, MCA agreed to split its commission on his income with GAC for five years. Dorsey was said to have been pleased with the deal, until he realized he should have taken less cash and a percentage: it would not be long before Sinatra was making a great deal of money.

Dorsey and Sinatra were both the kind of men who did not want to be seen to be bested. They had respect for each other's talent, and in fact they subsequently worked together; but when they were in the mood they could snarl at the memory of the battle of the lawyers. Sinatra always resented having to sign a bad deal to get out of Dorsey's clutches, and then having to depend on lawyers to get him out of the deal; saying something nice about Harry James, he would be reminded of Dorsey and become angry all over again. For Dorsey, to a large extent it was just business; he claimed that he had demanded a bad deal from Sinatra because he didn't want him to leave and didn't think he would go for it. Asked what he thought of Sinatra, Dorsey once said, "He's the most fascinating man in the world, but don't stick your hand in the cage." It was Dorsey himself, no doubt in a mischievous mood, who perpetuated some of the gangster nonsense in an article in *American Mercury* magazine in 1951, in which he claimed to have been visited by tough guys. (That magazine had been a favorite of American intellectuals in the 1920s and 1930s, but by the 1950s had fallen on hard times and was read by the paranoid anti-communist right, who disliked Sinatra.) In August 1956, Sinatra sang with the Dorsey band at the Paramount Theater in New York City (on the screen was the latest Sinatra movie), and Dorsey told the band, "I showed him all his shit. Everything he does, he got from me." That claim was not unjustified. The kid who didn't even graduate from high school had learned about more than music from Dorsey; he'd learned about business, and about promoting himself and his work. Dorsey had perhaps been a more useful father figure than Marty Sinatra ever was, and Sinatra admitted that Dorsey had been like a father to him, but he had grown up to be the kind of man who resented anybody who looked like a father. It is an irony that he may also have picked up more irascibility and a greater tendency to a quick temper from Dorsey as well, as though he were not already arrogant enough.

As he had done when he left Harry James, before he left the Dorsey band he introduced Dick Haymes, who was following in his footsteps. And then at last, from the autumn of 1942, not yet twenty-seven years old, Sinatra was his own boss. As with the so-called American century, even greater triumphs lay ahead, and even more trouble.

Chapter Four

King of the Hit Parade

In retrospect, it is remarkable how often Frank Sinatra was to be found at the center of things. The sort of fame he seemed to want was incompatible with privacy anyway, but his image often dovetailed neatly with what was going down in the realm of popular culture.

The early 1940s marked a turning point in the history of popular music, and not just because Sinatra left the Dorsey band. The Swing Era began after he had decided to become a singer while still a teenager, so that his generation of young vocalists was supported by jazz-oriented dance bands. This era, with its stars, its personalities and its fans, was the era when he himself became famous and would always be closest to his heart, yet he did as much as anybody to bring it to an end. In 1942 the Swing Era was becoming middle-aged, and the era of the pop singer was on the way, Sinatra soon its first and biggest star. But Sinatra wasn't thinking about any of this; his immediate problem was making a living, and he couldn't even make records for a while, because in August 1942, the same month he got his freedom from Dorsey, the musicians' union went on strike against the record companies.

The music press had paid surprisingly little attention to the big change in his career, and he needed bookings. He was already acquiring a reputation for being prickly, but he was also an effective hustler; he had cultivated radio stations, deejays, music publishers and songwriters for years. Several of the songs he had recorded with Dorsey were songs associated with Bing Crosby, and in some cases he actually recorded them before Crosby did, because in his single-minded pursuit of Crosby's stardom he was courting writers like Jimmy Van Heusen and Sammy Cahn, who wrote for Crosby. Sinatra had people in his corner because of his enormous talent; they believed in him. His staff of friends, hangers-on and gophers in the early 1940s was called the Varsity, and included songwriters, boxers/bodyguards, a sportswriter, Axel Stordahl and Manie Sacks, as well as Nick Sevano, Hank Sanicola and Ben Barton, who was a partner with Sanicola in Sinatra's music publishing company. And soon he had a new press agent.

Sinatra's solo career took a few months to get started, and his booking agency, GAC, was not too impressed with its new star at first. He sang one song in a film called *Reveille with Beverly*, and he guested on radio programs, but he was not setting the world on fire. Then Sinatra's handler at GAC talked Bob Weitman, the manager of New York's Paramount Theater, into catching Sinatra's act at a theater in Newark, New Jersey, where there was a lot of audience reaction when he walked out onstage. Weitman thought it might be local New Jersey enthusiasm for a home-grown celebrity, but he was impressed enough to book Sinatra as an "extra added attraction" for the New Year's show at the Paramount, which included a film (*Star Spangled Rhythm*, a musical potpourri featuring most of Paramount Studio's payroll), and the Benny Goodman band, which then had Peggy Lee singing with it.

The Paramount Theater was one of the shrines of the Swing Era, and Sinatra was frightened when he went to work on December 30; he knew this was an important gig. After the Goodman band had played for a while, Goodman announced in his careless way, "And now, Frank Sinatra." When Sinatra came through the curtain a wall of screaming crashed over everybody onstage, so that Goodman, frozen in the act of giving the downbeat for the next tune, looked over his shoulder and blurted out, "What the fuck is that?" Sinatra laughed, and his fear left him. Sooner or later, one or two of the girls passed out in the aisles, and the phenomenon of the swooning fans immediately began to get media coverage.

Sinatra's press agent was Milt Rubin, who was connected with Broadway columnist Walter Winchell. Winchell in retrospect was one of the biggest frauds in the history of journalism, but at the time he had a lot of people in his pocket, and if you were in Winchell's pocket nobody else was of any real importance. Sinatra needed his own press agent, and Manie Sacks recommended George Evans, who handled Glenn Miller and some of the other big acts of the era. Evans went to the Paramount and, walking down the aisle to get closer to the stage, he noticed the girls in the audience moaning, and recognized the publicity value of it. It is true that he paid some girls and trained them to orchestrate the action, but he had to be careful not to be trampled by the ones who wanted to moan, scream and swoon for nothing. Evans took advantage of the fact that the kids were on vacation from school, keeping the excitement whipped up, and the Paramount's business didn't fall off after New Year's Day, traditionally a slow time, but remained very good. And this was only the beginning: Evans invented words like "Swoonatra," which the press were only too happy to pick up, and Frank Sinatra was soon becoming one of the most famous entertainers in the world. Something new seemed to be happening.

And yet it wasn't really new at all. All these stories have been told many times, but some details have always been left out. When Sinatra had been added to the bill at the Paramount, Benny Goodman is supposed to have said, "Frank who?" But the truth is that Goodman was so self-centered he could hardly remember the names of the sidemen in his own band. (In another version, it was comedian Jack Benny who was asked to tell a few jokes and introduce Sinatra, and said, "Frank who?") As far as the screaming and the swooning are concerned, Crosby, Rudy Vallee, Rudolph Valentino and a great many others had caused mini-riots in their time, including Goodman himself: on his first appearance at the Paramount in March 1937, less than six years earlier, a theater full of kids went nuts over the bespectacled clarinet player and his band. The nineteenth-century piano virtuosi Franz Liszt (in Europe) and Louis Moreau Gottschalk (in the U.S.A.) inspired ladies who threatened to harm themselves if their burning passions were not assuaged. Yet in each case there *was* something new: the big modern grand piano with its rich sound was new in the mid-nineteenth century, and Liszt and Gottschalk were superb players and composers of passionate, Romantic music; the image of Valentino in his desert robes looks corny today, but seventy-five years ago on screen it was a romantic fantasy come to life; in the mid-1930s Benny Goodman was the leader of a big jazz band full of hot soloists and swinging arrangements that sounded to its audiences like something very new indeed. And it is not too much to say that Frank Sinatra was the ultimate interpreter of American popular song, which by the 1940s had reached a peak, with George Gershwin already dead, while Jerome Kern, Cole Porter and Irving Berlin had already done much of their best work.

During the 1920s, the so-called Jazz Age, young people had supposedly become liberated, the "flappers" bobbing their hair, smoking in public and so forth; and then the country had been struck with a terrible economic depression. In the 1940s a new generation was ready to pick up where its parents had left off, and furthermore had heard more songs and seen more films than any previous generation. In the 1940s teenagers were in fact a new phenomenon of adolescents catered to by the newly powerful broadcasting and filmmaking industries; they had churning hormonal juices, like every generation of young people, but they also believed absolutely in romantic love. Every teenaged girl who screamed at a Sinatra gig expected that someday soon she would meet Mr. Right, fall in love, get married and live happily ever after; all the songs Sinatra sang reinforced that worldview, and he sang them not only with a passion that seethed just beneath the surface, but also, somehow, with complete integrity.

Frankie's fans knew that he lived the ideal, with a pretty wife and a baby daughter (and Franklin Wayne Emmanuel Sinatra, named after FDR and Manie Sacks, was born in January 1944). They didn't know that he screwed every woman he could get hold of. They didn't know about his compulsive habits—his constant hand-washing, and changing his underpants several times a day—or his intolerable temper, his need to blame anybody, the nearest person, for anything that went wrong; or his hero worship of gangsters. They didn't know that his mother was a monster who had taught him almost nothing except selfishness. But they would have known, if they had thought about it, that he was capable of feeling guilt, even if he would deny the guilt and push it away, blaming it on someone else; they would have known that he was aware of his own limitations, even if he tried to hide them; and, if they had known about his sex life (so insatiable that he used hookers when he ran out of starlets and bar-girls), they would have known that every time he made love he thought, however fleetingly, that the woman in front of him was the most desirable creature in the world.

For as a famous man once said, you can't fool all of the people all of the time, and Frank Sinatra did not fool a huge worldwide audience for over fifty years. It was both blessing and curse for him that he too believed in romantic love and in living happily ever after, in spite of his own inability to live up to any sort of recognizable ideal. He himself was at once the ultimate romantic and the archetypal rebel, and enough of an artist to value the words enough to sing the songs well enough to drive the teenagers crazy, and that is how he eventually supplanted Bing Crosby as the nation's favorite singer. Crosby, too, was selfish, a rotten husband and father and an incessant womanizer, but he allegedly hated to sing or say the words "I love you" on a record or in a film. Sinatra didn't mind saying it: his passion may have been unreliable, even dangerous, but it had an admission of vulnerability in it, so that we could love the art, if not the artist.

When Sinatramania began, commentators made fun of the fans and their swooning; but that was another era, and it must be remembered that the songs Sinatra sang were respectable songs. American popular music had African and ragtime elements in it, but the songs we now call standards were also deeply influenced by the European operetta style, their structure musically credible; the lyrics and rhyme schemes were often intelligent, written by people who had not grown up listening to advertising jingles. And while the songs were about romantic love, they were also, not far beneath the surface, about sex: everybody knew what you were permitted to do once you were married, and where "baby makes three" came from. The phenomenon, which seemed new at the time, of crowds of screaming bobby-soxers having to be held back by cops outside the Paramount Theater was explained by teachers, preachers, psychiatrists and other professional explainers: mass hysteria, wartime nostalgia for the boy-next-door, and so on. Jokes about Sinatra's skinny frame became a cliché: he was called "hoe-handle," and it was maintained that if he stood sideways he disappeared behind the microphone stand. But when he touched the stand the girls went mad. (Evans told him to stroke it.)

The theory was that he looked vulnerable, and that the girls wanted to mother him, but thirty years later, one of the bobby-soxers, Martha Weinman Lear, described the sociologists as yo-yos, and wrote that "Whatever he stirred beneath our barely budding breasts, it wasn't motherly...the thing we had going with Frankie was *sexy*. It was exciting. It was terrific." In mid-1943, when he made his second appearance at the Paramount, some of the girls threw their underwear on the stage, a fact that was not widely reported in family newspapers. Writing in the *New York Times* in 1974, Lear recalled how the girls would have swooning parties at home, practicing how to faint; and she also remembered that the boys at school knew that Frankie was sexier than they were, "and that was why none of them liked him, none except the phrasing aficionados." There were young men who resented Sinatra, but there were others who knew a good singer when they heard one. There were those who wanted to know why Sinatra was not in uniform—there was a war on, after all—but he was finally classified 4-F because of his punctured eardrum, and Evans got Frank as many gigs as he could singing at war-bond rallies. Manie Sacks had got his boss, Bill Paley, to give Sinatra his own sustaining program (available cheaply to all the network's affiliated local stations to help fill up their schedules); he was paid $150 a week for *Songs by Sinatra*, and the response was good. The nation's chart show from 1935 (until 1959) was *Your Hit Parade*, sponsored weekly by Lucky Strike cigarettes; Frank joined that program in February 1943 and became its star.

But while Evans was busy authorizing Sinatra fan clubs all over the country, and arranging accidental meetings in the street with hysterical fans and cameramen, or organizing "Why I Like Frank Sinatra" contests, there was the very real worry about whether

Sinatra appealed to adults as he did to young people. So in April he made his first solo nightclub appearance at the Riobamba in New York, where teenagers could not get in. Once again he was billed as an "extra added attraction," and once again he took the place over for an extended engagement: the grownups may not have swooned, but they liked the way he sang the songs. Top of the bill had been a veteran master of ceremonies, Walter O'Keefe; when his engagement ended on April 9, O'Keefe announced from the stage that "a steam roller came along and knocked me flat. Ladies and gentlemen, I give you the real star...Frank Sinatra!" Paul Ross, an editor at *Billboard*, wrote a piece that was such a rave that his boss accused him of having been drunk. He dragged the boss to the Riobamba, and the next day the boss ordered larger headlines on the story.

That year Sinatra sang with symphony orchestras, raising money for them at a time when the war had hurt their box-office takings; in August he sang with the Los Angeles Philharmonic Orchestra at the Hollywood Bowl, a gig that was considered controversial: why should the "long-hair" classical musicians and venues make room for a pop singer? But again he was successful (though a soldier in uniform was heard to say, "I hope they won't forget to flush the Bowl"). In the autumn he sang at the Waldorf-Astoria in New York City, then one of the most famous hotels in the world, and made friends with society hostess and columnist Elsa Maxwell, an arbiter of manners who until then had disapproved of him. It seemed that he couldn't do anything wrong; he worked hard, and the money kept getting better and better: $2,800 a week for the radio program alone.

And more and more of the musicians were impressed. With Stordahl doing his arrangements, he worked with the very good dance band of Russian-born violinist Jan Savitt in 1943, and another fiddler in the band, John Garvey, later on the faculty at the University of Illinois, remembered his professionalism.

The musicians were skeptical until one day, at rehearsal, Sinatra and the orchestra were handed a new song. Sinatra just stood there with the lead sheet in one hand, the other hand cupping his ear, following along silently while the orchestra read through the Stordahl chart. A second time through he sang it in half-voice. The third time through he took over. We all knew then that we had an extraordinary intuitive musician on our hands.

But the music business keeps changing. During the early 1940s it was partly the war; rationing, conscription and many other factors made it difficult to keep a big band on the road, and later, after the war, the musicians' wages were too high, many of the dance halls had closed, and all the returning soldiers would be starting families and staying home to watch television. The Big Band Era seemed to be over as suddenly as it had begun, and just at this point, when modern jazz or "bebop" was being invented, when the vocalists were taking over from the bands, and when soldiers black and white, north and south, were listening to each other's music, many for the first time, there were very few records being made of all this transition, because the musicians were on strike against the record companies.

Union boss James Caesar Petrillo was a combative little man who liked behaving like a gangster, just as in Chicago his Local 10 of the American Federation of Musicians had been a violent and racist one. Petrillo was elected leader of the national union, and thought "canned music" was a problem, ordering the record companies to forbid records to be played over the radio. But the record companies had already tried that, and even the Supreme Court had ruled (foolishly) that copyright was not infringed by playing a record on the radio. The bandleaders didn't want a strike, because they knew that records were good for business; a committee appointed by Petrillo himself had investigated the problem and recommended against industrial action. But Petrillo ordered a strike anyway. It lasted two years while everybody lost money, and it was a nail in the coffin of the Swing Era, because vocalists (looked down upon by musicians) were not allowed to belong to the union, and soon began making records without any musicians.

In those days records were not as big a part of the business as they are now; live music was far more important. Nevertheless, the fact that for two years the fans could buy new records by the singers, but not by the bands, accelerated a phenomenon that was already under way. During the Swing Era the emphasis was on the bands: when you heard a record or a live performance on the radio you were listening to a tune chosen by the bandleader, and arranged by somebody who was effectively a composer, who knew what a sheet of music paper looked like and what to do with it. The singer, if there was one, was a member of the band. But soon, especially with increasing prosperity, fans would go to the record shop and buy the latest release by their favorite singer, no matter what the song was, no matter who had arranged it or produced the record, and the arrangement was meant to be a setting for the star, played not by a working band but by a bunch of studio musicians on salary. Not only did the fans get less musical value for money, but the power to decide what they heard on the radio and on the jukebox was passing from the bandleaders and the music publishers to the deejays and the A&R men at the record companies.

At the beginning of this process of dumbing-down the listeners, Bing Crosby and Dick Haymes (both on Decca, where the boss was Jack Kapp, who never missed a trick) made records *a cappella*, backed by vocal groups, with no musicians at all. There were a lot of singers around; everybody made V-disks (for "Victory"), available only to GI jukeboxes, and often dubbed from radio broadcasts; one of Sinatra's was a novelty about the competition, "Dick Haymes, Dick Todd and Como" ("I'll soon become a wreck / They're breathin' on my neck"). Todd was a Canadian baritone who did not stay the course, but all the singers got a boost during the strike at the expense of the musicians they had always worked with.

Sinatra stayed out of the recording studio for nearly a year; as a good Democrat from a working-class family, he probably didn't want to cross the picket line. But the strike went on too long, the federal government's labor-relations department unable to make Petrillo behave himself. And meanwhile the record companies were reissuing older material: Columbia pressed up "All or Nothing at All" with a new label, as "Frank Sinatra with Harry James and his Orchestra." Recorded in September 1939 and first released in July 1940, in June 1943 it began to sell a million (and became another Sinatra performance to be sent up in a Warner Brothers cartoon). In July Sinatra recorded the first of nine tunes backed only by the Bobby Tucker Singers, seven of which charted in *Billboard*. In early 1944, three more of the old records with Harry James charted on Columbia, and Victor reissued the January 1942 recording of "Night and Day" with Axel Stordahl (this time on the full-price RCA label), which was a hit for the second time.

The *a cappella* records with the Bobby Tucker Singers make interesting listening today; they are beautifully sung, Sinatra superbly confident, his terminal vibrato sweet without cloying; he sounded like all the other boy singers, but he was first among equals, a boy singer but also a grownup. "Close to You" had words by Al Hoffman and Jerry Livingston, for decades two of the most successful of Tin Pan Alley hacks, and was published by Sinatra's Barton Music Corporation. There were two songs from *Oklahoma!*, a smash hit that was revolutionizing Broadway; they had an operetta flavor, but also revealed Sinatra's dramatic side. The biggest hit was "I Couldn't Sleep a Wink Last Night," while "A Lovely Way to Spend an Evening" was from Sinatra's first starring film role, in *Higher and Higher*. (Like Crosby in his first film over a decade earlier, and Elvis Presley over a decade later, he played a singer coping with stardom.)

The second Sinatra frenzy at the Paramount Theater occurred just when "All or Nothing at All" was hitting the charts in mid-1943; the *a cappella* records were all made in the following six months, and then there was a hiatus in his recording for a year. When he came back to the Paramount on October 12, 1944, for three weeks, 3,600 fans in the theater wanted to sit through all five shows, while Times Square outside was jammed with 30,000 fans who couldn't get in: traffic was stopped, windows were broken and literally hundreds of police personnel got overtime pay during what came to be known as the Columbus Day Riot.

The engagement was marked by visits backstage by friends old and new; Marion Schreiber came by to see her old friend. Fred Tamburro stopped in to ask Sinatra to lend him money so he could buy a tavern, and Sinatra turned him down. Apparently Tamby was still there when Buddy Rich turned up and told Sinatra that he wanted to start his own band; on the spot Sinatra offered to lend Rich money to get started, and Tamburro lost his temper and had to be prevented from physically assaulting Sinatra. Many years later he complained about what a poor friend Sinatra had turned out to be, and here perhaps is one of the keys to Sinatra's difficult behavior: Tamburro was the sort of fellow who thumped Sinatra when he, Tamburro, seemed to be the boss, and who later wanted to be treated as though he deserved a favor when Sinatra was doing well. Similarly, Harry James was the sort of boss who would not stand in the way of an ambitious young talent, while Tommy Dorsey wanted to keep his claws in deep. Perhaps it is no wonder the quality of Sinatra's mercy was often strained.

Finally in November Petrillo's strike was over, and Stordahl and Sinatra could do their jobs properly, starting with four recording sessions at the end of 1944; Sinatra's first studio session on Columbia with Stordahl yielded a *Billboard* hit with "White Christmas" (the first version to rival Crosby's perennial 1942 hit), backed with "If You Are But a Dream," words written to a classical tune by Anton Rubinstein (and again with an operetta feeling). "There's No You," by Tom Adair and Hal Hopper, gave rise to more "skinny Sinatra" jokes; and "Saturday Night (Is the Loneliest Night in the Week)" was written by Jule Styne and Sammy Cahn, two of Sinatra's pals. The next session included "I Dream of You (More Than You Dream I Do)" by Marjorie Goetschius and Edna Osser, and three more Styne-Cahn tunes: "I Begged Her," "I Fall In Love Too Easily," and "What Makes the Sunset" were all from Sinatra's new movie, a musical extravaganza: *Anchors Aweigh* co-starred Gene Kelly, who taught Sinatra to dance, and was one of the biggest film hits of the year.

"Saturday Night" and "I Dream of You" were issued back-to-back; the second record from these sessions to hit the charts, and provide a paradigm of what was happening to popular music. "Saturday Night" is a memorable pop song and a likeable record, but it is merely slick and competent. Something is missing: the soul, the spirit of the Swing Era (the essence of jazz, perhaps), is replaced by the dead hand of the studio. Stordahl was a good arranger, but this type of tune was not his forte, requiring more jazz feeling; the band was a crack team of musicians, but they did not play together every night, like the Dorsey band, sharing rooms on the road and listening to each other at every gig until they breathed together. Sinatra even sounds a trifle hesitant (though his phrasing is always wonderful: when he begins the second chorus with "But Saturday…" the slight hesitation on "but," so that he has to catch up on the next syllable, is magic. That was exactly the sort of thing that drove the fans wild).

"I Dream of You" is completely different, one of the first examples of the sort of pop record that would be regarded many years later as most typical of its decade. With the victory in the Second World War in sight, it seemed to have become an American century: we were sorting out the rest of the world for the second time and rebuilding our own industry into the bargain, at a fraction of the casualties suffered by other nations; soon to create a television industry, making more and more films in color, adopting the latest technology in every area, the sky was the limit when it came to the superficial sophistication of Manhattan towers and fashionable snap-brim hats for men. Our parents thought that everything would just get better and better: the McDonald brothers would open their first hamburger restaurant in San Bernardino in 1949, and in 1951–52 NBC-TV would become the single most valuable advertising medium in the country, with all its prime time sold even before the season began. Business was good, and our pop music reflected a childlike optimism "I Dream of You (More Than You Dream I Do)" sounds like a silly title, but again, the song is a good marriage of words and melody, and the sheer innocence in the song and in Sinatra's delivery is hard to resist, and the lavish sound of what amounted to a symphony orchestra seemed impressive at the time: if a big band was good, a full-sized orchestra must be better. No pretense at jazz feeling or danceability is made on "I Dream of You"; the writing for the lower strings is straight out of Debussy's *La Mer* (c. 1905), and none the worse for that. Coming from Frank Sinatra and Axel Stordahl in 1943, it was a better than average example of the kind of music the nation was going to hear a lot of.

"I Begged Her" is another uptempo number, probably arranged by George Siravo, who was better at this type of number than Stordahl; the singer sounds more at ease, but the ultimate ease found on the best records by the working swing bands is still not there, and a string section including a harp is no substitute. A striking thing about the pop records of the 1940s is the absolute distinction between swingers and ballads, as though it never occurred to an arranger that a ballad could swing; and the ballad style of Stordahl-Sinatra was where the future of pop seemed to lay.

Stordahl was one of the nicest people in the music business, putting up with Sinatra's temper tantrums with complete unflappability, and he was also good at his job, which was supporting Frank Sinatra; but the next ten years would hear a lot of Stordahl-Sinatra arrangements, and they began to have a sameness about them. It could be that Stordahl simply did not have as much musical personality as Paul Weston, or as much skill at writing a countermelody as Percy Faith; on the other hand, the arrangements were limited by the three-minute length of a ten-inch 78: recording technology would soon increase by leaps and bounds, which would make a difference. And perhaps it took a whole generation of musicians awhile to get used to working in a studio rather than on the bandstand. Arranger-conductors such as Nat Shilkret, Al Goodman, André Kostelanetz, David Rose and others had recorded pop songs in a symphonic style, but with the Stordahl-Sinatra sessions of the 1940s that style came into its own, and the stage was set for Weston, Faith, Gordon Jenkins, Robert Farnon and several more to make a new kind of pop history.

Not many people ever heard this kind of music live, except on the radio, because the studio orchestras did not, could not, tour the country the way the dance bands had; it was now studio-bound music. This was an ominous development in the history of technology versus musical values, but among the compensations at the time was that the best musicians in town were on tap. When Sinatra and Stordahl relocated to the West Coast, Stordahl's concertmaster was violinist Felix Slatkin, one of the best in the business. Many years later, talking about the golden age of studio pop, Paul Weston recalled that in the 1950s his fiddle section consisted of the first violinists of all the best orchestras on the West Coast, to say nothing of the Swing Era veterans who were working in the reed and brass sections of the Hollywood studio orchestras: as an arranger who was about to hear his own work recorded, Weston could hardly wait to get to the studio. The best arrangers could provide a setting for a song and singer that could be admirable in itself without distracting attention from the star, but too often the result of large forces and lots of studio time (which became more and more expensive) was merely grandiose product. As in every kind of pop through the decades, the most successful were imitated by the second-rate.

The Sinatra session of December 3, 1944, included "The Charm of You," another Styne-Cahn song from *Anchors Aweigh*, while "Ol' Man River" and "Stormy Weather" were big production numbers cut on twelve-inch 78s: in the band were Ernie Caceres and Hymie Shertzer in the reed section, Billy Butterfield in the trumpet section and Johnny Blowers on drums, all veterans of the Swing Era. But the next two sessions resulted in eight standards, as though Manie Sacks, Sinatra and Stordahl were already thinking in terms of an album, whether they knew it or not. A storage album with Sinatra's picture on it was issued in 1945, for the fans to keep their 78s in, but albums with records already in them were still such a small part of the market that the *Billboard* album chart was established only that year.

The British musician and journalist Benny Green has made the point that Sinatra was not simply the successor to Al Jolson and Bing Crosby, "but the culminating point in an evolutionary process which has refined the art of interpreting words set to music. Nor is there even the remotest possibility that he will have a successor. Sinatra was the result of . . . a set of historical circumstances which can never be repeated." This needs a caveat: we are talking about pop singing here, not Schubert's *Die Winterreise*. But within certain limits Green is right. The songs, as much as we like them, are about sexual desire in disguise, a modern misconception of romantic love, not about life and death or the nature of existence. But they are enduringly popular around the world, and if the type of songs Sinatra championed can never be written again, Sinatra himself is similarly unique. His successors have been Jack Jones, Vic Damone, Steve Lawrence, Julius LaRosa and so on, good voices all; perhaps Tony Bennett is almost Sinatra's equal as a saloon singer. All of them would admit that they could not supersede Sinatra, but only compete with him. In the future there would be other equally fine but completely different troubadors, many of them writing their own songs; but there could never be another Sinatra, because the so-called golden age of American songwriting and the Swing Era which popularized the standards were both historical flukes.

Before the Second World War the concept of the "standard" did not exist. A new Irving Berlin or Cole Porter song was simply a new pop song; nobody knew that some of them would still be loved decades later, let alone which ones. Sinatra did as much as anyone to choose the songs which we now regard as standards, beginning in the 1940s. In fact, two songs from the sessions of late 1944 and early 1945, "She's Funny That Way" and "When Your Lover Has Gone," from 1928 and 1931 respectively, might have been forgotten, except that Sinatra liked them and kept singing them; and with his phrasing he resuscitated a 1901 chestnut, "Mighty Lak' a Rose." The authors of these remained obscure, except for Richard Whiting, co-writer of "Funny"; the rest of the songs from these sessions were by the likes of the Gershwins, Rodgers and Hart, and Jerome Kern, and Sinatra fans could allow their songs to be chosen for them with some confidence. The singer and the songs were coming together.

Sinatra recording sessions in March and May 1945 were a more typical mixed bag, including "I Should Care," a lovely song co-written by Cahn, Stordahl and Weston, and Johnny Mercer's "Dream (When You're Feeling Blue)"; with Stordahl's orchestra and the Ken Lane Singers, "Dream" almost harks back to the huge success of "I'll Never Smile Again," speaking of which, "Put Your Dreams Away (For Another Day)" was also written by Ruth Lowe: it was Sinatra's closing theme on the radio, published by Sinatra's company. Others were two hits from Rodgers and Hammerstein's new show *Carousel* and a version of "Over the Rainbow." Unusual sessions in May included four tracks with a black gospel group, the Charioteers, accompanied only by a small proto-jazz sextet; two of these were spirituals and two pop tunes, one of which charted briefly, and none of them were reissued in any format for nearly fifty years.

Too often Sinatra's studio experiments seem to have been thrown away, like another two tracks from May, with a thirty-two-piece orchestra arranged and conducted by Xavier Cugat. Born in Spain in 1900, Cugat grew up in Cuba and later invented the kind of watered-down Latin American style that was thought to be sophisticated in downtown New York. "Stars in Your Eyes" (a Mexican song called "Mar" with English words) and Cugat's own "My Shawl" are good tunes, but the slushy arrangements throw away their rhythmic essence, and Sinatra does not sound very involved.

But the second half of the year found Sinatra and friends consistently ahead of the pack. Songs for his children included "Nancy (With the Laughin' Face)," written by Phil Silvers and Jimmy Van Heusen. They had presented the song to Sinatra to mark Little Nancy's fourth birthday; a studio recording was made that remained unreleased, but a V-disk version was much liked by the troops as a song about what they were fighting for, so a new studio recording was released and became a top-ten hit. More standards included "The Moon Was Yellow" and "I Only Have Eyes for You"; there was a beautiful "Day by Day," written like "I Should Care" by Stordahl, Weston and Cahn; and "Oh! What It Seemed to Be," from pianist-bandleader Frankie Carle, was Frank's first number-one *Billboard* hit made under his own name, at the top for eight weeks. He must have been ecstatic.

And there were recording sessions with one of America's most interesting musicians. Alec Wilder (1907–80) was an eccentric, a loner who lived in a hotel and liked traveling on trains. He was a first-rate musician who was too long-hair for the jazz musicians and too lightweight for the classical world; he would have found a niche in Europe, but in the U.S.A. fame and fortune require a commercial pigeonhole. He wrote wonderful songs; "I'll Be Around" is the best known, but a great many others are loved by singers, and words are still being written to his tunes. It was Wilder who arranged the first nine *a cappella* Sinatra sides for Columbia, with the Bobby Tucker Singers. He also wrote, in 1972, a definitive book about what we now call standards: in *American Popular Song: The Great Innovators 1900–1950*, the craftsman examined the work he most admired, too modest to include any of his own.

Wilder's old schoolfriends included Mitch Miller, a world-class soloist on oboe and English horn who was also becoming a record producer in the 1940s, and Goddard Lieberson, who later came from the classical division at Columbia Records to be president of the whole company. For a Sinatra session in November 1945 Wilder arranged his own "Just an Old Stone House" and Willard Robison's "The Old School Teacher," a couple of sentimental, almost countrified tunes. Miller conducted the arrangements, which bristled with woodwinds, French horn, and so on, like chamber music: Wilder sounds a bit like an American impressionist. The musicians probably included Miller, Julius Baker on flute and Harold Goltzer on bassoon; Baker, for example, was then principal flute of CBS Radio's symphony orchestra, and eventually filled that role in the New York Philharmonic. Neither of these tracks was worth anything in the marketplace, one of them not even released at the time.

Meanwhile, Sinatra amused himself backstage at various gigs with a portable record player, and among the things he had come across were off-the-air recordings of two of Wilder's instrumental pieces. He liked them, but Manie Sacks did not intend to record them commercially, so Sinatra insisted on conducting them for a recording session, thus lending his name to Wilder's music, which most of his fans wouldn't care a fig about. He had never conducted and was not good at reading music, but he memorized six of Wilder's pieces and he knew how he wanted them to sound: in December 1945 he recorded four "Airs" for solo instruments, a "Slow Dance" and a "Theme and Variations": for six sides of three twelve-inch records, he conducted a chamber orchestra with soloists and a harpsichord. Some of the musicians were skeptical at first, but he won them over; the records have never made much money, but they are still winning listeners fifty years later.

As if that wasn't unusual enough, Sinatra and friends made still more history in the second half of 1945. In two sessions, one in July and one in December, Sinatra and Stordahl recorded eight more standards, this time for an honest-to-gosh album.

Albums were rare in those days because they were expensive: an album was several 78s in a cardboard holder (the album) for which the buyer usually had to pay extra. But *The Voice* was not only his first album, it was virtually the first concept album. To be

Left The Harry James band played Atlantic City in the summer of 1939; in the front row here are Connie Haines, James and Frank Sinatra. This was Frank's first big break; Harry and Frank were both young, skinny, ambitious and struggling. Connie later followed Frank to the Tommy Dorsey band, but they didn't get along; she became a popular vocalist too, but in a more extrovert style. (Frank Driggs Collection)

Below Trombonist Tommy Dorsey (left) was already one of the most successful bandleaders of the era when he hired drummer Buddy Rich, arranger Sy Oliver, the Pied Pipers and Frank Sinatra, all in late 1939 and early 1940. Jo Stafford of the Pipers and Frank are on each side of the microphone; Jo was a superb singer who later said of Frank, 'He didn't sound like anybody I'd heard before. And he was sensational.'
(Frank Driggs Collection)

Above Frank left the Dorsey band and
went solo during a musicians' strike
against the record companies; he couldn't
make records, but his public appearances
soon caused pandemonium. Here he is
clowning with Benny Goodman in 1943;
Goodman actually sang on a couple of
his own records, but they were not in
direct competition: Frank couldn't play
a note. *(Corbis/Bettmann/UPI)*

Right Frank made news when he
opened at the Paramount Theater
with Goodman and the bobbysoxers
screamed, but nobody knew whether
he could attract a wider audience.
It was this engagement at New
York's Riobamba club in April 1943
that clinched it: kids couldn't get in,
but the grownups packed the place. His
art appealed to song-lovers of all ages.
(Frank Driggs Collection)

Linton Weil's

Riobamba
151 E. 57th ST.
WALTER O'KEEFE
SHEILA BARRETT
SPECIALLY ADDED
First Cafe Appearance
FRANK SINATRA
His voice has thrilled millions
Russell Patterson's
Magazine Cover Girls
BRANDWYNNE'S MUSIC
CHAVEZ and His
Rhumbas

Complete Revue
for DINNER at 8
Then at 12 and 2:30 A.M.
Res: Fred Chiaventone
PLaza 8-1960

Bing Crosby had been Frank's idol since childhood; Crosby continued having more hit records than Frank during the 1940s, but his style was being superceded. They sang together several times, as here on the radio in 1945; Crosby said, 'Frank Sinatra is the kind of singer who comes along once in a lifetime – but why did it have to be my lifetime?' *(Frank Driggs Collection)*

Above Frank's Columbia records inaugurated a new era in pop; here they were recording 'Laura' in 1947 at Liederkranz Hall in New York, a legendary recording venue in that golden age. Frank always loved musicians and got along well with them; the tall bald fellow is arranger/ conductor Axel Stordahl, Frank's main man during this period. *(Redferns)*

Below Frank won jazz magazine polls too; in December 1946 he recorded 'Sweet Lorraine' with the Metronome All Stars. Nat Cole (on the right) was then famous as a pianist leading a trio; on this date he played piano and sang 'Nat Meets June' with June Christy. The guitarist on the left is Bob Ahern. *(Frank Driggs Collection)*

Above At a recording session, the boys in the control booth are (left to right) Frank's press agent George Evans, A&R producer Bill Richards, Frank, and recording engineer Harold Chapman. Note the fish-eye Evans is giving Frank: his hands were full keeping his most famous client out of trouble. *(Frank Driggs Collection)*

Below Making the pro-tolerance short film *The House I Live In* in 1944. Frank came from a generation that loved ethnic jokes that would be considered offensive today, but he always hated racial and ethnic intolerance. The picture was written by Albert Maltz, who was later blacklisted during the McCarthy era, and won a special Oscar for director Mervyn LeRoy. *(Frank Driggs Collection)*

Above By 1948 Perry Como (a former barber) was hot competition, with several hit records every year, but Frank never minded competing with real talent. Here they are clowning in the MGM studio barber shop; no photos exist of Frank's tonsorial results. *(Corbis/Bettmann/UPI)*

Main picture Frank admitted that the hardest work Gene Kelly ever did was probably teaching him to dance. *Take Me Out To The Ball Game* (1948) was the least successful of the pictures they did together, and it was still a delight. *(Kobal Collection)*

The tempestuous love affair and brief marriage of Frank Sinatra and Ava Gardner was one of the biggest gossip-column stories Hollywood ever had. They were well matched: strong personalities who didn't take any nonsense, they both liked to drink and smoke and stay up late. In fact they were so evenly matched that their love ended in a draw, but Frank was never the same again. *(London Features)*

fair, the Liberty Music Shop had made concept-type recording sessions with the excellent Lee Wiley singing first-rate songs (virtually a Gershwin songbook, for example) and backed by all-star groups of jazzmen, as early as 1939. That was a labor of love; there was no money in it, and major labels were content to sell "singles." But eight superb love songs by Sinatra were irresistible. "Someone to Watch Over Me," "You Go to My Head," "These Foolish Things (Remind Me of You)," "I Don't Know Why (I Just Do)," "(I Don't Stand) A Ghost of a Chance," "Why Shouldn't I?," "Try a Little Tenderness," and "Paradise" were made with just nine musicians: four strings and a rhythm section, and a flute on the first four and Miller on oboe for the rest. The guitar (George Van Eps on the first four) played a prominent role, adding to the sound rather than simply strumming away in the background, and Stordahl's writing for the string quartet was a chance to be less slushy: the harmonies were more exposed than usual, so more affecting. The result was not just a set of several 78s, but an album in a more modern sense. The *Billboard* album chart had been established early in 1945, and Sinatra's first album was number one barely a year later, the first of seventy-four hit albums including *Duets II* in 1995. (The total number of chart albums includes compilations and reissues, but no other recording artist has continued charting with *new* albums for half a century.)

Early in 1945 Sinatra had parted with radio's *Your Hit Parade*. The president of the American Tobacco Company, George Washington Hill, had a $20 million advertising budget which was important to the network, so he usually got his way (he was later immortalized in a novel called *The Hucksters*); but Sinatra had moved his family to the West Coast from Hasbrouck Heights in New Jersey, and Hill refused to pay for the cost of musicians, studio time and telephone lines so that Sinatra could broadcast from California. There was no question of Hill moving the show to the West Coast, because this eccentric millionaire, who didn't really like any song later than 1910 anyway, wanted to supervise the show himself. He wanted the arrangements to resemble jolly marches; he thought Sinatra slowed it down too much and he also didn't like the way Sinatra entertained the live broadcast audience between songs: Hill wanted to get his money's worth by making the audience listen to the cigarette commercials. So Sinatra got a release from the contract with Hill, and in September 1945 began two seasons of half-hour *Songs by Sinatra*, sponsored by Old Gold cigarettes, who were willing to broadcast him from wherever he happened to be each week. This was one of his best broadcasting experiences, for he was able to do as he pleased, as well as using Stordahl and the Pied Pipers (June Hutton, who soon became Mrs. Stordahl, had replaced Jo Stafford in the group). In one October program, his guest was Tommy Dorsey, and the broadcast went like this:

> *Sinatra*: My old boss! Hadn't seen him since '43! Would he speak to me? I said to myself; would he be glad to see me? I just had to find out. So I ups to him and I says, "Hi Tommy!" And gee, he was so sweet! Why, he turned to me and said,
> *Dorsey*: "I knew you'd come crawlin' back one of these days...!"

In fact, 1945 had been a very good year indeed, and Sinatra had no need to crawl anywhere, but the joke was still a good one.

Sinatra's first period of stardom was now reaching a plateau. In the next two years, 1946 and 1947, he often sounds more like Crosby than he ever did in the earliest years; the singing is never less than good, the phrasing always thoughtful and often uniquely so; yet sometimes he is crooning. Along with his radio work, films and everything else, in these two years he recorded no fewer than 124 studio tracks, not counting alternative takes, which would have been enough for a dozen twelve-inch LPs, if they had been available at the time. Sinatra was never afraid of work, but this was too much recording.

Apart from a handful of Christmas songs, there are a few artsy numbers like "Where Is My Bess?" (George Gershwin), "Lost in the Stars" (Kurt Weill), and "Soliloquy," from Rodgers and Hammerstein's *Carousel*, which is nearly eight minutes long and used two twelve-inch sides. "Soliloquy" is a partly speech-song piece about being a father; Sinatra wanted to record it precisely because it was artsy, and did a perfectly good job of it. But then there was "The Dum-Dot Song." Columbia, by 1945 again becoming the biggest record label in the U.S.A., had to have a full product line, and most artists had to record the occasional children's song (Brahms's "Lullaby," called "Cradle Song," was on the other side of "Nancy"). "Denny inna dum dot" meant "penny in the gum slot," but children's records should be childlike, not some hack's idea of childish; one is embarrassed to note that "Dum" was published by Sinatra Songs.

Sinatra may have been a sensation, but Bing Crosby was still the bigger star. Crosby recorded every kind of song there was, from phony Irish and Hawaiian songs to "San Fernando Valley" (from a Roy Rogers movie); in mid-1945 he had a hit with Xavier Cugat. Sinatra not only recorded with Cugat but threw in "Home on the Range," believe it or not, as well as the maudlin "I'm Sorry I Made You Cry," from 1918, while "I Want to Thank Your Folks" wasn't much better, and "I Have But One Heart (O Marenariello)" was sung in both English and Italian. Crosby was very good with money and fast becoming very rich; no doubt it was the aspiring businessman in Sinatra who sang too many songs published by his own company: in early 1946 he recorded his own mushy turkey called "From This Day Forward," exceeded in its embarrassment quotient only by "Something Old, Something New," another Barton song from the same session, in which we are to imagine a horny bridegroom singing about the contents of the honeymoon suitcase. "None But the Lonely Heart" is an early Tchaikovsky song, from Opus 6; nearly everyone seems to have recorded it, although it repeatedly failed to reach the hit parade. Just to make sure we knew it was Tchaikovsky, Stordahl's arrangement absurdly threw in a bleeding chunk of the Sixth Symphony, from sixty-eight opuses later.

Of course there are better records, too, from 1946–47: "How Cute Can You Be" and "Could Ja?" are not bad pop songs, and Barton songs at that, the latter title reminiscent of "Wouldja for a Big Red Apple," one of Johnny Mercer's first songs. "Five Minutes More" was a Styne-Cahn song and Sinatra's second number-one hit; "Mam'selle" was a film song and his third number-one, in 1947. There were a lot of standards, new and old: "Blue Skies," "Always," "Among My Souvenirs" and "Why Was I Born?" from the 1920s, as well as "Begin the Beguine," "September Song," "That Old Black Magic," "I Concentrate on

You," "Stella by Starlight," "Almost Like Being in Love," "Falling in Love With Love," "They Say It's Wonderful," "If I Had You," "That Old Feeling," "The Nearness of You," and more. "My Romance" and "Tea for Two" were duets with Dinah Shore, and a marvelous "All of Me" was arranged by Siravo. "Ain'tcha Ever Comin' Back" was another Weston-Stordahl song, "Where Is the One" at the very end of 1947 was a wonderful Alec Wilder song, and there were a bunch of new offerings from Styne and Cahn: "The Things We Did Last Summer," "Guess I'll Hang My Tears Out to Dry," and two of their best, from the film *It Happened in Brooklyn*, "It's the Same Old Dream" and "Time After Time."

One of the things that made "Five Minutes More" a Sinatra hit was its intimacy: it was recorded with only ten men. Sinatra fans are permanently disappointed that he did not make more small-group recordings. In December 1946 he made two tracks with the Page Cavanaugh Trio, just piano, bass and guitar, like the Nat Cole Trio, and they blew it. The setting should have been perfect, but the songs were badly chosen; "You Can Take My Word for It, Baby" and "That's How Much I Love You" are little more than novelties, and the latter speeds up the tempo after about two minutes as though they can hardly wait to get it over with. That year he won both the *down beat* and the *Metronome* polls in the male singer category, and the day after the Cavanaugh session he made "Sweet Lorraine" with the Metronome All Stars: Frank Sinatra singing with nine pieces that included Charlie Shavers on trumpet, Coleman Hawkins on tenor sax and no fewer than three stars from the Ellington band is almost more pleasure than a Sinatra fan can take, but there was only the one track. In late 1947 there was "It All Came True" with an eight-piece group, Alvy West and the Little Band, not a very interesting arrangement, and again only the one track. "A Little Learnin' Is a Dangerous Thing" at the end of the year was a two-sided duet with Pearl Bailey and a septet with the great Billy Kyle on piano, but the record was just a novelty, too long and full of corny wisecracks. In late 1948 and early 1949 there were four tracks with the Phil Moore Four, actually a quintet: Cole Porter's "Why Can't You Behave?"; "Bop! Goes My Heart," co-written by Jule Styne; Burke and Van Heusen's "If You

Stub Your Toe on the Moon" (a Crosby hit); and "Kisses and Tears," by Styne and Cahn. The results were fine, with Moore's piano and Robert Bain's guitar sometimes playing in unison, and clarinet obbligato from Marshall Royal; but the easygoing jazz-flavored records were probably not commercial and not played much on the radio. And the object was to have hit records, difficult in a market that was changing.

Frank Sinatra was not really in charge of his life or his career, and he was heading for a logjam, for a number of reasons—perhaps again, broadly speaking, because he was always in the middle of everything. It wasn't just the music business that was changing, but the whole culture. The other Styne-Cahn songs from *It Happened in Brooklyn* are a case in point—"I Believe" and especially "The Brooklyn Bridge." "I Believe" is an uptempo number about believing that wishes come true; and both tracks, by the way, are very well played, as though the musicians were learning how to relax in the studio, so that the message of the lyrics is easy to take, and Sinatra seems to swing with extra ease.

When the Brooklyn Bridge was completed in 1883, it was the largest suspension bridge ever built, and the whole world had been following its progress for years: a span of nearly 1,600 feet was held up by four main cables of wire rope which had been spun on the site. It was not only an engineering marvel, but was seen as a symbol of human progress, a modern work of art and a cultural icon. Over sixty years later Jule Styne and Sammy Cahn wrote

Like the folks you meet on,
Like to plant my feet on
The Brooklyn Bridge.

What a lovely view from,
Heaven looks at you from
The Brooklyn Bridge.

Sinatra sings about the wind in her strings, the clouds in her hair; and "If you've been a rover / Journey's end lies over / The Brooklyn Bridge." Styne, Cahn and Sinatra were three talented men in their prime and at the top of their professions, and they shared a number of things: Styne was the oldest, born in London in 1905, educated in Chicago and soon working in New York; Cahn was actually born in New York, in 1913—they were both Jewish—and Sinatra was also big city, East Coast, and a member of a minority group, an Italian Catholic. They all believed in the kind of progress symbolized by the Brooklyn Bridge without even thinking about it. They would have taken for granted that the journey's end of the bridge was the Manhattan end; they probably all made jokes about Cleveland, Ohio, while Bing Crosby came from a place much like Cleveland.

Everybody knew that Bing Crosby was an Irish Catholic, yet Crosby was not an outsider. He was the guy next door, from Spokane, Washington, in the far Northwest, as far from New York as you can get in the U.S.A.: when Crosby was born there, in 1904, Washington wasn't even famous for apples yet. Sinatra may have been the singing sensation of the 1940s, but, next to his three number-one *Billboard* hits in that decade, Crosby had five in 1944 alone: our popular culture is what we want to believe at a given time in our history, and America was still Crosby country. Of course Crosby was no bumpkin; during the later 1940s he was in the vanguard of tape recording for studio and broadcast work, not just because he had an interest in the Ampex Corporation or because tape's sound quality was better, but so he could prerecord his radio programs and get back to the golf course. Furthermore he was perhaps not a very nice fellow, but Crosby's folksy persona was the one America wanted, and the facts didn't matter. While Americans in general believed in the progress symbolized by the Brooklyn Bridge, somehow one cannot imagine Crosby, America's hero, singing a song about a big-city East Coast engineering marvel; Sinatra on the other hand would straddle the generations, beginning with brash optimism, then growing old less-than-gracefully in an era that would laugh at you if you suggested celebrating a bridge.

One difference was that Sinatra never bothered playing a role. Crosby kept his secrets until he dropped dead on a golf course, whereas whatever difficulties Sinatra was having were there for all to see.

In a sense the whole country was becoming studio-bound, and needed wise guys like Sinatra to struggle against the rising tide of conformity. Since 1900 many factors had tended to knit the country together: the infrastructure of the railroad, the telegraph and the postal service was already there, and then the cultural stuff—baseball's World Series, New York City's Tin Pan Alley (where all the hit songs came from), the cinema, and finally broadcasting—meant that Americans were all enchanted with the same artifacts. As these businesses grew bigger and more profitable, the executive types began to take over from the innovators, the mavericks and the artists themselves. Crosby could misbehave all he liked behind the scenes, while his interest was in making money; he would never remind us how the American dream was being compromised, but would ride the system while pretending to ignore it. On the business side, for example, while the cancer of suburban Los Angeles replaced groves of fruit trees, Crosby was one of the first into frozen orange juice. Sinatra by contrast would conduct his partying and his love affairs as he saw fit, daring anyone to disapprove, and he would kick against the system: if a studio boss was going to call the shots, then Sinatra would damn well sooner or later have to be the boss. For all his shortcomings, and whether he knew it or not, Sinatra was showing us what kind of country we lived in, if we wanted to see. In the late 1940s Sinatra had pushed his luck and his confidence as far as he could, spending money as fast as he earned it, making too many records, balling too many chicks, often behaving like a fool, and soon there was trouble in paradise.

Nancy Sinatra wrote in her first book about her father (in 1985), "If a person doesn't allow his dark side to surface, he's probably not in control of it." That is self-serving rubbish. Apart from the music, admittedly the only reason we have ever heard of him, few show-business figures have ever been less in control of themselves than Frank Sinatra; the endless stories about his childish behavior would be boring if it were not for the way he consistently ended up back on top. One of the keys to Frank Sinatra is that he could never keep his mouth shut. For example, after he had won over the audience at the Hollywood Bowl with the Los Angeles Philharmonic in August 1943, he said, "I understand there has been a controversy out here over whether I should appear at the Bowl at all. Those few people who thought I shouldn't, lost out in a very big way." A harmless-enough indulgence, perhaps, but this studied banality reveals his lack of education and his appalling judgement, as though he thought that all he had to do was open his mouth and everyone would listen. He was so successful in those years that the smart thing to do would have been to accept the success without any comment on it; but he could not even pretend to possess any humility, and success just made things worse. In 1944, tired and cranky during the filming of *Anchors Aweigh*, he yapped to a reporter:

> Pictures stink and most of the people in them do too. Hollywood won't believe I'm through, but they'll find out I mean it. It's a good thing not many of these jerks came up as rapidly as I did. If they had you couldn't get near them without running interference through three secretaries.

Apart from the fact that this rant does not appear to have any coherent meaning, these are the words of a spoiled brat, and it's not true that any publicity is good publicity. Sinatra repeatedly had to apologize for this sort of nonsense, causing press agent George Evans (and Jack Keller, Evans's partner on the West Coast) endless trouble. When Sinatra went on his first United Service Organization tour, after the war was over, he cared about entertaining the troops, and he won over the audiences by allowing himself to be a straight man for his friend Phil Silvers. But when it was over he needlessly and gratuitously insulted the military personnel who ran the USO, describing them as "shoemakers in uniform," throwing away the goodwill he had acquired on the tour.

And then there were the columnists. The dean of the gossips was Walter Winchell, but he and Sinatra never tangled, perhaps because they recognized each other: both had thin skins, both saw themselves as underdogs, and in those days they were on the same side politically, supporters of Franklin Roosevelt. The rest of the media reptiles, Hedda Hopper, Louella Parsons, Lee Mortimer, Westbrook Pegler and the others, were a lot of loud-mouthed trash, and could have been humored or even ignored, but at the time they had a lot of power because studio bosses were afraid of them, and Sinatra could not resist getting into trouble. He liked to send snotty telegrams: when Parsons printed stories about Sinatra's bad behavior on a film set, he sent her a long foolish telegram, whereupon he was twitted by another Hollywood columnist, Erskine Johnson, and walked into the trap, threatening Erskine that he would "see that you get a belt in your vicious and stupid mouth." While he provided the columnists with juicy tittle-tattle, the irony was that nobody could be more vicious and stupid than Sinatra; even his friends were afraid of his temper. But the gossip columnists were the sort of people who found others' lives more interesting than their own, and were basically cowards; they never picked on anybody with any influence. Sinatra was only a singer, they thought, never reckoning that in the end he was tougher and nastier than any of them.

Nowadays every half-baked pop star and bit player pronounces on the subject of politics, but it is well to remember that Sinatra was going out on a limb in 1944 when he revealed himself to be a Democrat and a supporter of Franklin Roosevelt. He even went to the White House to meet the president, and was as thrilled as a kid. Meanwhile, Pegler and most of the others were Republican sympathizers, prominent in the Right-wing newspaper empire of William Randolph Hearst; and the Right in those days was incredibly frustrated because it had not won a national election since 1928. The Democrats seemed to have the monopoly on all the decent values, so the Republicans stupidly allowed themselves to be left with the monopoly on bigotry, and there was no doubting Sinatra's hatred of that. He had made a short film, *The House I Live In*, in which he talked to some kids about tolerance and sang the title song (co-written by Lewis Allen, the same left-wing poet who wrote Billie Holiday's "Strange Fruit"). The film was shot in one day at RKO, and distributed free to cinemas; it was written by Albert Maltz, and won a special Oscar for director Mervyn LeRoy. Sinatra also toured high schools and community centers to talk to young people about tolerance, and, in the American political spectrum of the time, if he was opposed to racial and religious intolerance he must have been ipso facto pro-communist. Yet he seemed not to have any tolerance for himself: he caused an unnecessary fuss by skipping one of his anti-bigotry gigs to attend a boxing match. It was as though he could be at peace with himself only when he was actually singing; when the music stopped he needed to be in trouble or at the center of a fuss. And the fuss was accumulating.

A serious Sinatra problem was his choice of friends, and this was something that went straight to the heart of his identity as Dolly Sinatra's pride and joy. He had been surrounded by violence and corruption since he was a child; true, the violence was usually at one remove, and even when he himself threw a punch he would have several of his burly friends around to protect him if things went wrong. But his father and several of his relatives had been boxers, and the idea of violence, the proximity of it, was a thrill. He invested in the boxing career of one of his Varsity sidekicks, and for years he went to the Friday-night fights at Madison Square Garden every time he could; part of the attraction was being in the audience with the gangster types. And the corruption was a part of everyday life. The cancer in the body of the American dream was influence; influence was what Dolly Sinatra had acquired and peddled; it was influence that got Marty his job as a captain in the fire department, and that got Frank some of his earliest singing jobs.

Several generations of American families, driving from the Midwest to the East Coast, perhaps on their way to see some national monuments and to celebrate the land of the brave and home of the free, drove across a corner of New Jersey and noticed that that state's part of the national highway system was below the standard of the rest. The pavement had more cracks in it, grass grew in the cracks and the verges at the side of the road grew tall with weeds. Everybody knew that this was because a lot of the federal money that the state of New Jersey was supposed to be spending on its part of the highway system went into the pockets of criminals. Indeed, for a hundred years it is doubtful if any public-works project of any kind took place in the Tristate area (comprising parts of New York, New Jersey and Connecticut) without lining the pockets of crooked contractors and politicians. The same has been true in Chicago's Cook County, in Los Angeles and many other parts of the U.S., just as money for earthquake relief in southern Italy disappears into similar pockets in that country. It is a shame that Sinatra's understanding of "the house we all live in" did not extend to the true cost of corruption, but then corruption equals influence equals power, which is about all he had learned from his mother.

There was a time when a certain amount of corruption may have been necessary in the governing of American cities, because the aristocracy of previous generations might have allowed immigrants in the slums to die in the thousands of disease and starvation; but after a certain point the buying and selling of cops and public officials was institutionalized, or Americanized. This was during the unbelievable stupidity of Prohibition, the period of 1919–32 in which members of the species *Boobus americanus* (H. L. Mencken's phrase) tried to prevent each other from doing as they pleased in a so-called free country, and then needed to organize a trade in illegal booze: hence organized crime. Prohibition made it more fashionable to drink, and probably resulted in more alcoholism rather than less; it was followed in 1937 by another federal prohibition, of marijuana, the poor person's intoxicant, this time without consulting the voters, and leading more or less directly to today's horrendous drug problem, with still more violent criminals now running entire countries in Central America. Not only did the U.S.A. invent modern organized crime, but it has tolerated it, glamorized it, and even sentimentalized it ever since. When Prohibition was repealed at the end of 1933 the criminals found their way into labor unions and into every aspect of the entertainment and leisure industries, beginning with the cinema projectionists: in the early 1930s if you wanted to join a union the boss's goons might beat your head in; by the late 1940s if you didn't want to join a union, the union's goons beat your head in. This was progress in America.

Frank Sinatra was acquainted with criminal elements from an early age in New Jersey; there was the syphilitic Willie Moretti, and then the Fischetti family's youngest brother Joe. In early 1947 Sinatra's troubles began to multiply exponentially when he went to Miami and then to Cuba with Fischetti, and met Charles "Lucky" Luciano there, a top gangster who had gone to prison in 1936. Luciano was not so persona non grata that he had not been asked to help run Italy from his prison cell after Mussolini's downfall; the dictator had got the Sicilian criminals under control, and the first thing the Allies did was set them loose again. Luciano's reward for his help was probation, accompanied by deportation from the U.S.A., and some people suspected that he was to be allowed quietly back into the country. Sinatra in his foolish way had walked into a nest of hornets; then he flew on to Mexico City to meet his wife; and, after he had left Cuba, yet another right-wing columnist, Robert Ruark, who was also in Havana, realized that Luciano was there, and obligingly printed rumors of a Sinatra connection. In fact the unsubstantiated rumors came to the columnists from government sources, such as Harry Anslinger's narcotics bureau. Anslinger disliked Sinatra because he was in favor of tolerance and therefore a "pinko," and some of Sinatra's friends were musicians, some of whom must be marijuana smokers; Anslinger was such a crackpot that he eventually had to be removed from office. But the gossip columnists got away with all the finger-pointing they wanted to do, no matter how silly the story, no matter where the evidence came from.

Also early in 1947, Sinatra wrote to *The New Republic*, supporting Henry Wallace for president: Roosevelt's former vice president was mounting a left-wing challenge to President Truman, and people labeling themselves as "Progressives" were always suspect in American politics. The same year, Sinatra was named as a pinko in testimony to the House Un-American Activities Committee by Walter S. Steele, a right-wing stooge who also thought the Campfire Girls were "communistic."

It is by now well known that Sinatra has consorted with gangster types. He always liked to have his own circle of acolytes—the Varsity, the Rat Pack, the Clan, whatever—and if he admired mobsters because they were more powerful than he was, this was the legacy of his mother's values and politics, to say nothing of American history. And you did not get to be one of the biggest names in American show business, appearing in places where liquor is sold and later becoming the biggest headliner in Las Vegas itself, without associating with the kind of people who were allowed to run these places. It seems a bit hard to try to blame the dark side of the American way of life on a singer, but Sinatra remained his own worst enemy.

Columnist Lee Mortimer had been sniping at Sinatra for

months, describing his fans as morons, and then repeated the stories about Luciano. (Mortimer was receiving "unofficial cooperation" from the FBI, which was passing on Anslinger's rumors, even though Anslinger was J. Edgar Hoover's rival in building federal bureaucracies with which to guard public morals.) When Sinatra met Mortimer in a Hollywood nightclub in April 1947, he knocked him down, was charged with assault, and tried to lie his way out of it, saying that Mortimer had called him a dago. All this was safe enough; Mortimer was not a big fellow, and Sinatra may or may not have had the help of his minders. But the incident cost him court costs and a settlement, and fibbing about it was foolish. There was some sympathy for Sinatra, and a lot of people enjoyed seeing someone like Mortimer get punched in the head; Sinatra was an underdog because he behaved liked one, however much money he was making, and even as the columnists unsheathed their knives their heyday was almost over, though nobody knew it at the time. But the bad publicity and obnoxious behavior began to have a cumulative effect on his business.

An engagement at the Capitol Theater in New York City in the autumn of 1947, for example, was surprisingly unsuccessful (an unfavorable review being substituted for a favorable one in a New York Hearst-owned newspaper). Also on the bill were the Will Mastin Trio, and Sinatra saw to it that young Sammy Davis, Jr., became the star of that act; 1947 was also the year he recorded "I've Got a Crush on You," of which Alec Wilder said that he had improved on Gershwin's original in almost every way. But times were changing; the cultural and demographic effects of the war and of changes in the music business were also coming down. A young white Baltimore woman who worked in a shoe store, Deborah Chessler, was writing songs, but couldn't get them sung the way she wanted them; then in September 1948 the Orioles, a black singing group, had a number-one hit in the *Billboard* black chart with her "It's Too Soon to Know," which Griel Marcus described in retrospect as the first rock 'n' roll record. After August 1946 Frank Sinatra did not have a record in the top five of the *Billboard* pop chart until 1954; in 1952 and 1953 he had no hits at all.

Frank Sinatra was a more typical American than most people

could admit, finding any number of ways to exacerbate the national extremes of license on the one hand and puritanism on the other. He fell in love too easily, or, to put it another way, he had more women than most men could fantasize about. Once he got to Hollywood he stayed out all night with the likes of Lana Turner, the "Sweater Girl," and Marilyn Maxwell, a statuesque alabaster beauty; he was not only unfaithful to Nancy, but was never going to be faithful to anybody. Yet he sought that romantic ideal that so many of us have believed in and that he exalted in his songs. At one point he wanted a divorce so that he could marry Maxwell, but Evans worked frantically hard to break up each affair before it became too public or seriously threatened the Sinatra marital status, because in those days his fans not only idolized him but idyllized his family life. In June 1948 his third child, Christina, was born; he had moved his family to the swanky Holmby Hills part of Beverly Hills, and just as Evans might have been breathing a sigh of relief came the rock on which they all foundered. The years from 1949 to 1952 were the most difficult of Sinatra's life, and at the center of his problems was a woman, the one person whom he could never dominate. Her name was Ava Gardner.

She was born in North Carolina in 1922, one of seven children of a tobacco sharecropper; a very beautiful girl from childhood, she had a strict upbringing, and later caught up for lost time. Ava had soon been married to actor Mickey Rooney and bandleader Artie Shaw: She and Rooney were nothing more than children when they were married; Rooney thought he was playing house, going off to play golf and leaving one of the most beautiful women in the world at home alone to be a housewife. Shaw was an intellectual snob who did his best to make Ava feel stupid, and lost his temper when he caught her reading Kathleen Windsor's best-seller *Forever Amber*, because he thought it was trash. (It was, but he later married Windsor.) Ava was seeing Howard Hughes when she first met Frank Sinatra in 1946, and she didn't like him; she thought he was arrogant, but she was no cream puff either. Charlton Heston described her when she was boozing (in his memoirs, *In the Arena*) as "mistress of the slash-and-burn technique; destroy everything in sight, wait till they sweep away the ashes and rescue the children, then start again."

Ava soon recognized the passion in Sinatra; he was dangerous, but at least he wouldn't treat her like a piece of wax fruit. Both under contract to MGM, they saw each other often enough, and within a couple of years embarked on a stormy, passionate relationship that lasted for several years. But it was doomed. In some ways they were completely incompatible: she liked to walk into a room and kick off her shoes and relax; he liked to make sure that the ashtrays were symmetrically arranged on each table. But mainly they were too much alike. They both liked to smoke and drink and stay out all night; they were both serious about their work and despaired of ever being fully in charge of their careers; they were each poorly educated and acutely aware of it; they each wanted to be fully in charge of their personal lives, and could not resist bringing out the worst in each other.

Big Nancy had put up with Sinatra's tomcatting for many years, but now Nick Sevano wasn't there anymore to lie on Frank's behalf. (Nancy had got him fired, but he had gone to work for Dorsey, and later came back to Sinatra's business orbit after Nancy was gone.) Soon not even George Evans could keep things under some kind of control. The Sinatras had been separated once, and got back together; when Sinatra was lighting like a bee on every flower he could find, he may have thought he was in love each time, yet there was ultimately no reason not to go home. But when Louella Parsons published her memoir in 1961, she remembered Nancy's downfall: "A woman can and has been able to handle a dozen rivals, but I never knew a woman who could handle just one." With Ava, Sinatra was in the grip of something a lot stronger than he was; being her lover was not only a sexual passion, but a personal challenge. Now Sinatra was clearly an adulterer and Ava a home-wrecker, though she was just as clearly telling the truth when she pointed out that Frank's marriage had failed long before she came along.

If you can't meet another person halfway, you can't have a relationship unless the other person is a doormat, and neither Sinatra nor Gardner was doormat material. They fought and made up like a pair of cats. Earl Wilson, a Broadway columnist Sinatra usually got along with, later described the affair as "a two-year soap opera with screaming fights heard round the world." It must have been early in their relationship that, according to Kitty Kelley, they got a little drunk and drove around Palm Springs shooting up the place with a pair of .38 revolvers; there was a fair amount of damage and a passerby got nicked by a bullet. Jack Keller got a phone call in the middle of the night and spent a lot of money buying everybody off so that this incident did not get in the papers, but it was followed by arguments and angry telephone calls as Evans tried to break up the romance. Sinatra, behaving badly as usual, reacted by demanding that Evans fire his partner Keller, but Evans refused, so (according to Kelley) Sinatra fired Evans. They soon made it up; Sinatra went to New York to see Evans before the end of 1949 (according to John Howlett), but it was only a few days later, in January 1950, the morning after an argument with a reporter about Sinatra's love life, that Evans died suddenly from a heart attack. He was only forty-eight years old and he had done more for Sinatra than anybody except his mother; he was almost the only person who could stand up to Sinatra and tell him off, and now he was gone. For once Sinatra was shocked, but still he had learned nothing.

Evans's funeral made Sinatra late to a hotel gig in Houston. He had insisted that Ava accompany him there (which he later admitted was a dreadful mistake, but he was so much in love that he was unusually out of control), and then made a fuss when a photographer from a local paper wanted to take his picture. The fuss (and the love affair) got into the papers, and Nancy had finally had enough humiliation: on Valentine's Day she announced that there would be a legal separation, though she was still opposed to a divorce.

Meanwhile, Ava was under contract to MGM, and she had asked the studio's permission to leave Los Angeles to go to Houston even though she wasn't working on a picture at the time; the studio said no, but she went anyway. It may seem strange nearly half a century later that a grown woman had to ask her boss's permission to go somewhere, but this was another era. The morals clause in the MGM contract began, "The artist agrees to conduct himself with due regard to public conventions and morals...." And once upon a time the morals clause had been a serious business. In 1938 an article in *Photoplay* called "Hollywood's

Unmarried Husbands and Wives" exposed the romances of Barbara Stanwyck and Robert Taylor, Paulette Goddard and Charlie Chaplin, Constance Bennett and Gilbert Roland, and Carole Lombard and Clark Gable, all MGM stars who were virtually living in sin while officially they were just friends. The magazine's line, for the benefit of secretaries and librarians everywhere, was that "the best way to hunt happiness when you're in love in Hollywood or anywhere else is with a preacher, a marriage license, and a bagful of rice." Louis B. Mayer's reaction to the magazine article was to push through Gable's divorce so he could marry Lombard before shooting of *Gone With the Wind* began, and to rush Taylor off a film set to his wedding. ("All I had to say about the whole thing was 'I do,'" Taylor said later.) Ava arrived in Hollywood in 1941, and at the end of that decade, the result of the hypocritical marry-go-round was that, just to mention Ava's friends for example, Gable got married again when he was drunk, David Niven and Mickey Rooney married their second or third wives, Taylor, director John Huston, and Artie Shaw were all in the divorce courts, and Mayer himself was dumping his wife for actress and singer Ginny Simms.

There had always been stars who refused to take any guff from the studio. When Mayer once asked Tallulah Bankhead about her lesbianism, she replied, "You mean like so-and-so?"—naming one of the studio's biggest stars—and that shut Mayer up for a while. The fan mags weren't going to print anything about lesbianism anyway, and nobody could tell Bankhead what to do, but at least she wasn't committing adultery. Meanwhile, however, pushing people into marriage against their will was not doing the institution of marriage any good; the handwriting was on the wall for the morals clause, and for that matter the studio system itself would not last much longer: Sinatra would do his bit to tear that down, too. At the end of the twentieth century perhaps both the marriage and divorce rates have peaked, and if fewer people get married in the next century, maybe marriage will mean more than it has since the time of the morals clause. Far be it from me to suggest that Frank Sinatra was single-handedly forging a new moral code, but once again he was in a sort of vanguard: his passionate, selfish, badly-behaved quest for some kind of personal fulfillment was the wave of the future. If the Depression was over, the Second World War was won and the Atomic Age was here, the generation that had won the war was going to make its own mistakes, and that generation had some sneaking admiration for Frank Sinatra, who carried on shooting holes in his own career.

Louis B. Mayer had been a Sinatra fan since he was moved to tears, it is said, at Sinatra's singing of "Ol' Man River" at a benefit for the Jewish elderly in 1945. When Mayer bought Sinatra from RKO, the singer said later that he went from $25,000 a picture to $130,000. Sinatra's MGM pictures included *Anchors Aweigh* (1945), *It Happened in Brooklyn* (1947), *The Kissing Bandit* (1948), *Take Me Out to the Ball Game* and *On the Town* (1949); in addition he did a cameo in *Till the Clouds Roll By* (a biopic of Jerome Kern in 1946, singing "Ol' Man River" again) and was lent to RKO for *The Miracle of the Bells* (1948, the one where he played a priest). The RKO *Bells* and the MGM *Kissing Bandit* are two of the worst pictures ever made, but four of the MGM pictures are still delightful musicals, three of them also featuring Gene Kelly. Being under contract to MGM was like being a member of a family and, sure enough, it was too good for Frank. In 1949 Mayer fell off a horse and was hospitalized; Sinatra cracked on a film set, "He didn't fall off a horse. He fell off Ginny Simms." Mayer heard about this banal and vulgar remark, but didn't laugh, and Sinatra's MGM career was suddenly over, just as other things in his life weren't going so well, either.

He had rejoined *Your Hit Parade* on the radio in September 1947, co-starring with Doris Day for the first couple of months, and had his own way, compared to earlier in the decade: he got more choice of material, could broadcast from wherever he wanted and had Stordahl as his music director. But it was the nature of a chart show that he had to sing the same songs over and over, and it must have been embarrassing that there were no big hits by Frank Sinatra in 1948 (he recorded "Nature Boy," but Nat Cole's version was number one). Not only were Frank's records not selling very well, but something strange was happening to the hit parade: "Woody Woodpecker" was number one for six weeks (yes, the theme from the Walter Lanz cartoon), and others like "I'm Looking Over a Four-Leaf Clover" and "Too Fat Polka"

("You can have her/I don't want her/She's too fat for me") were not exactly Sinatra's type of material. It especially griped him that a harmonica group could get a huge hit (the Harmonicats, with "Peg O' My Heart") but he couldn't. When he left *Your Hit Parade* for the last time in May 1949 he landed a series called *Light-Up Time* (again for the American Tobacco Company), broadcast every weekday afternoon for fifteen minutes and repeated in the evening; on that show he could sing what he wanted.

He also guested regularly on other people's programs, and was always successful on the radio. Though he probably never exceeded the overall standard of the *Songs by Sinatra* programs for Old Gold in 1945–47, there are quite a few broadcast tracks available on unofficial CDs these days, and he always sounds relaxed and swinging. He resisted appearing on television, and when he finally guested on a Bob Hope show, and then had his own TV series starting in 1950, his instinct turned out to have been correct. Musical shows on TV were at first little more than deejay shows with pictures and were not very successful. They had to become variety shows, and Perry Como, Dinah Shore, and Dean Martin later turned out to be very good at hosting such programs, but Sinatra's arrogance and his lack of gift for comedy did not come across well on the small screen. In fact, his complete unwillingness to cooperate was transparent. On a film set he could just about get away with refusing to do umpteen takes until everyone was satisfied, but television was different: it was broadcast live in the 1950s and required rehearsal, and Sinatra refused to rehearse. Meanwhile, things went from bad to worse for Sinatra at Columbia Records, partly because the record industry was in a state of flux and nobody really knew how it was all going to turn out.

Sinatra's second album, *Songs by Sinatra*, was released in April 1947, a compilation of sides recorded between late 1944 ("She's Funny That Way," "Embraceable You") and early 1947 ("I Concentrate on You") and was spoiled only by the inclusion of the dopey "I'm Sorry I Made You Cry." (Not that it wasn't well chosen for the album: the sentimentality of a song from 1918 was still acceptable in 1947; his fans probably swooned themselves half to death imagining him gently helping them back onto their pedestals. Little did they know that he rarely apologized to anybody for anything.) His third album (not counting a Christmas set) was *Frankly Sentimental*, released in mid-1949. Like *The Voice, Frankly Sentimental* was more a concept album than a compilation. It included "Guess I'll Hang My Tears Out to Dry," by Styne and Cahn, recorded in mid-1946; but the rest was all made in the second half of 1947. An August session included "That Old Feeling," "If I Had You," "The Nearness of You" and Sinatra's first recording of "One for My Baby," all arranged in the chamber-group style of the tracks on *The Voice*, with only four strings; the last of these made it onto the new album. "Laura" was recorded in October with the full Stordahl orchestra; then on two dates in November there were more chamber sessions, from which "Spring Is Here," "Fools Rush In," "When You Awake" and "It Never Entered My Mind" were earmarked; and "Body and Soul," from another November session with the full orchestra and including solo trumpet from Bobby Hackett, completed the album. The reason it was not released for more than a year was probably that Columbia knew they were going to introduce a completely new kind of record.

The plastic microgroove long-playing record required entirely new pressing and playback technology, and was a huge gamble; it was also one of the best-kept industrial secrets of the era. In June 1948 Columbia's laboratory wizard, Dr. Peter Goldmark, demonstrated the new product at a famous press conference; a photograph was released showing Goldmark standing next to a tower of 78 albums over six feet high, and holding a small stack of LPs in his arms having the same playing time. One of the first ten-inch pop LPs, released that month, was a straight reissue of *The Voice*, at a time when there were no privately owned record players in the country that could play it. (It was issued in a pink paper sleeve; later that year the heavier cardboard LP sleeve was introduced.) When *Frankly Sentimental* came out the following year it was released in both 78 rpm and LP formats.

In December 1948 Columbia began marketing seven-inch 33 rpm singles—the first one was a Sinatra record—and continued releasing them for two years. In 1949 RCA introduced its entirely unnecessary 45 rpm record, having instructed its engineers to come up with a new system that was incompatible with Columbia's new product. The 45 was limited to the seven-inch size, but with a new record changer: the hole in RCA's record was 1.5 inches wide and the record-changing mechanism, contained in the fat spindle of the player, was quick, positive and quiet. The public decided in favor of three-speed record players, so RCA's new machine faded, but not before the 45 rpm "doughnut" had been established as the medium for singles. The "battle of the speeds" went on for years; 78s continued to be made (in decreasing numbers) for most of the 1950s; the original cast recording of *South Pacific* was a huge hit in 1949, spending 400 weeks in the *Billboard* album chart, and record shops had to stock it in all three formats, which used a lot of space. Some small record labels went to the wall, unable to invest in the new technology; Blue Note, already a well-established jazz label, was almost put out of business by the new necessity to produce artwork for album covers. But as the 78 began to lose favor, microgroove records allowed larger selections in record shops and larger collections at home, and transformed the record business utterly. The introduction of the album as we knew it for the next forty years would transform the career of Frank Sinatra. But it took awhile.

Meanwhile, the reason for the furious amount of recording activity near the end of 1947 was that James "Little Caesar" Petrillo had announced another of his musicians' union's strikes against the record companies, just as the Swing Era was effectively over anyway. No fewer than nine famous bands disbanded at the end of 1946, and everybody knew an era had ended; paradoxically, 1947 turned out to be the best year the American record industry had had since 1922, which is a measure of how much damage competition with radio and then the Great Depression had done since then. People were buying a lot of records, but nobody really knew what kind of music the public wanted.

The only studio tracks Sinatra recorded during this period were two Irving Berlin songs from the MGM musical *Easter Parade* in March 1948, overdubbing Stordahl's backing tracks, which had been recorded before the strike started; and one *a cappella* item in April. By now all the major studios had gone over to tape-recording, which made overdubbing and editing easier, but Sinatra did not like this monkey business; neither did Jo Stafford or Dinah Shore or any of the singers who had come up during the Swing Era, because they were singers, not switches or buttons on a studio console. Rosemary Clooney once had to prerecord a vocal for a backing track to be added later; Mitch Miller assured her that the result sounded fine, but she knew that if she had known what the arranger was going to do she would have phrased it differently. The coming decades of increasing studio technology would leave these artists cold, because too much production resulted in cold records. Sinatra liked to keep the studio technology at bay, staying in control as much as possible and sounding as though he was having more fun on the radio, because the broadcasts were effectively live gigs. On "It Only Happens When I Dance With You" he sounds ill at ease, as though he might have asked for the tempo to be speeded up if he hadn't been stuck with the track as Stordahl had recorded it. He had more fun with "A Fella With an Umbrella," an uptempo tune; he even contributed a rare bit of scatting during the instrumental bridge, while standing there alone in front of the microphone with no orchestra to look at.

The *a cappella* item was a complete success. "Nature Boy" was a strange song and a sensation of the year, composed by a proto-hippie called Eden Ahbez. The song had an almost oriental sound, possibly based on a Yiddish song, "Schweig Mein Hartz" ("Be Calm My Heart"), and the pseudo-philosophical lyrics were at least opposed to the creeping mechanization that seemed to be overtaking the world. Nat "King" Cole had the big hit version, recorded with Frank DeVol's orchestra on Capitol before the strike started, but Sinatra must have liked it, because he'd been singing it quite a lot. The strike made it harder for anyone to cover it, but in fact it was the sort of material that lost nothing for being backed only with the Jeff Alexander Choir, and when Sinatra's record reached the top twenty, Cole's was still at number one. (The main *Billboard* chart is a retail chart; if jukebox and radio plays are factored in, Sinatra's "Nature Boy" was probably the equivalent of a top-ten hit.)

With the end of the strike, he recorded nearly 100 titles between December 1948 and September 1952, and some of them of course were quite wonderful; but the industry was cranking out a lot of product, in a management style later described by a record company executive as "throwing a lot of shit at the wall to see if any of it stuck." For example, the first tune Sinatra recorded when the strike was over was "Sunflower," a Mack David ditty which became the Kansas state song; even Sinatra's version had a slight country flavor (its resemblance to "Hello, Dolly!" was confirmed in a court case many years later). There were six hit versions of "Sunflower," the biggest (by Russ Morgan's band) on the other side of "Cruising Down the River," which had won a songwriting contest at London's Hammersmith Palais ballroom in 1945 and was an American number-one for seven weeks in 1949. These were knees-up party tunes, virtually novelties, and this was the sort of thing that was increasingly successful on the radio in the U.S.A.: Now that the dance bands weren't broadcasting from ballrooms all over the U.S. and live music seemed to be dying, the records played on the radio were increasingly created to fit snugly between the advertising jingles, and they were not Frank Sinatra's type of songs.

Another ominous trend was that the songs that should have been Sinatra's type of songs were not. Rodgers and Hammerstein were writing smash-hit shows such as 1948's *South Pacific*, from which Sinatra recorded "Some Enchanted Evening" and "Bali Ha'i," but the former was too arty, sung onstage by Ezio Pinza, a bass from the Metropolitan Opera (though Perry Como had a pop hit on it), while the second had a desperate quasi-Hawaiian treatment in Sinatra's version. Irving Berlin's *Miss Liberty* flopped in 1949, but Sinatra recorded two songs from it: yet another song called "I Love You," and "Let's Take an Old-fashioned Walk." But both were in waltz time. The latter was particularly charming, except that the arrangement got in the way a little; the words were typically catchy Berlin: "Let's take an old-fashioned walk/I'm just bursting with talk/What a tale could be told/If we went for an old-/fashioned walk." The record was a duet with Doris Day, who was a better singer than she ever got credit for; but like a lot of pop culture in the 1940s, from musical films to Bugs Bunny cartoons, the song harked back to a Tin Pan Alley where boys wore straw boaters and girls wore starched pinnies, and everybody was so sweet and pure that it's a wonder any of them ever had any children. This was not Sinatra's neighborhood.

Frank Loesser's "Once In Love With Amy" was sung in *Where's Charley?* by the much-loved Ray Bolger (who had played the Scarecrow in *The Wizard of Oz* in 1939); Sinatra recorded it, but Bolger's version, unusually, took a twelve-inch 78 into the top twenty. "While the Angelus Was Ringing" was a French song that became a huge country hit ten years later as "The Three Bells." "That Lucky Old Sun" was a huge hit in 1949, but Frankie Laine's record was eight weeks at number one; neither Sinatra's nor Louis Armstrong's reached higher than the top twenty. All of these were superbly sung; "The Right Girl for Me" (from *Take Me Out to the Ball Game*) was so sweet it made your teeth hurt:

> She'll have a simple, sweet appeal
> That wins my affection;
> She'll be the kind who'll make me feel
> She needs my protection...
> If my heart says, "Come in,
> Darling where have you been?"
> She's the right girl for me.

It is remarkable the way Sinatra almost made the words work, but it just made you long for a better song. There were songs by Burke and Van Heusen, by Styne and Cahn, and another Cahn-Weston-Stordahl effort, but they just weren't very memorable. "It Happens Every Spring," from a film of the same name, was one of the best songs from this period, and it didn't even chart; "The Hucklebuck," from the same session, was a dance-fad tune based on a Charlie Parker riff ("Now's the Time"); this was a top-ten hit and a nice record as novelties go, with the Modernaires vocal group and a laid-back beat, but without much for Sinatra to do. In fact, in retrospect, the golden age of American songwriting was coming to an end.

But before Sinatra's Columbia career wound down completely, his luck got even worse. Manie Sacks resigned and went to RCA to take over the popular-music division; Sacks had been Sinatra's friend and champion for nearly a decade, but losing him wasn't the worst part. The worse part was that Sacks was replaced by Mitch Miller.

Miller had been producing classical records at Keynote, which was taken over by Mercury, formed in Chicago in 1946–47 by a booking agent and the son of a plastics manufacturer. Mercury had hit the ground running, with money to invest; the label picked up the Harmonicats and schmaltzy pianist Jan August from even smaller independents, broke Frankie Laine and Vic Damone from cabaret to the big time, and struck pay dirt with Patti Page, a singer on local radio. Mercury invented the promotional tour, sending Laine on a series of one-nighters in the Midwest to promote his new records, and was one of the first to lease the 45 rpm system from RCA: the sound of Patti Page singing close harmony with herself, made possible by overdubbing, was associated in the public mind with the new high-tech 45 single, though the 78 sounded exactly the same. Miller had hits with all of Mercury's artists, an immediate success as a pop producer.

Although Miller had come from a classical background, he had been listening to jazz and pop ever since his student days with Alec Wilder, and was clever at using new technology. He had been hand-picked by conductors like André Kostelanetz and Leopold Stokowski to play oboe and English horn on recording sessions, and had turned down a job in the New York Philharmonic because it didn't pay enough; he had played on so many recording sessions that he was very good in the studio at getting a balance and recording a take while other producers were still fooling around. Even while he produced records at Mercury, Miller's playing was still in demand on a freelance basis; at a Sinatra recording session, in fact, a perfect take was said to have been spoiled because it was a few seconds too long for a ten-inch 78 side, and Miller was heard to growl from the back of the band, "We'd make it fit over at Mercury." Perhaps Mercury had more up-to-date equipment for cutting master disks, and Miller, like Sinatra, was never one to keep his mouth shut.

Miller had recorded some of the most famous oboe and English horn parts in all music, such as in Sibelius' "Swan of Tuonela" and Dvořák's "New World" symphony. He told interviewer Ted Fox about playing for Stokowski, "This man had a kind of magic. I can't explain it. It was one of the most exciting experiences, like meeting a strange, beautiful woman, and you knew all about her and she knew all about you. The phrasing came—I did what he wanted without him saying anything."

When Sacks left Columbia, it was not a bad idea to poach Miller from Mercury to replace him. Miller had been largely responsible for the *Charlie Parker and Strings* album on Mercury/Clef in 1949, a high-profile album with a great jazz genius, but the only good thing about that album was Parker: a chance to do something unique had been thrown away because Jimmy Carroll's arrangements were lackluster. In fact Miller needed someone with Stokowski's artistic sensibility to tell him what to do. On the other hand, to be fair, Miller's lack of taste was just what pop music required in the early 1950s, which is why he became one of the most commercially successful record producers in history, just as American culture began to perfect its ability to pander to the most common denominator. One of Miller's hits at Mercury had been Frankie Laine's record of "Mule Train," an obnoxious novelty complete with whip-crack sound effects; this was number one for six weeks in late 1949, making two huge hits for Laine that year; Laine and Vic Damone followed Miller to Columbia.

It was the month before Miller arrived at Columbia that Sinatra recorded a cover of "Chattanoogie Shoe Shine Boy," a big hit for country star Red Foley in 1950. Everybody was still thinking in terms of hit singles, and Sinatra hadn't had a top-five hit for eighteen months. In the next couple of months he tried duets with Rosemary Clooney and Jane Russell, a phony country song called "When the Sun Goes Down" (published by Sinatra Music and co-written by Walter O'Keefe, the comic from the Riobamba in 1943), and a silly tune called "American Beauty Rose," given a dixieland feeling by Miller (this was intended to recapture the success of "Five Minutes More"). Then Miller decided that Sinatra hadn't recorded enough "rhythm songs," by which he meant uptempo arrangements, which was true enough. So in April 1950 seven tunes were arranged and conducted by George Siravo to add to "It All Depends on You" from the previous July, to make an album called *Sing and Dance With Frank Sinatra*, released on 78s and on LP in October.

The rest of the tunes were "Should I (Reveal)," "You Do

Something to Me," "Lover," "When You're Smiling," "It's Only a Paper Moon," "My Blue Heaven" and "The Continental," and the band included Billy Butterfield on trumpet, Babe Russin and Hymie Shertzer on reeds, Alan Reuss on guitar, Phil Stevens on bass and Johnny Blowers on drums. This was a hip crowd, and the album has been regarded by some as among Sinatra's best work of the Columbia period. It is hard to dislike. The tunes are all good ones (from 1926 to 1934), the arrangements, taken one at a time, are fun, very well played (and well recorded); there are some good solos from the sidemen. But the band sounds disappointingly four-square (especially on "You Do Something to Me" for example), as though somebody had just noticed that dance bands had been playing in 4/4 for some years and thought it might be a good idea to try it. The arrangements are formulaic; there are plenty of clever details, but they are cute for their own sake, having nothing to do with the tune. The trumpets use that Swing Era *jeek-jeek-a-jeek* sound a lot, as though Siravo had been taking lessons from Benny Goodman's worst records.

Somebody once calculated that at one point in 1946 Sinatra had been doing as many as forty-five shows a week, singing eighty to a hundred songs a day; and this was a singer who admitted that he smoked and drank too much and never slept enough. In 1950 he was doing three shows a night at the Copacabana (where his voice gave out completely, almost the only time in his career when he had to stop and rest whether he liked it or not), plus five radio shows a week, as well as recording sessions and the occasional benefit. His voice was so tired that at the sessions, Miller said, he ended up recording tracks for Sinatra to sing over later. Much of the album was therefore dubbed, if Miller is correct, which is probably one of the things wrong with it. On the finished product, though, Sinatra went for some spectacular notes and hit them just fine, and the one thing about the album that foretold glories to come was the way he seemed to be taking it easy while the band did all the work. That's a sneaky way of swinging.

But in the broadcasting-jukebox milieu of the era, none of the sides charted, and neither did the album. Sinatra's biggest hit in his last four years at Columbia was a folk song in 3/4 time, "Goodnight Irene," written by Huddie Ledbetter, better known as

Leadbelly. Some producers copied other people's hits, especially black hits, arrangement and all, note for note; Miller never did that, and in fact preferred to make his own hits, but "Goodnight Irene" was a cover of a big one, a Decca record by the Weavers, a folk quartet led by Pete Seeger. The Weavers had the advantage of Gordon Jenkins arranging an orchestra and chorus: Dave Kapp didn't want them on Decca, but Jenkins snuck them into a recording session. It may seem odd to accompany a folk song in such a way, but Jenkins was no fool; he began his arrangement with a solo violin playing the second half of the chorus, establishing the front-porch nature of the song right away. Miller's arrangement began with the Mitch Miller Singers. Sinatra had recorded on Columbia with the Bobby Tucker Singers, the Modernaires, the Pied Pipers, the Ken Lane Singers, the Norman Luboff Choir and so on, but he had probably never heard anything like Miller's sing-along chorus: loud, stiff and unyielding, like a group auditioning for a chance to be satirized by Stan Freberg.

There was nothing wrong with "Goodnight Irene"; it's a lovely tune of its kind, the sort of thing that went well on the radio but was much less offensive than, say, "If I Knew You Were Comin' I'd've Baked a Cake," one of the other big hits of 1950. But it was simply not Sinatra's type of material. The first disk-jockey programs had only started around 1935, for dancing to records (e.g. *Make-believe Ballroom*), but by 1950 they had gained such momentum that what you expected to hear on the radio was either a soap opera or somebody playing records, and during the decade of the 1950s radio drama disappeared in the face of competition with television. When the jocks took over completely, "top forty" was born, and this process was already well advanced when Sinatra's career seemed to be crumbling. The jocks played records that grabbed the attention for three minutes, and neither lyrics nor phrasing were particularly valued. In the last six months of the year, Sinatra made some nice records—"April in Paris," "I Guess I'll Have to Dream the Rest," "Nevertheless (I'm In Love With You)," "Let It Snow! Let It Snow! Let It Snow!"—but they weren't hits.

Meanwhile, Miller pitched a couple of pseudo-folk songs at Sinatra, but he refused to record them, so Miller gave them to a kid named Al Cernick he'd discovered, and "My Heart Cries for You" / "The Roving Kind' (adapted from old French and English songs respectively) was a huge two-sided hit for Cernick, whose name had been changed to Guy Mitchell. Miller's jolly waltzes and whooping French horns became something of a trademark as Mitchell had hit after hit with "My Truly, Truly Fair," "Sparrow in the Tree Top," "Belle, Belle, My Liberty Belle" and "Pittsburgh, Pennsylvania."

Meanwhile Miller was pulling the same tricks with Frankie Laine ("Jezebel") and amplifying a harpsichord on Rosemary Clooney's Armenian-flavored "Come On-a My House." He once allegedly put bagpipes on a Dinah Shore record, trying anything to grab the listener's attention, and the result was so awful that deejays broke the record over the air. But he also grabbed the best country songs and made them pop crossovers, giving Boudleaux Bryant's "Hey Joe!" to Frankie Laine, and Hank Williams songs to Laine, Tony Bennett and Jo Stafford. Trying to have a hit record in the early 1950s was like banging away in a shooting gallery with a hundred other blindfolded people, nobody having any idea where the target was; Miller had no taste, but he was probably a riot at a party with a lampshade on his head, and a significant number of his records were hits.

Once when Jo Stafford had to sing along with a prerecorded track, which she hated to do, Miller came down from the control booth and started dancing a jig in the studio. "What the heck are you doing?" asked Stafford. Miller explained that he was trying to cheer her up, get her in the mood; she told him to get back in the booth where he belonged. Miller meddled in every detail of every session; Sinatra claimed to have finally forbidden Miller to attend his recording sessions at all, which Miller later denied. But Sinatra's hatred for Miller became one of the cornerstones of his life. It wasn't Miller's fault that Sinatra's old market was gone and the music business had changed forever; it is possible to argue that if the radio hadn't had Miller's records to make hits out of, the standard might have been even lower. Miller was supposed to have been a musician, some will say, and should have known better; but his job was to make money for Columbia, and he made it the number-one label in the U.S. Miller pointed out that Sinatra's contract gave him final choice over the material and over each release; Paul Weston said that Sinatra's career was crumbling at the time, his confidence was low and Miller was having hits with other people; and anyway, Miller was hard to refuse: like a Hungarian in a revolving door, he could enter behind you and exit in front, and some of the junk the artists refused to record was even worse than some that they did.

A Sinatra recording session in January 1951 began with a dreary ballad called "Faithful," a plea for sexual-marital fidelity, which was rich coming from Sinatra; and his Columbia contract ran out in September 1952 with "Why Try to Change Me Now," which was more realistic. A session with his old boss, Harry James, was a failure because the tunes were dumb: "Castle Rock," for example, had three hit recordings that year, but it was only a jump-band riff that didn't need any words. Another date had three songs from Rodgers and Hammerstein's *The King and I*, arranged and conducted by Stordahl, on which Sinatra lavished all the acting talent he possessed, changing his timing and his feeling completely for each tune, from the sadness of looking back to say "Hello, Young Lovers" to the star-crossed lover himself in "We Kiss in a Shadow" and the innocent bravado of "I Whistle a Happy Tune." "I Could Write a Book" was lovely; "I Hear a Rhapsody" was overarranged; "Walking in the Sunshine," written by Bob Merrill, was a good-natured outing, not much of a song but better than Merrill's big hits (the aforementioned "If I Knew You Were Comin' I'd've Baked a Cake," and then "Doggie in the Window"), and likewise "Don't Ever Be Afraid to Go Home" (by Hilliard and Sigman) is as much fun in Sinatra's version as it could possibly be.

One of Sinatra's biggest successes of the period was "I'm a Fool to Want You," written for a radio drama; Sinatra changed a few words, and when the writers (Jack Wolf and Joel Herron) heard him sing it they wanted him to record it so badly that they gave him a piece of it. It has always been taken for granted that he put all his grief over Ava Gardner into his performance, and it became one of his all-time classics. The other side was the infamous "Mama Will Bark," a duet with Dagmar, a celebrity on account of her measurements; she was famous for showing more cleavage than anyone else on television. What the novelty with a tango beat is about is hard to say; either Mama is a dog or the dog's name is Mama, but she will bark if the boy tries to get his hands on the girl's prominent features. Sinatra drew the line at barking like a dog and Miller had to hire someone else to do that, but it was this record more than anything else that Sinatra held against Miller. And yet Sinatra's professionalism almost carried it off: he had, after all, been appearing onstage with Dagmar (and Jackie Gleason), and he has as much fun as he can with this mindless junk, as well as with "Tennessee Newsboy" and "Bim Bam Baby." He is creditable on "The Birth of the Blues," "Azure-Te (Paris Blues)" and a few other things, but not even he can do anything with "Luna Rossa (Blushing Moon)" or "Feet of Clay," which sounds like a stand-up comic in a Lebanese nightclub trying on a tearjerker just for the hell of it. Good or bad, none of the records were the big hits both Columbia and Sinatra wanted.

It was a year after the legal separation from Nancy that Sinatra recorded "I'm a Fool to Want You," in March 1951; in May she finally agreed to a divorce. Some say that Nancy at last gave up not only because Frank wasn't coming home this time, but also because the passionate and very public Sinatra-Gardner affair was getting some public sympathy, and Nancy was beginning to look like a spoilsport. But others say that she never should have agreed to a divorce, and eventually she would have got him back. Many women of today would ask what would she want him back for, after everything she'd been through, but the fact is that she carried a torch for the rest of her life. Some of their friends also said that she wouldn't have lost him in the first place if she had developed with him, and that he went out alone a lot because she didn't like parties, but it seems hard to blame a mother and a homemaker for not being able to stay out all night. The truth is simply that Nancy was a nice Italian girl who fell in love with the wrong man.

Frank and Ava continued to fight constantly, Sinatra's temper the worst problem. It is hard to avoid the conclusion that his passion for her only exacerbated his inability to have a proper relationship with anybody; he could not expose his vulnerability except in a song. (Yet according to Sammy Cahn, his flatmate of the period, he would call up Nancy and cry on her shoulder, moaning "You're the only one who understands me.") In July Sinatra and Gardner went to Mexico, followed everywhere by photographers; on their return to Los Angeles their car nearly ran someone over at the airport. In September he attempted suicide, or at least had an accident with pills. Finally, at the end of October, Nancy's divorce was granted, and after still more quarrels, Sinatra and Gardner were married on November 7, in Philadelphia, at Manie Sacks's brother's house, having tried unsuccessfully to throw the press off the scent. They both remained insanely jealous, Sinatra worried about her former husband Artie Shaw and Gardner incensed at the thought of Marilyn Maxwell, yet neither could avoid rubbing the other's nose in the grief. She admitted it: "We both had a terrible tendency to needle each other's weaknesses."

And nearly a year after the marriage, "Why Try to Change Me Now" was arranged and conducted by Percy Faith, only one tune from a session split with another singer, and Sinatra was finished at Columbia; they didn't want him anymore and he didn't want to stay there. Since getting the boot at MGM he had made two films: *Double Dynamite* at RKO was a flop, Groucho Marx and Jane Russell looking better on-screen than Sinatra; *Meet Danny Wilson* from Universal was also a flop, but in retrospect was a clue and a warning of what was to come next. Danny Wilson was an unpleasant little nightclub singer who didn't want to take any nonsense from anybody, and some critics thought they saw a dramatic actor emerging; but, true to form, Sinatra had managed a bitter, nasty quarrel with his co-star, Shelley Winters. In 1952 the studios didn't return his calls, his television series was cancelled, and then even his booking agency dropped him, complaining that he owed them money, too. He was the greatest singer in the world, in his opinion, but he didn't even have a recording contract; and on top of all that his wife's career was going great guns: she was flying off to Africa to shoot *Mogambo* with Clark Gable and Grace Kelly, and since he didn't have anything else to do anyway, he went with her, so they wouldn't have to stop fighting at all.

Frank Sinatra looked like he was down and out, but there is an advantage in being at the bottom. The only way you can go is up.

Chapter Five

Maggio, Oscar and Nelson

A mong the noteworthy novels published in the U.S.A. in 1951 were *The Catcher in the Rye* (J. D. Salinger), *The Caine Mutiny* (a Pulitzer Prize for Herman Wouk), and *From Here to Eternity* (James Jones). Whatever their relative literary merits, all three were definitely post-war fictions: the Catcher, schoolboy Holden Caulfield, sought his own identityin a world that had become very confusing; *Mutiny* was about a paranoid super-patriot in the U.S. Navy, while Jones's novel seemed perhaps the most controversial of all at the time. With victory in the Second World War still very recent, the book was about bored and sexually frustrated military personnel in Pearl Harbor at the time of the Japanese attack: it not only featured sex, but adulterous sex at that, and few of the characters seemed to have anything heroic about them. Yet we knew that these ordinary people had gone on to win a war against the Japanese Empire.

One of the characters in *From Here to Eternity* dies before the end, missing out on the victory. Angelo Maggio is a skinny little guy, noisy and irritating, but full of energy and with a good heart; he is beaten to death by a bully because his pride will not allow him to submit. Frank Sinatra had campaigned in the past for non-singing roles, but Ronald Reagan played the returning serviceman in *John Loves Mary*, and John Derek was the slum kid on trial for murder in *Knock on Any Door* (playing opposite Sinatra's friend Humphrey Bogart); the role Sinatra did get was one he'd have been better without: the priest in *Miracle of the Bells*. But he knew beyond doubt that landing the role of Maggio would be the sort of timing that occurs once in an actor's career, if he's lucky. As he put it, "I knew Maggio. I went to high school with him in Hoboken." He would do anything he could to get that role.

There were a couple of factors in his favor. For all their problems and notoriety, Sinatra and his bride were well liked by other show folk; if his career seemed to be in trouble, her box-office success was increasing, and she went to work pulling strings on his behalf. Columbia Pictures had bought the rights to the novel, and both Frank and Ava were acquainted with the boss there, Harry Cohn. Ava went to see Cohn's wife, Joan, to beg for the part for her husband, while, according to Arnold Shaw, Cohn actually owed Frank a favor. In 1949 Columbia had made a comedy with Lucille Ball, *Miss Grant Takes Richmond*, and Frank was booked to appear at the Capitol Theater; as a favor to Cohn, Frank requested that picture to be shown on his bill, so that it got a Broadway premier. (Subsequently, according to Shaw, Sinatra fell ill before the engagement was completed and had to spend a few days in bed; Cohn kept him company while he recovered, but was then worried about his image as a tough bastard: he warned Sinatra, "You tell anyone, and I'll kill you!")

But landing the part was more difficult than pulling strings. Sinatra looked like box-office poison. *Meet Danny Wilson* had flopped (whether it was any good or not is beside the point) and Universal had not exercised its option to use him in another film. He had ruined his own deal with the CBS television network, refusing to rehearse and making problems on the set, so that the sponsors had canceled after thirteen weeks instead of three years. He tried to keep Ava from going to Africa to make *Snows of Kilimanjaro*, and threw a tantrum when the shooting lasted longer than ten days. (His judgement was so bad that he even tried to blame the press for the failure of his marriage to Nancy.) The miracle is how anybody ever allowed him to make another film; but he knew his career was on the line, and he was not above begging.

He pestered Buddy Adler, the producer, for a screen test for the part of Maggio. He went to see Cohn, and offered to do the part for $1,000 a week for a few weeks of shooting, though he had been getting $150,000 per film. Cohn's wife put her case for Sinatra, and even Jonie Taps, Tommy Dorsey's favorite song-plugger, who was now a vice president at Columbia, pushed for a screen test. Finally Cohn told Frank he might be considered for a test, and then it was a matter of seemingly endless waiting.

Sinatra's last recording date at Columbia Records (no connection with Columbia Pictures) was in September 1952; he was over $100,000 in debt for taxes, and somebody joked that the government would either put him in jail or recognize him as a foreign power. Columbia Records may have lent him the money to pay his taxes, because when he left there he was over $100,000 in debt to them. At the beginning of November, his career at rock bottom, he flew with Ava to Kenya, where shooting for *Mogambo* was to begin. They celebrated their first wedding anniversary on the Stratocruiser; he gave her a flashy diamond ring, and sent her the bill. (Later she cracked, "It was quite an occasion for me. I had been married twice but never for a whole year.")

The film set, in the Kenyan bush, was hot and dusty, and Ava did not get along at first with director John Ford. When the British governor of Kenya and his wife visited the set, Ford asked Ava what she saw in her "one-hundred-and-twenty-pound runt" of a husband, and she replied, "Well, there's only ten pounds of Frank but there's one hundred and ten pounds of cock." Ford was aghast, but the governor and his wife roared with laughter, and that was the beginning of Ford's respect for Ava, reinforced by her professionalism as an actress. But she did not feel well (it turned out she was pregnant), and Sinatra was bored and restless.

Sinatra went back to New York for a club date. His reviews were good, but a reporter who talked to him found him "a restless, unhappy man in his middle thirties who wants very much to reestablish himself and who wants to be an actor, not just a singer playing himself." Back in Africa he finally received a telegram offering him a screen test for the part of Maggio. He jumped on the first plane to Hollywood (Ava paid for all the plane rides, too) and Adler was astonished to see him thirty-six hours after sending the telegram. When the test was arranged, Adler handed Sinatra a script, but he had read the part so many times he didn't need it. It was the last test of the day and Adler wasn't going to bother to attend, but then he got a call from the director, Fred Zinneman: "You'd better come down here. You'll see something unbelievable." Zinneman had already filmed the test, and made Sinatra do another take without any film in the camera; this time even Adler was impressed. But Cohn was out of town, and anyway they were also testing Eli Wallach, a first-rate Broadway actor who had never made a film. Sinatra flew to Africa yet again, knowing that he'd done a good test but worried that he'd lose the part to Wallach, and Ava and Clark Gable did their best to cheer him up.

They also tested a comedian, Harvey Lembeck, but he wasn't right. Wallach was the best of the three, everyone agreed, but then the money came through for the production of Tennessee Williams's new play, *Camino Real*, to be directed by Elia Kazan, and there was no way Wallach was going to turn that down; he went back to Broadway (the play flopped, and Wallach made his first film a few years later). But Wallach's test for the part of Maggio was so good that Cohn, Adler, Zinneman and scriptwriter Dan Taradash couldn't make up their minds whether to go with Sinatra or test somebody else, so Cohn asked his wife for her opinion. She agreed that Wallach was a great actor, but there was no doubt in her mind. "He's not skinny, and he's not pathetic, and he's not Italian. Frank is just Maggio to me." And the picture was going to be expensive, with Burt Lancaster, Deborah Kerr, Donna Reed and Montgomery Clift already cast, and location shooting in Hawaii required, and Cohn could have Sinatra cheap. So Sinatra was offered the part of Maggio for $8,000.

He knew this was a turning point in his career, and now all his arrogance came back. His relationship with Ava was always tempestuous, but it was most tolerable when he was down and he really needed her; the rest of the time he was unbearable and sometimes she hated him. He left Africa again and a few days later, at the end of November, Ava flew to London for an abortion, making two of his children she'd aborted that year (there had been one in May). She already knew a thing or two about being unhappily married, and she must have felt that having children of this marriage would be a mistake, as well as a bad career move. She was as complicated and as temperamental as he was, but she had more self-knowledge. As Arnold Shaw put it, referring to one of his bouts of swearing loudly at newsmen in public,

> It was at moments like these that the man she loved—attentive and affectionate as Mickey Rooney had not been, outgoing and tender as Artie Shaw had not been—reminded her of all the roughnecks she had ever known, from the vulgar tobacco workers and poor white trash of the North Carolina hamlet where she had been born, to all the sharpies and wise guys of the Hollywood Hills.

He came back to Africa for Christmas, and they went to Paris together for a few days in January, but they squabbled constantly. He thought that everything would be all right as soon as he had finished shooting his part in *From Here to Eternity*, but the love of his life was hanging by a thread that would soon break.

In March and April 1953 the forty or so days of shooting took place. Montgomery Clift was a drunk and a drug addict, but he was also a very good and serious actor; Sinatra had never seen anyone work so hard on a film set, but the work habits didn't rub off. Nevertheless he learned a lot. He and Clift and James Jones spent a lot of time getting drunk together and crying on each other's shoulders. At the same time, the other, even more important upturn in Sinatra's fortunes was taking place.

His old friend Manie Sacks had tried to get him a recording contract at RCA, but the A&R department there didn't want him; the William Morris Agency had taken him on at the end of 1952, but couldn't sell him. Finally Capitol Records offered a contract. Capitol was then a ten-year-old independent label, so successful that it was virtually a major, the only important label located on the West Coast; such Capitol artists as Les Paul and Mary Ford, Nat Cole and Kay Starr, were having hit after hit. Furthermore, the label was hip and cared about music, having been formed by two songwriters, Johnny Mercer and Buddy DeSylva, and a major West Coast record retailer, Glenn Wallichs. In the early days they had cramped offices upstairs from Wallichs's record store, and Paul Weston, one of Capitol's first music directors, has a great many stories about the joie de vivre there. Weston, Mercer and the others would be listening to test pressings of records they'd just made, and Wallichs, the businessman, would be on the telephone, saying, "Hey, turn it down, you guys; I'm trying to set up a distributor in Philadelphia." The others would say, "Aw, forget about that; come and listen to this!" In the first half of the 1950s Capitol recorded the big jazz bands of Benny Goodman, Woody Herman, Charlie Barnet, Stan Kenton and Duke Ellington at a time when such bands did not seem to have a future and almost never had hit records; and furthermore, Capitol's technology was first-rate: during this period it was making records as good as any in the world.

Producer and music journalist Dave Dexter wanted Sinatra at Capitol, knowing what a fine singer he was and that only the right combination of songs and arrangements was needed. Even so, apart from Dexter, it took the influence of Axel Stordahl's wife, June Hutton, then a Capitol recording artist, and pianist Dick Jones, a Capitol producer who had played at the Sinatra-Gardner wedding, to bring off a deal. And Capitol wasn't taking any chances: the initial contract was for one year only, no advance was paid, and Sinatra would be responsible for the cost of the recording sessions. Having signed with Capitol, Sinatra angrily rejected Dexter as his producer, because Dexter had once made a mildly disparaging remark about one of Sinatra's Columbia disks in *down beat* magazine. (Dexter eventually co-produced a Sinatra session, and never stopped admiring him as an artist, but many years later still referred to him privately as an "evil, foul-mouthed bastard.") So it was former drummer Voyle Gilmore who supervised the Sinatra sessions in the early Capitol years.

Gilmore was not particularly a Sinatra fan at the time, but probably knew from the start that he wanted to get away from the lushness of the Stordahl-Sinatra classics. In Sinatra's last couple of years at Columbia he had used several other arrangers and conductors as well as Stordahl, but used Stordahl on his first Capitol session, early in April 1953, recording four tunes. "Lean Baby" (arranged by Heinie Beau) and "I'm Walking Behind You" were issued back-to-back; the former was a nice riff by Billy May with dopey words added, and the latter was a new ballad from England by Billy Reid. When the *Billboard* pop charts of the period are compiled (Best Sellers, Juke Box and Disk Jockey), the ballad was a top ten in May, but Eddie Fisher's recording of the same song was number one for seven weeks.

Even so, a hit with Sinatra first time out was not bad going, and by then there had already been two more recording sessions. The issue of Stordahl was soon resolved: with a pleasant boyish tenor voice, Eddie Fisher wasn't half the musician Sinatra was, but with five top-ten hits in a little over six months he was the hottest artist in the business, and Stordahl accepted an offer to conduct Fisher's new TV show. Sinatra then nominated Billy May to arrange and conduct his next sessions, but May had to cancel because he was on tour with his own band; and so it was that Gilmore brought together one of the greatest teams in the history of popular music. From the sessions of late April and early May, Billy May got label credit for "South of the Border," but it was the ex–Dorsey arranger Nelson Riddle who had done it in May's style, with a lasciviously slurping reed section. Of the eight tracks recorded, three made it into the top twenty, but something new was happening. One of the nicest was a new ballad called "My One and Only Love," which didn't chart at all, but it didn't matter; and the tune on the other side of the single changed a lot of people's listening habits.

In mid-1953 I was twelve years old, and crazy about music. I was interested in jazz, but there was none of that on the radio; I liked what we called "popular instrumentals," like Percy Faith's "Delicado," because I liked the sound of an orchestra (I was looking for classical music, though I didn't know it yet). I liked Fisher and Jo Stafford and the others well enough, but I didn't have much money to buy records anyway, and I was bored half to death, because I couldn't find enough music to listen to: in those days there were many fewer radio stations than now, and almost no FM at all. In July I was hanging around in an ice-cream parlor in the resort town of Lake Geneva, Wisconsin; a radio was playing, and suddenly there was the most amazing brass fanfare, some interesting harmony from the reeds, and then Sinatra began singing, slowly at first, but expectantly, a familiar old song:

I've got the world on a string...
Sittin' on a rainbow...
Got the string around my fi-i-inger...

(stringing out the word "finger," teasing me, though I didn't know what I was waiting for) and then, *Pow!*—the band came in swinging, two-beat style, perhaps influenced by Sy Oliver, and everything was all right: every note in the right place, the best kind of playing because it sounded like it was being improvised on the spot. I knew who Frank Sinatra was; I had heard him on the radio since I was little. He was somebody my mother liked, and the press didn't. He was supposed to be a loser, always in some kind of trouble, but now I knew that that must have been wrong. Sinatra has always cared what people say about him, even when it's his own fault, to the point of trying to stop people from writing about him; but with regard to his music, he has said that, whatever people say about him, nothing matters except that when he is singing he is honest. I knew that was true, listening to his new record: he really did have the world on a string, because he said so, and that was that. Feeling sorry for myself the way only a frustrated poverty-stricken almost-teenager can feel, I nevertheless felt better for the rest of that muggy July day, having heard that record on the radio, and over forty years later I still feel better every time I hear it.

When Frank Sinatra came out of the eight weeks of work on *From Here to Eternity* a new man, knowing he had done well in the best part he'd ever had, he also knew he was making good records.

In May he and Ava left on a tour of Europe; he had gigs booked in several cities, and she was shooting a film in England. They quarreled constantly. The picture, *Knights of the Round Table*, was a turkey, with Robert Taylor, who should have played one of the horses; *Ivanhoe*, also with Taylor, had been a hit the year before, and the studio was trying to cash in. Such costume dramas showed a profit in those years, but Ava must have known that the work had little value, while Sinatra knew that he was back on top again. Journalists were impressed with the new sparkle in his eye, and he got good reviews in England, but his domestic life actually got worse. "We were happy when he was on the skids," Ava said in August, but the truth was that they could never get along. He was insanely jealous when she was out of sight, yet he could not resist being seen and even photographed with other beautiful women, to make *her* jealous. It is true that his changing fortunes made him more arrogant than ever; he had to dominate a woman as though she were hired help, and Ava was the last person to put up with that. Their quarrels were so violent that the police sometimes had to be called, and neither could be the first to make a conciliatory move. They behaved like children, yet they must have been changed by their passion. They were each the other's greatest love, and, if they could not stay together, at least they had clashed memorably, doing their best to conquer each other. Their marriage did not last until its second anniversary in November, though he chased her around the world for a while longer; they were not divorced until 1957. But when they finally gave up the game, they each had some new, harder steel in their souls; having loved like that and lost is almost as good as having the world on a string. Many years later, Little Nancy asked her father if he would leave Big Nancy for Ava again, if he could do it over; and he answered that he would not. But that was whistling in the dark. He had never had any choice.

On the last day of filming *From Here to Eternity*, Sinatra had disagreed with the others over how a scene should be done, and Harry Cohn was so angry he sent Sinatra away before he'd even seen the final rushes; but he knew he had a hit on his hands. Sinatra returned to the U.S.A. to find showbiz agog over the film and his part in it. It opened in August in New York; it was unheard of to launch a major film during the summer holidays, but Cohn knew he didn't have to worry. It did record business at the Capitol Theater on Broadway, and Richard Watts wrote about Sinatra's performance in the *New York Post*, "Instead of exploiting a personality, he proves he is an actor by playing the luckless Maggio with a kind of doomed gaiety that is both real and immensely touching." A film guide now describes it as a "cleaned-up and streamlined version of a best-seller"; David Thompson, one of today's most interesting film critics, feels that the novel's robustness scared off the director—he describes Zinneman as "middlebrow"—and that Sinatra's performance is superficial.

Today's viewers can make up their own minds; the cultural artifacts of the past can seem to look different each time we see them. But in 1953 the picture and all its performances were dynamite. The poster photo of Burt Lancaster and Deborah Kerr having an adulterous snog in the surf became a film industry icon; *From Here to Eternity* was nominated for twelve Oscars and won eight, the most any picture had won since *Gone With the Wind* before the war; and all this for a picture with no gimmicks: it had no wide screen, no 3-D process and it wasn't even in color. All it had was a good story, a good script and good acting. And among the Oscar nominations was Best Supporting Performance (Male) for Frank Sinatra.

The night before the awards ceremony, in March 1954, he had dinner with Nancy and the children. They gave him a little gold medal with St. Genesius on one side (the patron saint of actors) and Oscar on the other. He was their Oscar, whether he won or not, and he knew it, but he had now reduced Big Nancy to the status of best friend; one can only try to imagine what she was feeling that evening. The next night his two eldest children accompanied him, and they had to sit through most of the awards: unlike nowadays, all the big ones came at the end. Some of the competition was stiff—other nominees for best supporting actor included Jack Palance for his demonic murdering gunfighter in *Shane*, and Robert Strauss for his scruffy, hilarious prisoner in *Stalag 17*. When Sinatra's win was announced, the ovation was one of the longest of the evening, because there's nothing Hollywood likes better than a comeback, and especially if it's a solid one: nobody voted for Sinatra because they felt sorry for him. Accepting the award he seemed to be at a loss for words, as though he really hadn't thought about what he would say: "If I start thanking everybody I'll do a one-reeler," was the best he could do.

Afterwards, he rang Nancy, and he rang his mother in New Jersey. Allegedly, he was overheard saying "Yes Mama... No Mama..." over and over. Dolly had long since given up on Nancy, who didn't take any nonsense from her; she liked Ava (they no doubt admired each other's guts) and had engineered at least one reconciliation after a violent quarrel. But no matter who Sinatra was married to or separated from, he still needed his mother's approval. There was a telegram of congratulations from Ava. She had been nominated too, for her part in *Mogambo*, the only nomination she ever had; she hadn't won, but she certainly knew how important his win was, and that she deserved some reflected glory. He later joked about the Oscar: "It was a dream that came true. It's quite a dream. I still have it three nights a week. I'd have it seven nights but I don't go to bed four nights a week." But at the time he was sharing a bachelor pad with composer Jule Styne, who often saw him sitting alone in a dimly lit room, surrounded by photos of Ava.

Already in February 1954, a month before the Oscars, a Sinatra record called "Young-at-Heart" was a hit. It was a song he didn't much care for, but four years earlier he had turned down "Mona Lisa," which turned out to be an Oscar-winning song and a huge hit for Nat Cole, so this time he took somebody's advice, and "Young-at-Heart" made number two in the *Billboard* retail pop chart, his biggest hit since 1946. Meanwhile he'd been signed to do a picture called *Pink Tights*, co-starring with Marilyn Monroe, who never showed up; he spent some weeks cooling his heels on the set of a film that was never made. His pals Styne and Sammy Cahn had written some songs for that film, and were similarly sitting around doing nothing, when the studio needed a song in a hurry for a film that was finished but had only just acquired its final title: *Three Coins in the Fountain*. They wrote a soupy ballad in a couple of hours, and then needed a demo to send to New York: in a wonderful story which Cahn never tired of telling, he conned Sinatra into doing it. Thinking he was going to make a demo as a favor with Styne on piano, Sinatra walked onto a soundstage to be confronted with sixty musicians and conductor Lionel Newman on the podium, and that recording is said to be the one used in the soundtrack. Be that as it may, the song won an Oscar; the number-one hit version was by the Four Aces, a vocal quartet that sang all their slow numbers with a shuffle beat, and all these years later I still hate the dumb song. Sinatra's Capitol studio version recorded with Riddle reached the top ten.

He continued having hits in the *Billboard* singles chart for over twenty-five years, but only nine more reached the top ten, and that didn't matter, because meanwhile something far more important and interesting was happening to the record business, something neither Mitch Miller nor Capitol Records nor Frank Sinatra could have anticipated. In 1947, when the long-playing record was introduced, Sinatra's biggest fans, the generation of the returning soldiers and their brides, were short of cash: some were going to college on the GI bill, and the rest were starting families. But by 1954 they were becoming more prosperous. Some of them still had their Frank Sinatra 78s, but now they were buying albums, not singles. They were buying Frank Sinatra albums.

To put things in perspective, most of the number-one albums in those days were the film soundtracks: in 1954–55 the biggest sellers were the scores from *The Student Prince* and *The Glenn Miller Story*; in 1955 the only vocalists who had number-one albums were Doris Day and Sammy Davis, Jr., and Day's album was soundtrack-related (*Love Me or Leave Me*). In 1956 album sales reached a new high; the number-one albums included three soundtracks, a Broadway musical original-cast album, and two albums each by Harry Belafonte and Elvis Presley: we were entering a new era. But between February 1954 and May 1957, Sinatra's first seven albums on Capitol, arranged and conducted by Nelson Riddle, all reached the top ten of the *Billboard* album chart; only *This Is Sinatra!*, a compilation of singles, did not reach the top five. In 1958 Sinatra albums on Capitol spent a total of ten weeks at number one (each staying in the charts over 100 weeks), while a two-LP compilation on Columbia, *The Frank Sinatra Story*, reached number twelve (his debt to Columbia had been repaid quickly, and his royalties on that back catalog soon amounted to $50,000 a year).

The baby boom's orthodoxy is that album sales became more important than singles only in the 1960s, but this was never true. Long-playing records always made more money than singles, and at a time when more albums were being sold than ever before, Sinatra was easily beating the competition. In the 1954–57 period no other singer, not even Nat Cole, Perry Como, or Bing Crosby, did as well; only Eddie Fisher had some hit albums. Back at Columbia, Mitch Miller's biggest artists, Frankie Laine, Guy Mitchell, Tony Bennett, Rosemary Clooney, and Johnny Ray, had no hit albums at all in this period; nor did Patti Page or Kay Starr or any of the other singles-sellers. Talk about a comeback: while Miller was having hit singles with noisy, witless junk and banjo-ridden nineteenth-century campfire songs ("The Yellow Rose of Texas"), Sinatra was reckoned to be the biggest-selling album artist of all by a wide margin during 1955–59, and for the entire decade of the 1960s he was beaten only by the Beatles.

All this emphasis on chart comparisons would be merely vulgar and pointless today, but in the mid-1950s the markets for singles and albums had diverged completely; even the recording sessions were usually different. Albums were a lot more expensive then, relatively speaking, and they were not impulse purchases, so the music that was made for them had to be of more lasting value. Sinatra was making records for grownups, people who bought records carefully and kept them and continued playing them for many years, and replaced them when they wore out: records, in other words, that are still selling forty years later. And it is not too much to say that Sinatra's enduring reputation as the greatest pop singer of the century could rest on these 1954–57 albums with Nelson Riddle.

Songs for Young Lovers and *Swing Easy* were both ten-inch LPs with four songs on each side, and both reached number three in 1954; later they had tracks added and were reissued in the twelve-inch format with six songs on each side. That worked well enough, but the original albums had been well planned, so finally the original running orders were restored on one twelve-inch LP with eight songs on each side. Because of the way song royalties were paid by the U.S. record industry, albums with seven or eight songs on each side cost more than those with only six, but people bought Sinatra's anyway. The romantic *Songs for Young Lovers* began with "My Funny Valentine," a song Sinatra had practically made his own, and was a nicely paced album, with two uptempo tracks ("A Foggy Day" at number three, and "I Get a Kick Out of You" halfway through), ending with "Violets for Your Furs." The lineup of the "chamber group" Columbia sessions was revived, the band including just two horns, a rhythm section and four strings, but this time the four strings were the Hollywood String Quartet: Felix Slatkin and Paul Shure, violins, Paul Robyn, viola, and Eleanor Aller Slatkin, cello. With Capitol's first-rate sound quality and a group that was also making legendary chamber-music recordings for Capitol's classical division, the result was pure class.

And when you turned the twelve-inch over, you got a different set: the band on *Swing Easy* was a fourteen-piece swing band that never got in the way, because Riddle's arrangements abolished the artificial distance between the ballad and the swinger. If it had seemed in the 1940s that a pop record had to be either a soupy ballad or a novelty, now Sinatra and Riddle demonstrated that ballads with strings didn't have to be soupy, and that love songs could be nicely uptempo without being frenetic, from "Just One of Those Things" to a remake of "All of Me," which had been one of Sinatra's best swingers at Columbia. And the boyish enthusiasm of 1947 had been replaced by mature skill: the illusion of swing was now fully and effortlessly accomplished. Confirmation that Sinatra was back at the top came with wins in both *Metronome* and *down beat* polls, while *Billboard* named him as top male vocalist, "Young-at-Heart" as best single, and *Swing Easy* as best album.

In the Wee Small Hours came next, often described as the first concept album: in fact it was only further proof that Sinatra (and Gilmore and Riddle) were thinking in terms of albums far ahead of most other recording teams. It was first released on two ten-inch LPs (confusingly using the same number with different pre-fixes), but was soon squeezed onto one twelve-inch, and that was the end of the ten-inch era. The sixteen songs about unrequited love and loneliness were nearly all recorded in early 1955, when he knew beyond doubt that his marriage to Ava had failed. Sinatra had known how his fans felt in 1941, when they were all young together; by 1955 a lot of people in that generation were finding out that living happily ever after isn't so easy after all, and Sinatra knew how that felt too, still there for the fans when they weren't kids anymore. For many years we have heard a lot about the baby boomers, but it was no picnic being the parents of the most priv-ileged generation in history: no wonder they bought Sinatra's albums. And the songs! Some were remakes, like Rodgers and Hart's "It Never Entered My Mind," which he'd recorded for

Columbia, and there were others he hadn't got around to before, like Alec Wilder's "I'll Be Around": he never seemed to run out of good ones in those years, and he sang them better than ever, because, like Billie Holiday, the older he got the more he knew what the words meant.

Often he inserted a syllable or dropped a word to make the song swing the way he felt it, and like all the greatest singers he often altered a melody line. Composers sometimes didn't like this; Cole Porter complained about the way Sinatra did one of his tunes. Mel Tormé, in his book *It Wasn't All Velvet*, tells of singing "Blue Moon" for the soundtrack of the Rodgers and Hart biopic *Words and Music* in 1948. The song as written goes like this:

> Blue moon,
> You knew just what I was there for,
> You heard me saying a prayer for
> Someone I really could care for.

This is a rare example of Rodgers and Hart writing a song that was hillbilly enough for Elvis Presley. Tormé wanted to sing: "You heard me saying a prayer.../For someone I really could care for," using his own rhythm to make the extra syllable fit in the last line. Rodgers didn't like it, but Tormé had his way, so that it sounded as though the words meant something to him, rather than as if he were reading them off the page. This sort of singing reached its peak in the 1950s, just as the songwriting had passed its peak; and Sinatra, who had learned to talk before he ever heard a radio, let alone a television, was the acknowledged master of it.

The song had to be sung as it was felt. When Billie sang "I'll Never Be the Same," she changed the words, singing "I'll never be the same all day" (no wise guy was going to break her heart), but on *Wee Small Hours* Sinatra sang it the way it was written: "I'll never be the same again." He made the clumsy word "again" sound perfectly natural spread across two notes, because he'd been a sucker for Ava and he'd screwed it up, and she would never be his again, and he would never be the same again. There was no room for bravado here: he could fool himself some of the time, but not when he had a song to sing.

It was immediately evident that Nelson Riddle deserved a lot of credit. His arrangements are equal partners with the singer, but never getting in the way. While the charts add up to a beautiful album, there is no sameness because they are also each tailored to the song. Here there's a muted trumpet solo from Harry Edison, there it's a reed section of Mahlon Clark, Skeets Herfurt, Babe Russin and Ted Nash, making a blend that any leader could have been proud of. "Mood Indigo" is unique to start with because it's a Duke Ellington tune, basically an instrumental with words added, and the words aren't really up to much; so while Sinatra makes the best that can be made of them, Riddle takes a post-modernist glance at the music of the century: here and there the reeds (including flutes, and in one passage combined with muted trumpets) sound like an unanswered question by Charles Ives; there's a passage for plucked strings that might pay homage to Bartók, a short passage of double time that echoes New Orleans jazz, and then the writing for saxes is first in the style of Billy May and then (appropriately) Ellington. Yet on several tunes, such as "Dancing on the Ceiling," there's only a quartet, because lying in an empty bed looking up at the movie in your mind is *lonely*.

There is enormous variety here, yet all adding up to an album with its own integrity. Startling evidence of the importance of Riddle's work is provided by comparing a session of December 13, 1954, with trumpeter and band leader Ray Anthony, and arrangements by Dick Reynolds, almost the only one of over forty Sinatra recording sessions at Capitol between April 1953 and April 1957 that wasn't directed by Riddle. "Melody of Love" was a 1903 waltz with 1954 words added; it was not right for Sinatra. The other tune recorded that day was a hey-look-at-me anthem, "I'm Gonna Live 'Til I Die," which Frankie Laine used in his cabaret act. The arrangement isn't bad, and it's well played, the studio band including many of the same people who played on Riddle's sessions; but it is one of those frenetic swingers that is somehow trying too hard. It would have made a fine souvenir of a stage show in some gin palace, but it would never fit on the albums Sinatra and Riddle were making. It was the last gasp of the pre-modern Sinatra; now, in his albums with Riddle, he had not only survived, but was singing better than ever.

Not that Sinatra's behavior had changed much. Also in 1954 Sinatra and Joe DiMaggio decided that Marilyn Monroe was having a lesbian relationship, so they hired a couple of goons and smashed down the door of an apartment in New York City, frightening some strangers half to death: they were in the wrong apartment. A lawsuit resulted, and Sinatra swore that he had stayed outside while the others smashed down the door; he was suspected of perjury, but it was decided that there was not enough proof. An eyewitness who had claimed to see him actually inside the apartment was mysteriously beaten up. (Years later, Sinatra had an affair with Monroe and then passed her around to his friends; the former baseball hero DiMaggio remained deeply in love with his ex-wife, and never forgave Sinatra.) But the albums Sinatra was making in the mid-1950s transcended all that. Items from gossip columns are as nothing compared to the flowering of the talent that had made him famous. As an actor, too, he was doing interesting work, though the level of inspiration could not be up to that of the albums, given the problems of the film industry during the 1950s, with fewer cinema tickets being sold each year.

One of the tunes from an early Capitol session, a torchy ballad called "From Here to Eternity," had been written for the film, cashing in as a minor hit. Sinatra was now a freelance actor and in demand; his next picture was *Suddenly*, a tight thriller (over forty minutes shorter in its released version than *From Here to Eternity*) in which he played a would-be presidential assassin. *Not As a Stranger* was a slow hospital melodrama in which Robert Mitchum and Sinatra were wasted, but again a solid acting job; both these were for United Artists. Meanwhile Jack Warner had an idea: he liked to raid his own locker, avoiding the cost of acquiring or developing a new property; Sinatra had a big hit record and Warner liked Sinatra, so he dusted off a piece of small-town hokum from 1938 called *Four Daughters* and turned it into a musical for Doris Day and Frank Sinatra called *Young at Heart*. The original had been a sensational film debut for John Garfield, but the remake got a lukewarm reception, too obviously a heartwringer cobbled together for its stars. Sinatra's character, a singer who needed somebody to love him, was probably the best thing about it, but it wasn't enough.

The Tender Trap saw him back at MGM, this time as the star; no dancing and no singing (except for the hit title song, behind the credits), and no competition with the magic of a Gene Kelly. The picture was a romantic comedy in the mainstream Hollywood style of the decade, with Sinatra as a Broadway playboy opposite Debbie Reynolds. The song, by Cahn and Jimmy Van Heusen, fell into the same category; it was a top-ten hit for Sinatra and nominated for an Oscar. Froth was big back then.

After the recording of *In the Wee Small Hours* Sinatra went to work on the set of *Guys and Dolls* for MGM, an incomprehensible disaster. Sinatra and Marlon Brando were miscast in each other's parts; Brando couldn't sing but he had all the best songs, and Sinatra couldn't stand Brando's working habits. The method actor had to think about it all day and then do it ten times; Sinatra said to writer-director Joe Mankiewicz, "Don't put me in the game, Coach, until Mumbles is through rehearsing." And the Damon Runyon–style dialogue was corny rubbish anyway. But Ava was in town; they were seen together here and there, and friends noticed a change in them: they could not live together, and had begun to give up on each other, yet they could not doubt the passion they had known. He was the closest thing she'd ever had to a man she could rely on; she referred to him as "Francis" or "my old man," and he fondly called her Mrs. Sinatra. The flame would never quite go out, but they had put down their torches; he had more time to spend with his children, and life went on. We have known love; we shall know love, or at least we can remember love. And the next album celebrated it.

Songs for Swingin' Lovers! was mostly recorded in January and February 1956, and became a hit album at the end of March: no time was wasted in those days. The title of the album has become mildly irritating; it was the beginning of swinging this and ring-a-ding that. Musicians who can swing don't have to talk about it, they just do it; and wasn't it around 1956 that "swinging" became a euphemism for suburban wife-swapping? But never mind the title: the album itself is one of the great pop documents of the century, celebrating the existential hope of romantic love with another fifteen of the best songs, in arrangements that are the best of their kind. With this album Sinatra and Riddle made themselves permanently the masters of their trade. There are wonderful individual tracks from almost all of Sinatra's career; but in retrospect it is impossible to exaggerate the importance of Nelson Riddle, because it was these albums and especially *Songs for Swingin' Lovers* (hereinafter I shall do without the exclamation point) that earned Sinatra his crown as our greatest singer of this kind of song. Henceforth he could have retired anytime, undefeated.

Among the many ways in which Sinatra had got older along with his fans, changing as they had changed, was that his voice had deepened and darkened. It had always been an attractive and distinctive voice, but it had now become even more so, the instantly recognizable Sinatra familiar now for so many years. Yet on *Songs for Swingin' Lovers* he actually sounds younger than he did in 1950. He taped the tracks for *Sing and Dance With Frank Sinatra* when his personal and professional lives were in a mess, while George Siravo's charts tried to recapture a Swing Era which was over; six years later, Riddle's charts were not retro music, but something new, and Sinatra was on his way up, not down, the love of his life behind him. As Bob Dylan would write a decade later, "I was so much older then; I'm younger than that now."

Along with the greater emotional understanding and experience, some might conclude that there was a slight falling-off of the technical mastery: but was there? During the 1940s his youthful intonation had seemed perfect; now the point was no longer to sing the songs perfectly, if it ever was. The more mature Sinatra was an even greater interpreter. Someone asked me, when I was starting to write this book, "Why does he always sing flat? Crosby never did; why does Sinatra sing flat?" I was startled: *Flat?* But when I thought about it, I was glad that I do not have perfect pitch to get in the way of my listening. In fact it is no accident that Sinatra warmed to Dorsey's trombone and to the violin of Jascha Heifitz (or that Riddle had been a trombonist): those are instruments that allow the player to make his or her own tonality, or microtonality. Henry Pleasants, a legitimate music critic who wrote a very good book about pop singers, put it like this:

While a note might not be, strictly speaking, out of tune, it could be just far enough off center for the listener to feel its resolution to be imperative, and to experience a sense of relief and satisfaction when it is resolved... the variance from true pitch is microtonal, and, because it is too slight, the average listener may be unaware of any variance at all. But he reacts to it.

Thus if on the first half of "Too Marvelous for Words" Sinatra sounds "flat," that's because he's almost talking the words. He's remembering that she was so marvelous that she's gone now, but the remembering (and the arrangement) has a bravura ending, and by the time he remembers just *how* marvelous she was, you doubt neither his knowledge of her nor his knowledge of tonality. He sings flat at the start, if that is what he does, because he is laconic, until the full memory of her hits him; he sings flat for the same reason Dexter Gordon has his own intonation on the tenor saxophone: because he is a great actor as well as a musician.

Almost every singer has critical pitches in his or her range where smoothness is a problem, where there is a seam or a join that can be "covered" by depressing the larynx. Pleasants points out that Sinatra knew how to do this, but usually didn't do it, not because the impression of the absence of technique sometimes seems central to pop music, but because the slight evidence of strain will suggest innocence, sincerity, loneliness, or whatever the song might call for. In other words, like every great artist, he knew how to use his own technical shortcomings in the service of the art. Al Jolson sang *at* you; Bing Crosby sang to himself, as though being overheard by the microphone; Sinatra used the microphone so well that it disappeared. The occasional sound of strain or tiredness, the touch of a New Jersey accent, what Arnold Shaw described as a counterpoint of toughness and tenderness: it is all there in Capitol's superb recorded sound of the mid-1950s, and honest mono at that.

During the 1940s the Sinatra vocal was like a jewel, and the Stordahl arrangement was a cushion of velvet or satin on which it reposed; during the Capitol years, the Sinatra version of a song became a modern work of art: now pointillist, now cubist, now abstract as the song and the mood demanded. Here he slipped across the bar lines like a magician; there he sang on the beat, sending the words home like hammer blows. The voice was smooth as smoke, but here and there allowed to crack with emotion. Sinatra has a great reputation as a swinger: if he is too much in control to swing the way a jazz musician swings, he is a great interpreter, and if a great arrangement allows him the illusion of swing, that is enough. (Are the songs not about an illusion, of love?) Riddle's studio band might sound on these tracks as though it was working hard, but Sinatra made it sound easy, and in that paradox is part of the illusion. Always there was that amazing ability to sing as many bars as he liked without breathing; and to continue the metaphor with visual art, the Riddle arrangement is the only possible frame for each picture. For Riddle was a designer, and each song is a story, with a beginning, a middle and an end; the frame is ornamented, yet never overstated (because Riddle is a master of dynamics), but reveals the song's structure. It is as though song and arrangement were composed together by a lovestruck Beethoven of pop.

The hit singles on the radio in the early- to mid-1950s may have been rubbish as the U.S.A. began to use its increasing prosperity to trash its own culture, but when it came to making albums for grownups, the veterans of the Swing Era (albeit confined to the recording studios) knew what they were doing: musical lessons had been learned, so that (for example) the playing of studio rhythm sections in the mid-1950s was much better than that of the white bands of the 1930s and 1940s. The rhythm section on the 1950 album *Sing and Dance With Frank Sinatra* is not that much different from the albums of a few years later, but the arrangements are different, and Voyle Gilmore's studio was probably a nicer place to work than Mitch Miller's. More to the point, the years between 1950 and 1956 were crucial: a few more years to absorb the rhythmic lessons of modern jazz, and to get used to studio work in the era of tape recording; the arrangement wasn't limited to the playing time of a ten-inch 78. Also, Sinatra liked to have an audience of friends and hangers-on in the studio, who would have been appreciative of the band's playing. In some ways it must have been almost like being back on the bandstand at the Palomar, or Roseland, or Glen Island.

Riddle's studio band included the best of the Swing Era's survivors, who could play anything, and a good thing, too: a map of one of the arrangements from *Songs for Swingin' Lovers* might look too crowded on a piece of paper, too densely populated, yet in the listening everything is cherishable. The bass clarinet, the bass trombone, the baritone sax, are used as springboards for phrases; Harry Edison's muted trumpet became famous from these sessions, not a part of the trumpet section as such, but heckling fondly from the sidelines, "filling in the windows" as Buck Clayton once did for Billie Holiday. (Sinatra reportedly insisted that Edison have his own microphone to play into.) Bassist Joe Comfort had played in Nat Cole's trio, later worked for Perez Prado, Harry James, and Billy May, and then played on most of the Sinatra-Riddle sessions, again and again lending harmonic sophistication as well as a superb beat: he played some well-deserved solo bits on "Too Marvelous for Words." The experienced pianist Bill Miller had joined Sinatra when he was at the bottom, in the early 1950s, and was still with him in the 1990s: his fills on celesta all over the Riddle albums are part of their beauty.

The celesta is an instrument that can easily become irritating, but not here. Similarly, flutes are often merely distracting in a jazz-based arrangement, but Riddle's flutes (in various registers and combinations) peep out from the shrubbery like a family of woodland creatures sneaking closer for a better look: indeed, the whole arrangement is like an affectionate audience, murmuring intelligent commentary. The sections of the band provide ghosts of countermelody, teasing us: What are we going to hear next? Or they point out the harmonic sophistication of the tune: again and again Riddle reveals what it is that makes a so-called standard a high-class piece of work compared to most of Tin Pan Alley's output. And there's the strings: it always comes as a little surprise to remember that, yes, there are strings on these tracks, because Riddle uses them not as a tax dodge, nor to saw away slushily in order to impress some booking agent, but as another section in the band, an equal partner with every other section, and with the singer. Where the strings actually carry the melody, proudly, rightly, as in the middle of "You Brought a New Kind of Love to Me," far from intruding, they make you wonder why every band didn't have strings. There's all this stuff going on, and it's all a joy, because each detail is a joy, and nothing gets in the way.

In early 1956 when *Songs for Swingin' Lovers* was recorded, the average age of the fifteen songs was just under twenty years. The oldest, from 1923, was "Swingin' Down the Lane," by Gus Kahn and bandleader Isham Jones, surely an early-modern use of that word "swingin'." Another old one, from 1928, was "Makin' Whoopee," a song one would not have expected: Isn't it slightly corny? But it was co-written by Walter Donaldson, one of Sinatra's favorite writers, many of whose songs can be effortlessly updated, as in this case. Sinatra's coolly knowing delivery and Riddle's setting, full of gentle joshing, was perfect for Sinatra's fans in 1956, who had made their whoopee and were now saddled with mortgages on houses in the suburbs: if their fathers had chuckled at Eddie Cantor's version in 1930, it was time for a new generation to see itself in the mirror.

The tempo of each tune is exactly right. If you notice that you've been seeing rather a lot of a certain person, and you think to yourself, "You're getting to be a habit with me," it should be a sort of expectant stroll, almost (but not quite) fast enough for a tap-dance: happiness might be just around the corner, but you don't want to hope too much. Milt Bernhardt plays a famous trombone solo on "I've Got You Under My Skin;" that arrangement, said to have been written in a hurry and greeted by applause in the studio, is the most successful of all, rising to a controlled frenzy before it is over, halfway through the album. It is followed by "I Thought About You," a little slower; then "We'll Be Together Again," the slowest track on the album; then "Makin' Whoopee" picks it up again: the perfect tempo of each track is matched by the programming of the set as a whole. *Songs for Swingin' Lovers* is one of those albums on which entire careers could have stood or fallen, and there was a lot more to come.

The month after *Songs for Swingin' Lovers* was recorded, and not quite fourteen years after the Capitol label had been formed, the famous Capitol Tower opened in Hollywood: the label was now so successful that it was able to build its own landmark, and the first Sinatra session in the new building was an instrumental album called *Tone Poems of Color*. He conducted a set of twelve original pieces suggested by colors, written by Riddle, Victor Young, Billy May, Gordon Jenkins, Alec Wilder, Elmer Bernstein, Jeff Alexander, and André Previn. This is the rarest of all Sinatra albums, even less well known than his 1945 recordings of Wilder's music. (On Capitol he also conducted an album by Peggy Lee in 1957, *The Man I Love*, with arrangements by Riddle, and one by Dean Martin in 1958, *Sleep Warm*, written by Pete King.)

Then, recorded in March and April 1956, together with a session from the following November, came *Close to You*, an album of ballads, again featuring the Hollywood String Quartet. With only a few extra solo musicians in addition to the quartet and the rhythm section, the chamber-music feeling was even more intimate than on *Songs for Young Lovers*. On that album there was a fresh and youthful feeling as the horns occasionally played chirpy bits in unison; on *Close to You* there is only one solo instrument on each track, no chirpy bits and no uptempo tracks at all. On *In the Wee Small Hours* the tempi were all slow, but with a full-sized orchestra; on *Close to You*, with a much smaller, yet tightly arranged group, the string quartet almost dominates the arrangements. Sinatra and Riddle were not only concentrating on making albums, but each album was different; they were too intelligent and restless to copy themselves, and *Close to You* took longer to make than any of their other collaborations.

Songs for Young Lovers was romantic; *In the Wee Small Hours* was about loneliness; now *Close to You* combined elements of those albums to make one about various unsettling aspects of love. Again there were a few remakes; the title song was revived from 1943 and "Everything Happens to Me" from the Dorsey years, but all the songs represented snapshots of emotions: "Love Locked Out," "It's Easy to Remember." "P.S. I Love You" was a Gordon Jenkins song from 1934, a hit for Rudy Vallee; it had been revived for a 1953 hit single by the Hilltoppers (another of those vocal groups with a slow shuffle beat) and was then recorded by Billie Holiday in 1954, and now by Sinatra. He would have remembered the 1934 Vallee hit; he knew about all the tunes: for this album he rescued another Walter Donaldson song, "I've Had My Moments," from a forgotten comedy film (*Hollywood Party*, 1935). The most unusual track on the album, at the end of the first side, was "Don't Like Goodbyes," by Harold Arlen and Truman Capote, from *House of Flowers*, a show that flopped on Broadway in 1954. Gerald Bordman has written, "An intangible gossamer grace rendered the show somehow untheatrical," and the same could be said of the song (arranged by Riddle without any rhythm section, just four strings and an almost inaudible French horn), and about *Close to You* as a whole: too good for the market. *Close to You* is a fine album, and it was a number-five hit in the *Billboard* chart early in 1957, yet compared to the other Riddle-Sinatra albums it remains obscure and often unavailable. The Hollywood String Quartet was credited on the cover, and to the average punter "string quartet" means "classical": a fair number of fans may have been put off over the years thinking that the album was another of Sinatra's high-toned experiments. Which of course it was: a wholly successful one.

Two songs from the recording sessions could not be fitted onto the original album, "If It's the Last Thing I Do" and "Wait 'Til You See Her," as well as a joke: "There's a Flaw in My Flue" (with a line "Smoke gets in my nose") was allegedly recorded as a prank, but nobody at Capitol noticed. All three were included on a CD edition of *Close to You*, itself out of print by 1995.

Meanwhile, *Songs for Swingin' Lovers* had hit the charts early in 1956, the same week as Elvis Presley's first album, which hogged the top spot for ten weeks. Presley was seen by much of the music business of the time as a fluke, a carnival sideshow freak, while his album marked the beginning of a wider market for albums: kids, country-music fans and African-Americans bought Presley, all people who had not bought many albums until then. (And remember that that was the last decade to see an appreciable number of hit musical shows and films: Presley was dislodged from the top by the original-cast album of *My Fair Lady*, which stayed there for fifteen weeks.) *This Is Sinatra!* was the compilation of singles (including film songs) which went top ten, but *Songs for Swingin' Lovers* actually stayed in the charts longer than Presley's debut, and as soon as *Close to You* had been recorded, a sequel to *Songs for Swingin' Lovers* was on the way.

Arranging, or orchestrating, has always been one of the most important yet unsung jobs in popular music. Few people have heard of Robert Russell Bennett, for example, who was not only a prolific American composer, but was responsible for the sound of Broadway, orchestrating many of the biggest hit shows between 1923 and 1960. During the Swing Era the arrangers for the big bands, whether writing a chart for a pop song or composing an original tune, would create what was effectively a tone poem, a musical miniature, except it was the kind of piece you could dance to. Jerry Gray, to name just one arranger, created two of the classics of the era: Artie Shaw's version of Cole Porter's "Begin the Beguine" (1938) and Gray's original "A String of Pearls" for Glenn Miller (1942). In classical music Mahler, Strauss and Shostakovich memorably orchestrated some of their own songs, but in that music the melody, harmony and orchestration are all part of an integral work of art, whereas in commercial music the chores were parceled out. Significantly, Duke Ellington was almost the only Swing Era bandleader who was also the composer and the arranger, and he is generally considered to have been the greatest of all. Nelson Riddle had started in the Swing Era, working for Tommy Dorsey, but in the 1950s it was still the case that the arranger was paid a flat fee for each chart: Riddle was probably paid around $50 for Nat Cole's "Mona Lisa," one of the biggest hits of 1950, and a hundred dollars a chart for *Songs for Swingin' Lovers*: $1,500 for writing an album that is still selling forty years later.

A Swingin' Affair was recorded in November 1956 (except for "No One Ever Tells You," made in April) and hit the *Billboard* chart in May 1957. It is the first of the Sinatra-Riddle projects that is not a masterpiece *qua* album: it is a marvelous set, beloved of Sinatra fans, and almost any track on it could have fit on *Songs for Swingin' Lovers*, yet as an album it doesn't hold up as well, perhaps because Riddle was working too hard. But perhaps Sinatra knew that he had made a masterpiece with *Songs for Swingin' Lovers*, and didn't exercise his usual judgement over the songs and the arrangements on the follow-up album; with Sinatra there was always the danger of the attitude that he could do no wrong.

A Swingin' Affair opened with "Night and Day," a song that has been associated with Sinatra since the 1942 session with Axel Stordahl, and he would record it again, but this Riddle arrangement became a famous one. (Sinatra's diction is incredibly good, as always: at the very beginning you can hear two separate letter "d" sounds in "and" and "day.") "I've Got You Under My Skin" from *Songs for Swingin' Lovers* had made such an impression that by this time the fans" favorite cliché was that Sinatra sounded like he was swinging hard, but it was the band that was doing all the work; "Night and Day" is a good example of this, but the new album was made with the cliché too much in mind: on half a dozen tracks the arrangement starts off interestingly, but the band works harder and harder only to stop rather suddenly, as though Riddle had run out of manuscript paper. "I Got Plenty o' Nuttin'" is one of these; indeed it almost harks back to the Swing Era: Sinatra sings the songs, then George Roberts's bass trombone introduces an exposition for the band which takes a third of the track before Sinatra comes back. "I Won't Dance" and "From This Moment On" also suffer from a too-relentless application of the formula, now become a two-beat treatment with the drummer playing a loud backbeat, almost as if they were trying to turn these standards into rock 'n' roll.

"Lonesome Road" was the opener on the second side of the LP; at nearly four minutes it is one of the longest tracks on the album, but it is a song from another era by Nat Shilkret and Gene Austin, and should have been left there, with its repetitious tune and corny lyric about "weary totin' such a load" (it had been shoved into the 1929 film version of *Show Boat*, mimed by Stepin Fetchit). What is this doing on an album called *A Swingin' Affair*? On "Stars Fell on Alabama," Sinatra changes the melody line slightly in a pleasing bit of interpretation, but also changes the lyric: "stars fractured 'Bama" should have been confined to live gigs; listening to it over and over on the record becomes tedious. But Rodgers and Hart's "I Wish I Were In Love Again" is right up Sinatra Street, with its unforgettably sardonic lyrics:

When love congeals
It soon reveals
The faint aroma of performing seals
The double-crossing of a pair of heels
I wish I were in love again.

"No One Ever Tells You" was a new song in 1956, and a good one; "If I Had You" was a remake from 1947 and "Oh! Look at Me Now" from the Dorsey years; both are fine, along with "I Guess I'll Have to Change My Plan." Altogether, *A Swingin' Affair* seemed to mark the end of the beginning of Sinatra's Capitol albums; in some places it is a brash showing-off kind of set. There is nothing terminally objectionable about it, but it is not as fine an album as it might have been, either.

During the recording sessions two versions of "The Lady Is a Tramp" were made, one for the soundtrack of *Pal Joey* and one for a single or an album; this was finally added to the CD issue of *A Swingin' Affair*, to make sixteen tracks altogether. Sinatra played with the lyrics on "Tramp" too; it has always been one of my favorite Sinatra tracks, and I am not one of those who objects to the word "broads" for women. We took it for granted as slightly vulgar slang in the 1950s, and when you met a woman in a bar you hoped she would have a sense of humor. But again, it begins to jar after you've heard it a few dozen times, and might have been better confined to a club act. Meanwhile, Riddle wasn't the only one who was working hard. While he was arranging nearly 140 tracks for Sinatra between April 1953 and March 1957, Sinatra also made a dozen movies, including *From Here to Eternity* but not counting cameos in *Meet Me in Las Vegas* and *Around the World in Eighty Days*, both in 1956. With around sixty film roles altogether during his career, after *From Here to Eternity* he had become one of the biggest box-office draws in Hollywood's history. Some of the later ones weren't very good, but every single one of them made a profit, which is all that matters in Hollywood.

After *Guys and Dolls*, Sinatra's next film was one of his best, a controversial picture about drugs called *The Man With the Golden Arm*. Sinatra had wanted the part of Terry Malloy in *On the Waterfront* in 1954; producer Sam Spiegel and director Elia Kazan wanted Sinatra, but Harry Cohn at Columbia was putting up the money, and he wanted Marlon Brando. Sinatra was furious. Then Brando got the better of the two male leads in *Guys and Dolls*, which was the worst mistake Sam Goldwyn ever made; but now, in Otto Preminger's version of Nelson Algren's novel about a small-time gambler who becomes a drug addict, it was Brando's turn to be furious: Sinatra snatched *The Man With the Golden Arm* from under Brando's nose by agreeing to do it without even seeing the entire script. Preminger liked working with Sinatra, and, in a postscript to the story, many years later Preminger was offered *The Godfather* by Paramount, and in turn offered the part of Don Vito Corleone to Sinatra, who turned it down. So Preminger turned the film down too, and of course when the film was finally made by Francis Ford Coppola, it was Brando who turned in one of the best performances of his career.

There is something strange about the careers of Frank Sinatra and Marlon Brando being so intertwined; except that they both appeared in *Guys and Dolls*, one wouldn't think of them at the same time. Brando can't sing, but is no doubt the greater actor; as many films as Sinatra made, we still think of him primarily as a singer. Yet both men had serious character flaws which kept them from doing much of the best work they might have done on the screen. Brando's absurd ego and his disgust with himself and with his profession has meant that only a handful of his films are really first-class work; Sinatra was too impatient with the nuts and bolts of filmmaking to become the really first-rate actor he might have been. If Brando is the greater actor, some of his disgust with Hollywood was justified; his self-directed western, *One-Eyed Jacks* (1960), might have been a masterpiece, but we'll never know: it was butchered by the studio before it was released. But the film industry does not make allowances for egos like Brando, Orson Welles or Frank Sinatra. Brando described his own profession as empty and useless; Welles was described as "an active loafer, a wise madman"; Sinatra could do as he wished, but the overall result of his film career was disappointing. Movies have to be made on an assembly line, like any other mass-produced commodity; they have to be movies that the public wants to see, and it was during the 1950s that Hollywood, competing with television, came up with the slogan "Movies are better than ever." As the competition for the mass audience became keener, movies were worse than ever, and there was even less room for the destructive ego.

It is really quite remarkable that some of Frank Sinatra's films are still watchable, and given the nature of filmmaking in the

1950s, even the best of them are touch-and-go. The chores in film-making are broken down and parceled out even more than in the recording studio, and Sinatra's nature would not allow him to take part in a collaborative process. He wanted to be the studio boss, telling everybody else what to do; but at the same time, he wanted to come in, walk through his role and go home, and if the film flopped, as with everything else in his life except his singing, it would be someone else's fault. Preminger liked working with Sinatra because Sinatra was reliable when it came to learning his lines and turning up on time; but when Sinatra wanted to fire an electrician who'd somehow got in his bad books, Preminger was the sort of professional who could quietly make it clear that he was the one who did the firing. Sinatra admired Preminger, and talked about how much he'd learned from him, but as with Montgomery Clift on *From Here to Eternity*, what he learned from the professionals never seemed to seep into his own attitudes.

The Man With the Golden Arm benefited from a score by Elmer Bernstein; the soundtrack was a hit album in 1956, and there were several hit versions of the driving main theme, the biggest by bandleader Richard Maltby. Preminger's treatment of heroin addiction was controversial at the time, even though he watered down the story and gave it a happy ending. (Nelson Algren was a writer who was deeply suspicious of Hollywood, but he loved the way Sinatra played his character, Frankie Machine, whose golden arm, by the way, had nothing to do with the drug, but referred to the way he dealt cards.) Sinatra's acting, including succumbing to heroin (with Darren McGavin wonderfully creepy as a pusher) and later going cold turkey, seemed like dynamite in the mid-1950s, but he never fully absorbed the lesson that he was at his best playing characters who were not quite in control of themselves.

In general, the richer and more powerful Sinatra became the worse his movies got. Each film has to begin with an idea, a proposal from someone or other; Sinatra's knack of picking good ideas of his own (such as it was) did not outlast the 1950s by much. It is interesting that many of his best pictures were in black-and-white. Producers liked monochrome because it was cheaper than color and kept the budget down (the reverse is true now, when everything is made in color). It may be that the extra pizazz color added to a picture was at odds with the sort of characters Sinatra played best. *Golden Arm* was in monochrome, and so was *Johnny Concho* in 1956, a well-made, small-scale western for United Artists.

Also in 1956 came MGM's *High Society*, which must have seemed like a good idea at the time, with Cole Porter songs, starring Grace Kelly, Louis Armstrong, Gene Kelly, and Crosby and Sinatra together on-screen and singing a duet. This was a musical version of a play, Philip Barry's *The Philadelphia Story*, and it doesn't hang together at all, as though they all knew it was fluff. "Now You Has Jazz" with Crosby and Armstrong was merely insulting, "Well, Did You Evah" was reclaimed from Porter's trunk for Crosby and Sinatra, and "True Love" for Kelly and Crosby was a hit single and nominated for an Oscar, but it must be the weakest song Porter ever wrote: the world in which he was at his peak was long gone. *The Pride and the Passion* in 1957 was another bad idea, for United Artists, a star-studded costume melodrama about a bunch of people dragging a big cannon across Spain in 1810, forty-five minutes longer than *Johnny Concho*, in blazing color, with Sinatra, Cary Grant and Sophia Loren all wasted.

But also in 1957 there were two better films. *Pal Joey* was in some ways a typical Hollywood version of a Broadway musical, tinkered with and mauled a bit, but the original show in 1940 (revived in 1952) had been controversial, because the hero was a heel and one of the two female leads was past her prime. The book was by novelist John O'Hara (from his stories first published in *The New Yorker*), the music by Rodgers and Hart, and the whole thing was ahead of its time. The original songs included "I Could Write a Book" and "Bewitched, Bothered and Bewildered"; the latter had made little impression in 1940, except that it was regarded as daringly suggestive. But suddenly in 1950 there had been nine hit singles on it, the first and biggest a fluke: an instrumental version by pianist Bill Snyder on a tiny independent label was the sort of serendipity that we used to get in popular music now and then, establishing the song as a standard and perhaps encouraging the show's Broadway revival in 1952. Gene Kelly had played Joey in the original, Harold Lang onstage in 1952, but it is hard to imagine anyone other than Sinatra in the part now. In fact, in his tempestuous private and public lives and in his art since sometime in the 1940s, among other things he had been helping to establish the anti-hero at the heart of popular culture: Joey is a shallow, selfish gigolo who wants to run a nightclub, but somebody else has to put up the money; in the film, Rita Hayworth plays the hard-bitten femme fatale, and Kim Novak the younger woman who loves Joey. It was typical of a Hollywood studio (in this case, Columbia) to drag in songs from other Rodgers and Hart shows: "The Lady is a Tramp," "I Didn't Know What Time It Was" and "There's a Small Hotel" all came from other sources, while an appropriate but lesser-known song from the original, "Take Him," was dropped. But the result was a soundtrack album that spent twenty-seven weeks in the *Billboard* charts.

The other interesting Sinatra film in 1957 was a monochrome effort for Paramount, *The Joker Is Wild*. It was much too long (nearly twenty minutes longer than *Pal Joey*), but it was the true story of another wise guy, with songs added: Joe E. Lewis was a nightclub singer in the 1920s whose throat was slashed by gangsters, whereupon he became an even more famous comedian. Despite all the rumors about Sinatra's involvement with the Mob over the years, *The Joker Is Wild* is a picture in which the hoodlums are definitely the bad guys; his acting job was creditable, although he does not make a convincing comedian. Among the songs in the picture was "All the Way," by Cahn and Van Heusen, which won an Oscar.

In the mid-1950s Sinatra was a member of the Holmby Hills Rat Pack, whose ringleader was Humphrey Bogart. Other members included Lauren Bacall (Mrs. Bogart), Mr. and Mrs. Sid Luft (Judy Garland), Hollywood agent Swifty Lazar, David Niven, restaurateur Mike Romanoff, and songwriter Jimmy Van Heusen. They were iconoclasts who got together for the purpose of laughing, drinking a lot and staying up late; and being an iconoclast was essential in the 1950s. The U.S.A. was making more films and records and broadcasting more entertainment than had ever been seen before, and most of it was junk; television was famously described by a federal official as "a vast wasteland." Teenagers who were jazz fans (or Sinatra fans) in the mid-1950s were hipper than those who listened to the Crew Cuts (this was the era when mainstream pop music finally got so bad that Stan Freberg couldn't satirize it anymore), and it was necessary to know that Ernie Kovacs and Sid Caesar were funnier than *I Love Lucy* or *Ozzie and Harriet*. This was the sort of thing the Rat Pack would have been good at. In-jokes, teasing and funny names for everybody were also de rigueur; Sinatra was called the Pope, or El Dago.

Not just anybody could call Sinatra a dago. Some people in Hollywood disapproved of the Rat Pack, perhaps because they were not included, but most of its partying was probably done in private, and Bogart was always in charge. He was a well-read man who was absolutely secure in himself, and was held in such affection that the more he insulted Sinatra or the press the better they liked it. When Ava Gardner was driving Frank crazy by playing around with a bullfighter, Bogart said to her, "I'll never figure you broads out. Half the world's female population would throw themselves at Frank's feet, and here you are flouncing around with guys who wear capes and little ballerina slippers." (She told him to mind his own business.) Bogart liked Frank, but considered him immature, describing him as "a kind of Don Quixote, tilting at windmills, fighting people who don't want to fight." When he remarked that Sinatra would define paradise as a place where there were plenty of women and no newspapermen, he added, "He doesn't realize it, but he'd be better off if it were the other way around." He also knew that Sinatra would be a better actor if he paid a little more attention to business.

Sinatra had been anxious to go to Spain to make *The Pride and the Passion*, because that's where Ava was; his contract stipulated that no one could be paid more than he was, but when he got to Spain he hated it and behaved obnoxiously the whole time, squabbling about things like the type of car that would take him back and forth to the set. Sinatra probably admired and looked up to Bogart as much as any man he ever knew, but showbiz would have to take Sinatra as he was. Billy Wilder liked Sinatra but refused to work with him, knowing that it would probably drive him crazy; Wilder was one of those who thought that if Sinatra stopped spreading himself so thin and concentrated on acting, "his talent on film would be stupendous. That would be the only word. Stupendous." Shirley MacLaine speculated that perhaps Sinatra was afraid to put everything he had into it, the way he did singing, because then he wouldn't have anyone but himself to blame if it wasn't good enough. The way he always wanted to go with the first take may also have been a sort of gambling, effectively a roll of the dice with each scene; in fact he was always word-perfect on the first take (he clearly took film more seriously than television), but it is the nature of filmmaking that there are a large number of things that can go wrong on a take. Some directors could cope with Sinatra well, and when he appeared in a film with Spencer Tracy in 1962 he was in his element, because Tracy was another one who wanted to get it over with on the first take. But on the whole Sinatra's attitude was never going to allow him to realize his potential as an actor.

Bogart died in 1957, the same year Sinatra had his last stab at a TV series. He was even worse in a television studio than on a film set; he probably didn't even like television, but the whole country was watching TV, so he wanted to be a star there too, and the money was very good. He signed a three-year contract with ABC which included tax advantages and a majority owner-ship in thirty-six half-hour variety programs, as well as complete control over the content of the shows, saying that this time he wouldn't have anyone to blame but himself if he flopped, and that was the way he wanted it. The result debuted in October, and was a disaster to equal that of 1952; again he refused to rehearse or cooperate in any way. He would not even learn his lines, but read them off the TelePrompTer. Television skits depend entirely on ensemble skills (which is what made *Cheers* so successful thirty years later, for example), and the shooting schedule for a weekly program is even tighter than that for a film. But Sinatra behaved like a hooligan, as though he willed himself to fail; indeed, some of the critics thought that he despised the whole business and was effectively insulting the audience. On one program his guest was his crony Dean Martin, and the pair of them stood around making in-jokes that might have gone down well in Las Vegas. The series was canceled, and as the director Jack Donohue put it, "There are quite a few performers who have no business on television each week, and Sinatra is one of them."

Nelson Riddle had done all of Sinatra's musical arrangements in his films; but back in the recording studio Sinatra turned to Gordon Jenkins for his next album, *Where Are You?* He may have concluded simply that he and Riddle needed a rest from each other, and that he did not want to fall into a rut, as he had in the previous decade with Axel Stordahl. Or he may have been jealous of the amount of credit Riddle was getting for the quality of their albums together. Crosby allegedly advised Sinatra not to rely too much on one arranger, but if so Crosby should have kept his mouth shut; he recorded countless duets and one-offs with everybody under contract to Decca, but he never made an album with anything like the stature of *Songs for Swingin' Lovers.* Riddle's feelings were allegedly hurt, but it was certainly not the end of their work together. Sinatra wanted to make an album lush with strings, and in that area Jenkins had quite a track record.

Serving various apprenticeships with bands and on the radio during the Swing Era, Jenkins had then become a managing director at American Decca, making hits with Louis Armstrong, Peggy Lee, Dick Haymes and the Andrews Sisters, as well as Pete Seeger's folk quartet, the Weavers. His hit songs (apart from the previously mentioned "P.S. I Love You") included "When a Woman Loves a Man" (memorably recorded by Billie Holiday) and Benny Goodman's closing theme, "Goodbye." (Jenkins probably made more money from these few hits than Riddle made from all his arrangements.) He was a composer manqué, and his *Manhattan Towers* was a landmark of the LP era, a corny impressionistic suite with songs (including "Married I Can Always Get"), instrumental passages and narration. He first recorded it for Decca in 1945 and for Capitol a decade later, and there were other recordings, as well as concert versions (one for Las Vegas added comics, dancers, everything but the hat-check girl). *Manhattan Towers* remains very much a period piece, but by the mid-1950s Jenkins had gone freelance, and his arranging was in demand. When it came to albums with strings he was as highly regarded as Percy Faith, Paul Weston and Robert Farnon. In April 1957, just as Jenkins began recording with Sinatra, his album with Nat Cole,

Love Is the Thing, entered the *Billboard* chart and stayed at number one for eight weeks: "When I Fall in Love" and "Star Dust" from that album were so sumptuous that they sounded like little symphonies, and "Star Dust" got so much radio play that it took a 45 EP into the singles chart.

Made in April and May, *Where Are You* marked several milestones in Sinatra's recording career. Voyle Gilmore was replaced as producer by Dave Cavanaugh, and this was Sinatra's first stereo album; the vastly improved sound quality over what Columbia could do ten years earlier with Stordahl is important. If you are going to use a large string orchestra, the arrangement, the song and the vocalist must complement one another, with nothing getting in the way, and the balance of the sound is crucial. Jenkins's orchestra included three French horns, some woodwinds, and twenty or twenty-two strings, with no trumpets or trombones; not only was the studio full of the best string players on the West Coast, but the sound and the balance were virtually perfect. Before long, a great many stereo recordings would be overproduced, often putting the vocalist too far forward; one thinks not only of some of Sinatra's later albums, but of Billie Holiday's *Lady in Satin*, made only a year later at Columbia: the recording unfortunately emphasized the harshness in her voice at a time when her health was failing.

For my taste, there is often a problem with the use of such lush string orchestras anyway. The arrangements are too likely to become settings of no value in themselves; this is the opposite of Riddle's best work, in which the charts are an integral part, so that each track becomes a miniature work of art. The arrangers for strings were rarely adventurous at all; the object was always to be in the best possible taste, which means not to offend anyone. The two Jenkins arrangements mentioned above, on the Nat Cole album *Love Is the Thing*, are relatively impressive precisely because they are more listenable than such arrangements usually are. Another notable arrangement of this type is Percy Faith's chart on "The Song from Moulin Rouge (Where Is Your Heart)," a big hit in 1953 (sung by the Canadian Felicia Sanders); it is interesting that Faith was primarily an instrumentalist, and allegedly disliked accompanying singers. At any rate, Jenkins's arrangements on

Where Are You do not draw attention to themselves. Sinatra's vocals make it a beautiful album for listening late at night; Nick Fatool on drums can hardly be heard, and the bassist (John Ryan) does a superb job of playing ever so slightly behind the beat. The album could also be used for romantic dancing, because the lesson of Tommy Dorsey's band playing so well at slow tempi fifteen years earlier had been learned, and this was one of the things that Stordahl, Faith, Weston, Farnon and Jenkins all had in common: they always drew superb playing from their studio bands.

Once again the songs are well chosen. *Where Are You* is an album by a middle-aged man who knows that he is a failure at love; he has gone past loneliness now. Ava Gardner said that she knew their marriage was over when he rang her up while he was in bed with another woman, saying that as long as he had the name he was playing the game: it passes understanding how such an insensitive man could reveal so much self-knowledge just by singing popular songs, but that is sometimes the way; the artist can't help it. "Where Are You" itself came from a so-so musical film called *Top of the Town* in 1937; it was co-written by Jimmy McHugh, who had spent a few years writing shows at the Cotton Club for Duke Ellington's band. Several of the tunes are remakes: "The Night We Called It a Day" from the Dorsey years, "I'm a Fool to Want You" and Alec Wilder's "Where Is the One" from the Columbia period. "Lonely Town" by Leonard Bernstein, with lyrics by Betty Comden and Adolph Green, is from *On the Town* (1944), and it is gratifying to see it reprised here: not only is it a lovely song, but MGM had foolishly dropped it from the score when Sinatra's 1949 film was made. The only quibble I would make, listening to this album nearly forty years after it was made, is that "Laura" and "Baby, Won't You Please Come Home" should each have had a slightly quicker tempo, which would have lent the album just a touch more variety; they could have been nearly twice as fast without destroying the mood. In the case of "Laura," the melody itself seems to demand more tempo, but the choice of "Baby" for this album is itself remarkable. This classic of Dixieland cabaret was co-written by Clarence Williams, who was born near New Orleans nearly sixty years before this recording was made, and as a closer for the album more could have been made of the tongue-in-cheek fact of having it there at all. But on its own terms, *Where Are You* must be counted as a successful Sinatra recording project.

Next came the *Pal Joey* soundtrack album, with arrangements by Riddle, then a Christmas album with Jenkins (complete with "Jingle Bells"), and then *Come Fly With Me*, one of Sinatra's most famous albums, with yet another arranger, Billy May. The concept album was already becoming old hat; anyone could throw together twelve songs after girls' names, or (in this case) twelve about travel, and *Come Fly With Me* contains a measure of banality; the fair view to take is that much of it was meant to be tongue-in-cheek. The market was also changing: In the mid-1950s the old-fashioned 78 rpm record represented one-quarter of sales but less than 20 percent of dollar volume, so the record companies began squeezing it out, and by 1958 Americans were prosperous enough so that most people had up-to-date record players and could buy albums as impulse purchases. Deejays were paying more attention to albums: there was more profit in promoting an album, so there were 1,800 deejays receiving free copies, compared to only 50 a few years earlier. The number of albums released each year was multiplying, and all this meant that quality began to slip. A lot of people would buy an album because their neighbors had bought it, and deejays were playing the title track of *Come Fly With Me*.

Sinatra was becoming seriously rich, and had a reputation as a ferocious swinger in his private life; or to put it another way, he was living the fantasy life that a great many Americans envied, the American dream coming true: the invitation to jump on his jet plane and hop down to Acapulco was not to be resisted in a country where we were increasingly encouraged to remain adolescents as long as possible. "Come Fly With Me" itself was of course written by Cahn and Van Heusen; their film songs were instant fodder for Muzak, the 1950s equivalent of Bert Bacharach in the following decade, but "Come Fly With Me" was too lighthearted to offend. The next track on the album, however, was a dreary waltz: Victor Young's "Around the World (In 80 Days)," from the 1956 film. "Isle of Capri," "Blue Hawaii," and "On the Road to Mandalay" are simply silly; the latter had to be left off the U.K. edition of the album because the words were by Rudyard Kipling and his estate objected. Ary Barroso's "Brazil" is thrown away: the opportunity to turn a samba into a four-to-the-bar swinger is lost because of the way Sinatra mostly chants the words instead of floating over the beat. "Moonlight in Vermont," "Autumn in New York," "Let's Get Away from It All," and a few others are fine, the latter revived from the big production with Dorsey in 1941; "April in Paris" is lovely, while it is tempting to speculate that "London by Night" reminded Sinatra of a few weeks in that city with Ava that should have been idyllic, but weren't. Then the closer, "It's Nice to Go Trav'ling (But It's Oh, So Nice to Come Home)" is a risible novelty by Cahn and Van Heusen:

> And the Hudson River
> Makes you start to quiver
> Like the latest flivver
> That's simply drippin' with chrome.

Adolescents quivered over American cars in those days, and they were dripping with chrome, but a "flivver" was Henry Ford's original Model T, from two generations earlier. What can these words possibly have been about? In fact this was a throwaway album, as American culture was becoming a throwaway culture. Sinatra indulged himself with kidding around: in one song a girl is wearing a meatball on her finger; in another he's going on a cruise for some exotic booze all the way to a bar in Bombay, but in a third he can hardly wait to get home to make a pizza. Voyle Gilmore was back as producer, stereo was still a new technique, and the early stereo sound of *Come Fly With Me* is loud and brash: people liked that in those days; it made their hi-fi sets sound good. Entering the charts in early 1958, *Come Fly With Me* was number one for five weeks, and in the top fifty for over seventy weeks. Among the number-one singles in the U.S.A. in 1958 were "Witch Doctor" ("Ooo! Eee! Ooo Ah Ah! Ting! Tang! Walla Walla Bing Bang!"), and Danny and the Juniors' "At the Hop" ("Let's go to the hop!" repeated endlessly to a frenetic beat): the singles chart had been turned over entirely to children, and

Sinatra's first number-one album since 1946 was an album for older kids.

Whatever you thought of the album, however, you could listen to the band. Sinatra and Billy May had known each other for nearly twenty years before they finally worked together, and nobody was more likely to arrange a tongue-in-cheek album than May. As a trumpet player and arranger he had contributed to the happiest of all the white swing bands, that of Charlie Barnet, in 1939–40, leaving to go with Glenn Miller because Miller could pay more, but working for Miller was not as much fun: May's chart on "Ida, Sweet as Apple Cider" was supposed to have a jive vocal by the band, but Miller wouldn't allow it. Miller's delightful version of "I Got Rhythm," recorded live in early 1942, is almost certainly a May arrangement, the band loping along and having such a good time with it that one wonders if Miller hadn't taken the night off. In the early 1950s May and saxophonist Al Klink liked to make wisecracks such as "Adolf Hitler is alive and well and playing Fender bass for Glenn Miller in Argentina."

But also in the early 1950s, May became something of an institution at Capitol, perhaps the only dance-band leader to have four top-ten albums in 1952–55, including *Sorta-May*, with such unusual fare as "Donkey Serenade" and "In a Persian Market." He also took care of all the little bits of musical humor and fill-in on the records and radio programs of satirist Stan Freberg, who memorably described May in his Hawaiian shirt at a recording session as looking like a porpoise at a luau. May admired the Sauter-Finnegan band, run by two of his colleagues from the Swing Era, Eddie Sauter and Bill Finnegan: It had a lot of humor and unusual instrumentation in its music, but it was a concert band rather than a dance band; May's arrangements for Sinatra's *Come Fly With Me* seem to have been inspired by it. The trademark Billy May slurping saxes make an appearance here and there; the muted trumpets sometimes squeak like mice, there's a vibraphone on one track, and tuneable drums can be heard, as well as a huge gong on "Mandalay." If the album is largely fluff, it is fun to listen to every ten years or so.

Sinatra appeared on the cover of *Time* magazine in 1957 as the highest-paid entertainer in the history of show business, said to be earning $4 million a year. He may have been able to take anybody to Acapulco who wanted to go, but his jet-set love life was not going so smoothly. Also in 1957 an actress he had been seeing took an overdose of sleeping pills, but recovered; and his pal Humphrey Bogart died of lung cancer. Bogart was the screen's favorite tough guy, but in fact had the kind of confidence allied with wit that meant he could do or say almost anything he wanted and get away with it. Sinatra had a much thinner skin. Before long he was running around with the widow, Lauren Bacall. He took her to the openings of *The Joker Is Wild* and *Pal Joey*, but he was afraid of getting serious, and so he should have been, after the disaster with Ava, who had only recently divorced him. And maybe there were guilt feelings involved; some thought that he had started romancing Bacall before Bogart died.

Bacall later wrote that when she first met Sinatra in 1945 she said, "They tell me you have a voice that makes women faint. So make me faint." He had to like that; her kind of attitude was what had made the Holmby Hills Rat Pack work. In March 1958 they became secretly engaged, but Swifty Lazar was in on the secret. Irving Lazar was a tiny, bald man, nicknamed Swifty by Bogart because of his ability to make deals; but the brilliant Hollywood agent was also a hopeless neurotic, and for years Sinatra and the others had played pranks on him. Sinatra once hired a plasterer to cover up the entrance to Lazar's clothes closet, so that at first he thought he was in the wrong apartment, and then he realized he couldn't get to his clothes, which was even worse. Perhaps Lazar was getting his own back at last when he shot his mouth off about the Sinatra-Bacall engagement. The next day it was in all the papers, whereupon Sinatra dumped Bacall and did not speak to her for several years; he not only rejected one of the most attractive, desirable, and intelligent women in Hollywood, but did it in as humiliating a way as possible. Ava was amused, and teased him about it. Two months later he began recording *Only the Lonely*, with Nelson Riddle, an album that was back up to standard.

Sinatra was getting used to loneliness, a fact of his life, and he now made an album dedicated to his fellow losers (allegedly, it was almost called *For Losers Only*). The practice was now established of having Cahn and Van Heusen write a title song, but this time the normally glib Cahn had some trouble. "Session after session without the glimmer of a line," wrote Van Heusen, who offered to change the melody here and there, but Cahn wouldn't allow it, and said later that he usually refused to write a lyric that came hard, but was glad he'd persevered with "Only the Lonely," and it is certainly one of their better ones. After a rest from each other, once again Riddle and Sinatra broke new ground together, and later when Riddle was asked which were his favorite albums he'd made with Sinatra, he unhesitatingly named *Songs for Swingin' Lovers* and *Only the Lonely*. There is a large orchestra, with lots of Riddle's instrumental felicities, French horns, woodwinds, trombone solos, and so forth, yet the album has a minimalist feeling. After the line "Pardon me, but I gotta run" in "Angel Eyes," two bassoons make what can only be described as a muttering sound, startlingly apposite; Joe Comfort is back on bass, and nails down "What's New?" with wonderful grace notes, while the same track (well over five minutes long) also has a pair of trombones, then an oboe during the instrumental bridge. And on the bridge in "It's a Lonesome Old Town," the strings behind the trombone solo are surreal in the upper reaches of the harmony: the town is not only lonely, it is empty and cold. Carroll Lewis on muted trumpet plays the role Harry Edison played on earlier albums, but he is his own man, more detached, resigned rather than sardonic.

"Willow Weep for Me" could have had a slightly quicker tempo; all the tempi are very slow, as on *Where Are You*, and in fact the first recording session for this album was aborted after three tracks: at the end of May they were remade and four more were successfully got down with Felix Slatkin conducting (Riddle was allegedly not that good a conductor, and a slow tempo is more difficult to conduct than a swinger). It was at the second session that Sinatra famously failed to negotiate Billy Strayhorn's "Lush Life," a difficult tune; after three attempts he can be heard on the master tape walking out of the studio and slamming the door.

Riddle was back on the podium in June. To me, Gordon Jenkins' "Goodbye" always sounded simply dreary when Benny Goodman played it (but that may be the influence of the awful Goodman biopic of 1955); here Riddle's arrangement starts with a fat English horn sound (which can be the most mournful sound of all), followed downwards by a cello, then a string bass played arco (with the bow): We think, What song is this? And then Sinatra reveals that it might be a pretty good song after all. (There were two basses at the session, Comfort and Edward Gilbert, probably to do the bowing here and there.) "Blues in the Night," by Harold Arlen and Johnny Mercer, had six memorable hit versions in 1941–42, and Sinatra may have recorded it with Dorsey, but if he did, that version is lost; Rosemary Clooney revived it in 1952. In 1958 Sinatra and Riddle have all the familiar accents in the arrangement, but they are now definitive: it is as though we know what the song means at last, and there is resignation instead of melodrama. Cahn and Styne's "Guess I'll Hang My Tears Out to Dry" is revived from the Columbia years, with a very affecting solo guitar accompaniment; and the somewhat lugubrious "Ebb Tide" gets a more convincing performance than one would have thought possible. "Spring Is Here" and "Gone With the Wind" are followed by a classic: the first recording of "One for My Baby" (Arlen and Mercer again) with Bill Miller's piano and minimal orchestral backing. Sinatra had recorded the song in 1947, but here it became his own; it was actually recorded in the studio with a single spot on Sinatra, just as he did it in clubs.

Listening to the CD edition of *Only the Lonely* all these years later, one would like to remix it; Sinatra's voice is too far forward, a little boomy here and there, which isn't fair to anybody. Capitol has added a couple of tracks to the CD edition of each Sinatra album to pad out the playing time; one appreciates that they would be criticized if they didn't do that, but the original albums were thoughtfully arranged and compiled, and in many cases they should be left alone. In this case, "Sleep Warm" from a session of September 1958 would work as a new closer by itself, but "Where or When" from the same session has a bravura ending which doesn't belong on this album at all. *Only the Lonely* remains one of Sinatra's mature classics, made at a time when Capitol still displayed a lot of good judgement. But Sinatra wanted still more control over his affairs, and began to resent being under contract to Capitol.

He never liked not being in complete control. When Columbia

began reissuing Sinatra's old records on long-playing albums, he seemed to resent it. The old Columbia sides made successful albums, but selling in a different market than the original 78s, a grownup market, which should have vindicated Sinatra; but by that time rock 'n' roll was making inroads into all the markets, and Sinatra's old hatred of Mitch Miller was rekindled. There are plenty of reasons to regret Miller, who hastened the process of turning the singles market into wallpaper for the ears, but Sinatra tried to blame all his troubles in those years on Miller, which was nonsense. The memory of the painful period when his career seemed to be on the skids still rankled, and he had to blame it on somebody.

Rock 'n' roll was just another genre, a fusion of hillbilly music and black rhythm-and-blues, but Sinatra loathed Elvis Presley and his like, writing for publication about this "most brutal, ugly, degenerate, vicious" form of expression, saying that "it smells phony and false." (It is interesting that "vicious" was one of Sinatra's favorite adjectives, while it would also be the best word to describe some of his own behavior.) The best rock 'n' roll was musically simplistic, but anything but phony, a joyous, raucous, uninhibited music allowing people who would not have been welcome at one of Sinatra's shows their own form of expression; furthermore, to the extent that rock 'n' roll rhythms and songs were sexually suggestive, they were at least not hypocritical about it. Sinatra's type of song was very often about sex, but obliquely so, while the sheer number of women in Sinatra's life represented a standard of vulgarity that the most jaded rock 'n' roller could not hope to exceed. Sinatra had done a great deal in the 1940s to break down the hypocrisy of the studio system and its morals clauses, but when the urban working class (both black and white) began to express itself through R&B and rock 'n' roll, he turned out to have a good line in hypocrisy of his own. The ABC network got some of its money back from the fiasco of the 1957–58 TV series when Sinatra hosted several one-hour specials; on the last of these, in 1960, he finally got high ratings by welcoming the despised Elvis Presley home from the army. Presley's ten-minute appearance brought Sinatra's program the highest TV rating recorded in five years; but perhaps this was an early example of a kind of confusion that began to affect his artistic decision-making.

Meanwhile, Miller also disliked rock 'n' roll, but had the good sense to declare that there was no such thing as immoral music. In a speech at a disk-jockey convention in 1958, he accused the deejays of abdicating their responsibility, of pandering "to the eight- to fourteen-year-olds, to the preshave crowds that make up 12 percent of the country's population and zero percent of its buying power." In fact Elvis Presley was setting sales records, and a lot of his output must have been purchased by adults, while Miller had done as much to cheapen pop music as anyone. But Miller's point was that the broadcasters were chasing the top forty and ignoring most of the music that was available in the marketplace, which was bad for music, and he was right. The deejays gave him a standing ovation, but the Storz broadcasting chain (sponsoring the convention) then banned Columbia Records. Broadcasters who were chasing the largest common denominator did not want to be called upon to separate the gems from the dross.

In those days Columbia was clean and was not bribing deejays (the practice known as payola), nor did the company have any direct connection with music publishing. But when Congress decided to investigate payola in 1958–59, Sinatra stuck his oar in, claiming that he had been forced to record substandard stuff at Columbia because the parent company, CBS, had some connection with BMI (Broadcast Music Incorporated). In fact, when the music licensing organization ASCAP (the American Society of Composers, Authors and Publishers) went on strike against the broadcasters in 1940, trying to force them to pay a much higher royalty rate for each piece of music broadcast, it lost the strike ignominiously; the broadcasters had clubbed together to set up a competing agency, and BMI saw to it that black and hillbilly songwriters and publishers, always ignored by ASCAP, got a fair piece of the action; and all this still rankled twenty years later. Congressmen were trying to get votes by investigating "dirty" songs, and the industry tried to use public concern about rock 'n' roll as a stick with which to beat BMI. But Miller had only to point out that Sinatra's contract at Columbia had given him complete control over what songs he recorded; that of fifty-seven tunes Sinatra recorded for Miller only five had been BMI songs, and two of those published by Sinatra's own BMI company; and that "Young-at-Heart," the soppy ballad that had been one of Sinatra's biggest hits ever, on Capitol in 1954, was a BMI song. The truth is simply that there was something in Sinatra, his childhood loneliness, his awful mother or whatever, which meant that if anything went wrong it must have been somebody else's fault, and when he shot his mouth off he often demonstrated poor judgement.

Capitol Records had been sold to EMI in 1955, a move which Johnny Mercer later regretted; Glenn Wallichs was still chairman, but the sale freed Sinatra from any feelings of loyalty he should have had to the company which had relaunched him as one of the most successful recording artists of the century. From early 1956, when recording began at the Capitol Tower, Sinatra's masters were produced by his own Essex Productions: Capitol still owned them, but Sinatra's royalties were paid to his corporation, which was a tax advantage. (There was a Bristol Corporation that served the same purpose in his film work.) In 1957 he had signed a new seven-year contract with Capitol, but immediately regretted it: he had realized that the way to have complete control and to keep more of the profit was to start his own record company. He wanted Essex to become his own subsidiary label, but he was ahead of his time once again: nobody had such a deal in 1958. So he began agitating to be released from his contract. He was no longer happy with Gilmore as his producer, and switched permanently to Cavanaugh, a saxophonist and arranger whom he had known for some years; and he began to threaten to withdraw his labor—to stop recording—which was really the only weapon he had.

But recording continued for the time being. The next album, made in December 1958 with Billy May, was *Come Dance With Me!*, in a straightforward Swing Era style: no fancy bits or knobs-on, just brass and reed sections answering each other, as in the good old days. With Conrad Gozzo and Mannie Klein in the trumpet section, Milt Bernhardt back on trombone, old friends Babe Russin and Skeets Herfurt in the reeds, and Shelly Manne or Irv Cottler on drums, the crew was well equipped, and the whole thing is reminiscent of the 1950 Columbia album *Sing and Dance With Frank Sinatra*, except that the rhythm section is less stiff; in fact some of the new arrangements were by Heini Beau. Along with George Siravo, Beau had often written this type of thing for Axel Stordahl to conduct at Columbia. He could write in the style of Billy May or whoever he was helping out, and May himself was often very busy and only too happy to buy a few charts from Beau. (May was also a self-confessed procrastinator: he often came to a recording session with work unfinished, but always pulled it off in the end.)

The trouble with *Come Dance With Me* was that, like all retro pop music, the main purpose of it was nostalgia. There is not a single solo on the whole thing, despite all the fine musicians on hand. If the rhythm section is less stiff, it also does not sound very involved. On most of the tracks there is a two-beat feeling on what are clearly supposed to be re-creations of the peak of the Swing Era, but it has none of the unique flavor of Sy Oliver's best work, while the driving four-to-the-bar rhythm section of a Charlie Barnet or a Woody Herman is missed, as though the cast was all too aware that they were recording for fans who were now pushing middle age. The combination of corn and May's wacky sense of humor on *Come Fly With Me* is also missing. "Saturday Night (Is the Loneliest Night of the Week)" and "The Song Is You" were remade, and "Day In, Day Out" was Sinatra's fourth recording of that tune for Capitol; he could do this sort of thing in his sleep by now, and all the accents are in the right place, but he does not sound terribly involved, either. "Baubles, Bangles and Beads" has some words added ("Them cool, cool beads") to fill out the dull originals. Cahn and Van Heusen wrote the title opener, which isn't up to much, and the closer, "The Last Dance," which is better, the only slow one in the set. *Come Dance With Me* is eerily out-of-date, the same way the earlier Columbia album missed the boat: the Swing Era, an era of bands on the road and playing for live audiences every night, was over. Still, a lot of Sinatra's longtime fans must have had a good time dancing to this album; *Come Dance With Me* won a Grammy as Album of the Year in 1959. Like the album itself, the Grammy might have been a bow to yesteryear.

Four appropriate tracks have been added to the CD edition of *Come Dance With Me*: all had been made a few months earlier for release as singles. DeSylva, Brown and Henderson's "It All

Depends on You" had been recorded for Columbia, while "Same Old Song and Dance," "Nothing in Common," and "How Are Ya Fixed for Love" are better-than-average Cahn and Van Heusen ditties, the last two duets with Keely Smith, who brings plenty of the right chirpy spirit. The irony is that the four added tracks are more fun than the rest of the album, without the labored feeling that comes with cranking out tracks for a retro concept.

Look to Your Heart was a Capitol compilation, top ten in mid-1959; then it was back to Gordon Jenkins for another loneliness concept, No One Cares, made in March 1959. No One Cares is similar to the earlier Where Are You: tasteful strings, choirs of harmonizing reeds and/or French horns, a firm rhythm section and (again with Cavanaugh producing) perfect sound balance. The songs are good ones and Sinatra's delivery heartfelt, more evidence that his artistry was instinctive or it was nothing. The songs on Songs for Swingin' Lovers were all standards that he loved to sing and that perhaps made him feel young again, and on that album he had Riddle's best work to inspire him. But "Why Try to Change Me Now," "Here's That Rainy Day" and the rest of the songs on No One Cares are simply better suited to him than "Something's Gotta Give," "Too Close for Comfort" and the rest of the jivers on Come Dance With Me. He is now a forty-four-year-old who has loved and lost, and knows that he has lost for good. Anybody who tried to best Sinatra in a business deal (or tell him what to do or drink him under the table or take his photograph without permission) would find out what a loser was, but when it came to love he was the prince of losers, and he knew it; there is no other explanation for the way he sings these kinds of songs, so that we do not need to hear anyone else sing them. Billie Holiday sang sad songs, but her sadness was existential, as though maybe it wasn't her fault, and anyway her bravery shone through. Sinatra is simply bereft.

"Cottage for Sale" and "Ghost of a Chance" are just lovely; "I'll Never Smile Again" is remade, after nearly twenty years. It is nice to hear the intro to "I Can't Get Started" ("Superman turns out to be flash in the pan"), and the verses are updated: "I've flown around the world in a plane / Designed the latest IBM brain..." Indeed, another line seems to hark back to the corny "Mandalay" pretense:

In Cincinnatti or in Rangoon,
I simply smile and all the gals swoon;
Their whims I've more than just charted,
But I can't get started with you.

Now there's an admission: he's got all the broads he wants, and he wants them and likes them and charts their whims up and down, but the one he wants most of all has been and gone, or maybe hasn't turned up yet, and maybe he even begins to suspect that she doesn't exist.

On this album there was no sense of the customer getting his or her money's worth. There were only eleven tracks on the original edition of *No One Cares*, none of them as long as four minutes, and one of them was Tchaikovsky's "None But the Lonely Heart," which should have been left in the previous century. The CD adds some interesting things: a slow version of "The One I Love (Belongs to Somebody Else)," which had been a semi-jiver in the Dorsey years, had already been added to some later LP editions; and "You Forgot All the Words (While I Still Remember the Tune)" is an obscure but thoughtful song co-written by Bernie Wayne, a craftsman responsible for tearjerkers like "Laughing on the Outside (Crying on the Inside)" and "Blue Velvet," which turns up every few years like a bad penny. Sinatra was always one to give a song a chance, but it was becoming harder to find them.

Then he laid down his gauntlet. He was now so rich and famous that his arrogance began to manifest itself outside the saloons of Hollywood and Las Vegas; Sinatra and his friends in what came to be called the Clan were providing much of the spice in the showbiz columns. In April 1959 he visited Australia, and was completely unprepared for the sheer feistiness of the Australian press; he did not make a good impression. (Ava Gardner was there, shooting *On the Beach*, and she did not make a good impression either, saying, "I'm here to make a film about the end of the world and this sure is the place for it.") Sinatra redoubled his effort to take complete control of his professional life; between May 1959 and March 1960 he did not make any recordings except tracks for the musical film *Can-Can*; and then his dispute with Capitol was settled: they agreed to let him go before his contract ran out in return for four more albums.

Nice 'N' Easy, made in March and April 1960 with Nelson Riddle, had an informal photo of a smiling, comfortable, casual Sinatra on the cover, instead of garish artwork or a designer's idea of hipness, and twelve songs, nearly all remakes that everybody liked to hear him sing: "That Old Feeling," "How Deep Is the Ocean," "Fools Rush In," "Embraceable You," "Mam'selle" (his number-one hit from 1947) and so forth; the album was irresistible and the biggest chart success of his career (in the nick of time, while Elvis Presley was in the army and the Beatles were popping pills in Hamburg). The title song was a new one, not by Cahn and Van Heusen for a change; it seemed to be about premature ejaculation ("The problem now of course is / To simply hold our horses"). It did not fit terribly well with the rest of the album, but got a fair amount of airplay as a single, which helped: the album was number one for nine weeks and in the chart for eighty-six weeks.

The following year, 1961, he would have no fewer than six chart albums: all in the top ten, four in the top five. He paid off some of his obligation to Capitol with remakes of the songs he had recorded for the Columbia album *Sing and Dance With Frank Sinatra* in 1950. *Sinatra's Swingin' Session!!!* with Nelson Riddle (and three silly exclamation points) included six of the eight tunes from the 1950 album (with more interesting arrangements), and *Come Swing With Me!* with Billy May included another. The album with May was a retread of *Come Dance With Me*, but a more appealing album, with a smoother rhythm section (Joe Comfort back on bass), some medium-tempo and a couple of slower tracks for variety (for example, "Sentimental Journey"). Again, several tunes are remakes from the 1940s: "Five Minutes More," "American Beauty Rose." More than half the tracks were arranged by Beau, including "That Old Black Magic," which swipes its intro idea from Artie Shaw's "Begin the Beguine," and "Lover," with a pungent bass trombone in its intro. The CD adds five appropriate tracks with May, Riddle, or Skip Martin, and on the whole the album's bow to the Swing Era was less self-conscious than most such efforts.

All the Way was a Capitol compilation album, but no fewer than three Sinatra chart albums in 1961 were the first three albums on his new label, Reprise, for which he had already started recording in December 1960. Sinatra had tried to buy Verve Records from Norman Granz, but the deal fell through; then he had already made two albums for his new label before he made his last original album for Capitol, which he didn't really want to make at all. *Point of No Return*, made in September 1961, saw the return of Axel Stordahl, whose skill had been so important to Sinatra from the Dorsey years right up until 1953; Sinatra was in a hurry, and most of the tracks were done in one take (there is a very audible tape splice at the end of "These Foolish Things," on the last word Sinatra sings: "remind me of *you*"). But a miracle happened. The songs, of memory and regret, were well chosen, such as "As Time Goes By," "September Song," Noël Coward's "I'll See You Again"; "I'll Remember April" is particularly fine, introduced with a unique rhythmic pattern set down by Comfort on bass, and delicate percussion, almost chinoiserie. The tracks vary in length from two and a half minutes to more than four for "September Song," and one is glad for tape recording and the long-playing record: no doubt there is something about not being limited to the playing time of a ten-inch 78 that can help to set the music free. These arrangements of Stordahl's somehow sound less self-conscious than the old Columbia 78s. Sinatra may have been feeling impatient, but he was incapable of not turning in a professional job in the recording studio, while Stordahl was glad to be working with his old chum once more.

Stordahl was ill with cancer, and died less than two years later, just fifty years old; he had spent four years in the mid-1950s with Eddie Fisher and made some other albums, but he hadn't done a lot of the kind of writing he had been used to doing with Sinatra. Yet their old working relationship reestablished itself immediately and, if anything, Stordahl had actually improved. His string writing was as reliable as ever, but everything else fell into place as well; even the rhythm section, rarely audible on the Columbia sides, had a reason for being, and the arrangements are more fun to listen to than the lushness of Gordon Jenkins. With producer Cavanaugh and Capitol's recorded sound deserving some of the credit, the album was a great success, remembered with pride by everyone who was there. The CD edition includes the four tracks from April 1953, including a forgotten early version of "Day In, Day Out," combining Sinatra's first and last Capitol sessions and all his Capitol work with Stordahl on one disk.

Meanwhile, Sinatra was still making two films a year. *Kings Go Forth* in 1958 was a wartime melodrama; *Some Came Running* a postwar melodrama the same year, like *From Here to Eternity*, from a novel by James Jones. Sinatra saw to it that his friend Shirley MacLaine's part in *Some Came Running* was made more dramatic, by way of solving a problem that Sinatra himself had caused: When the film got behind schedule, he tore twenty pages out of the script and said to an assistant director, "There, pal. Now we're on schedule." The writers and the director had to pull the story together somehow, and Sinatra had thrown out one of MacLaine's scenes, so she received the dramatically rewritten ending, which resulted in an Oscar nomination for her.

Next was a Frank Capra movie. Capra's feel-good films were thought to be out of fashion: Americans could no longer be jollied along by the likes of *Mr. Deeds Goes to Town* and *You Can't Take It With You* (both from the 1930s); even *It's a Wonderful Life* had fallen flat in 1947, and Sinatra was no James Stewart. But he had discovered a property that he liked, and hired Capra to direct an easygoing sentimental comedy. Capra had a hard time dealing with Sinatra's work habits, and some scenes had to be improvised to keep everybody fresh, but *A Hole in the Head* was a box-office hit and revitalized Capra's career. (The theme song from *Some Came Running*, "To Love and Be Loved," was nominated for an Oscar, and "High Hopes" from *A Hole in the Head* won the following year: both were written by Cahn and Van Heusen, and "High Hopes" was Sinatra's third Oscar-winning hit single in six years.)

Never So Few in 1959 was about wartime jungle action in Burma, while *Can-Can* in 1960 was a dull musical: the 1953 Broadway version had established "It's All Right With Me," "I Love Paris," and "C'est Magnifique" as new Cole Porter standards, but musicals don't always translate well to the screen, and Hollywood often botched it. The set of *Can-Can* was visited by Soviet premier Nikita Khrushchev and his wife, and the papers got a chance to describe Sinatra's charm for a change instead of his bad manners.

So ended the most successful decade, in artistic terms, of Sinatra's career. He was now one of the most famous people in the world, both as a singer and as an actor, but much of his best work was behind him. Dean Martin and Peter Lawford, two of his Hollywood pals, had co-starred in *Some Came Running* and *Never So Few* respectively; his next film, still in 1960, was *Ocean's Eleven*, an overlong caper movie featuring the Clan: Sinatra, Martin, Lawford, Sammy Davis, Jr., and comic Joey Bishop, with the action periodically stopping for in-jokes. Sinatra would become richer and more famous, but he would also show more bad judgement as his power to do as he pleased began to coincide with a general decline in the quality of American popular and political culture. In 1960 he made a mistake which in retrospect signals this decline, and ironically the mistake lay in *not* doing as he pleased.

The object of the Holmby Hills Rat Pack had been to have a good time, but when Sinatra had assembled his own team of acolytes there was no Bogart to keep an eye on him, and the only object was to follow the leader. Not as well-read as Bogart, Sinatra's Clan invented its own schoolboyish vocabulary: all women were of course broads; death was the "Big Casino"; an act that flopped was "bombsville." The *-ville* suffix could be added to anything, as in Sinatra's famous quote about his own work: "The audience is like a broad—if you're indifferent, endsville."

Sammy Davis was a talented, crowd-pleasing singer and dancer who adored Sinatra, with plenty of reason to be grateful: they had already been close friends for a decade, since Sinatra had plucked Davis from obscurity in a trio act with his father and his uncle, and helped him to become the biggest black star in American entertainment since Nat Cole. Dean Martin had known Sinatra since 1948, and was one of the few people who never took any nonsense from him, eventually retiring with his integrity more or less intact. Joey Bishop was a successful stand-up comic useful for his one-liners. Peter Lawford was a second-rate actor, a drunk and finally a self-confessed pimp for the rich and famous, but he had some social cachet, apart from his English accent: In 1954 he had married a sister of John Fitzgerald Kennedy, a Democratic member of the House of Representatives from the state of Massachusetts, who looked increasingly like a successful candidate for the White House. The Clan period became legendary; Shirley MacLaine has described it:

> When we made pictures at the same time that the Clan was appearing in Vegas, there was an energy there that has never been duplicated since. Two shows a night, seven days a week, for three months—while shooting a picture. Granted, these pictures were not award winners...but the spontaneous humor on the stage and the set was unparalleled. The director never knew what was going to happen or how a scene would be played on a given day. But it didn't matter.

No doubt it was fun at the time, but it *did* matter. In retrospect, all these years later, all that jive looks and sounds like self-indulgence. And the spontaneous humor was not as free and easy as it seemed. The fact is that Dean Martin, for example, was a lot funnier than Frank Sinatra. The jokes were corny, many of them around the subject of booze: "Frank, do you know how to make a fruit cordial?" "No, Dean, how do you make a fruit cordial?" "Why, be nice to him!" But Martin could pull off this sort of thing; Sinatra could not. MacLaine goes on to describe how Sinatra got tired of Martin getting all the laughs, so one night they exchanged roles; and, instead of laughing at Sinatra's punch lines, the audience laughed at Martin's straight man. Martin's easy persona and his sense of comic timing are the reason he was a success on television and Sinatra was not; it is remarkable that they remained friends for so long. But as Joey Bishop said after Martin's death at the end of 1995, "I remember him most of all for his honesty. He hated anything that was phony and would not partake of it. He was one in a trillion." Martin and the others were having fun; one suspects that, even when he was trying to be funny, Sinatra took it all too seriously.

When Sinatra was at the bottom in the early 1950s, the story goes, he was walking down the street when he came across a gaggle of teenaged girls who recognized him, and poked fun at him, making it clear that they were Eddie Fisher fans. He took it well, allegedly telling them that he liked Fisher's singing too. But a decade later Fisher was a sort of mascot of the Clan, and one of their favorite pastimes was climbing onstage during his performance, making a shambles of it with their pranks. Fisher did not have the wit to take part in the shambles, and looked out of place in his own act.

In November 1959 John Kennedy stayed at Sinatra's Palm Beach home for two nights after a big fund-raiser in Los Angeles, according to Lawford; in January 1960 Kennedy, by then a senator and running for president, attended a performance by the Clan at the Sands in Las Vegas during the filming of *Ocean's Eleven*. Relaxing away from the campaign trail, he enjoyed japes about race, booze, Italians, and the Mafia, as well as a cake pushed in Bishop's face and some of the others running around onstage in their shorts. Both Kennedy and his father, Joseph P. Kennedy, were fascinated by Tinseltown and its inhabitants; and both Kennedy and his father were incorrigible womanizers, who liked to hang out in Hollywood picking off film stars.

The Irish-American Joe Kennedy had got very rich over the years in shady activities of various kinds, including bootlegging liquor during Prohibition, which no doubt brought him into contact with even shadier characters. One of the great ironies in the history of American show business was the fate of the Keith circuit: Benjamin Franklin Keith and Edward Franklin Albee had a stranglehold for decades on vaudeville venues in the U.S.A., cheating the performers the whole time; after Keith's death, and when the death of vaudeville was written on the wall in the late 1920s, Albee was bamboozled out of his empire by an even bigger crook. Joe Kennedy made several million dollars from mergers that became RKO Pictures, including Keith's vaudeville palaces, which were already showing films. (There is even a story that the threat of a phony paternity suit helped the deal along, and that the woman involved later died mysteriously.) Actress Gloria Swanson was one of Joe Kennedy's mistresses; later he was a Nazi sympathizer as Ambassador to the Court of St. James in London on the eve of the Second World War; and later still he was intent on buying the White House for his second son, as the first had been killed in a plane crash. Joe Kennedy and Frank Sinatra had something in common apart from shady friends and chasing skirt: emotionally they were both immigrants, getting even with the establishment, and winning the White House would be the last laugh. But in 1960 something almost came between them.

Sinatra had already survived the wrath of the paranoid anti-communists of the late 1940s, but there were other victims who were not unscathed. The House Committee on Un-American Activities had been formed in 1938, partly in reaction to Franklin Roosevelt, whose radicalism during the Depression had extended to creating the Works Progress Administration, for example, to give some of the unemployed some useful work to do. This sort of thing was seen as creeping socialism, which in the U.S.A. was thought to be the same thing as communism. In 1947 the Chairman of HUAC (or the House Un-American Activities Committee, as it became familiarly known) was J. Parnell Thomas of New Jersey, whose education in the arts had begun with the question, "Which WPA payroll is Christopher Marlowe on, New York or Chicago?" The Committee's senior Democrat was John E. Rankin of Mississippi, fond of using words like "kike," "nigger," and "Jew-boy" in debate on the floor of the House. In 1947 the Committee was investigating the film industry, one of the best ways of attracting column inches in the newspapers, and a group of craftsmen who refused to answer questions about their politics past or present were cited for contempt of Congress and sent to prison for a year. Only the most fanatic of film buffs ever would have heard of them, except that they went down in history as the Hollywood Ten. (J. Parnell Thomas, by the way, was soon sent to prison for taking kickbacks from federal employees, serving time in the same federal slammer as some of his victims.)

Seven of the ten were screenwriters; the others were directors and producers. All were blacklisted on release from prison and could not work at their chosen professions, although blacklisting itself was supposed to be against the law. Director Edward Dmytryk recanted and went back to work, but all had paid their dues. One of the screenwriters was Dalton Trumbo, who published a pamphlet in 1949 called *The Time of the Toad*, a title taken from an article by Émile Zola, in which Zola claimed that he purchased a toad in the market each morning and swallowed it whole and alive, in order to make himself immune to the mendacity of the French press of the 1890s. The time of the toad in Germany, wrote Trumbo, began in 1933, when the new Chancellor in that country decreed the discharge from the civil service of all "who have participated in communist activities... even if they no longer belong to the Communist Party or its auxiliary or collateral organizations," and those who have "opposed the national movement by speech, writing, or any other hateful conduct" or have "insulted its leaders."

Those were the days in Germany when respectable citizens did not count it a disgrace to rush like enraptured lemmings before the People's Courts and declare under oath that they were not Communists, they were not Jews, they were not trade unionists, they were not in any degree anything which the government disliked—perfectly aware that such acts of confession...rendered all who would not or could not pass the test liable to the blacklist, the political prison, the crematorium.

"As a matter of general policy," Trumbo went on, the House Un-American Activities Committee "has flouted every principle of Constitutional immunity, denied due process and right of cross-examination, imposed illegal sanctions, accepted hearsay and perjury as evidence, served as a rostrum for American fascism... acted as an agent for employer groups against labor..." And on and on, all too true. Informer Harvey Matusow had named many names, including those of the Weavers, the folk group discovered by Gordon Jenkins; having wrecked their career, he later confessed that he'd made it all up, and got five years for perjury. The unfreedom and the lies could not live forever, though; Trumbo subsequently won Oscars for his original story for *Roman Holiday* in 1953, allowing somebody else to take the credit, and under a pseudonym for his work on *The Brave One* in 1956, a story about a boy and his pet bull. In 1960 Kirk Douglas and Otto Preminger produced *Spartacus* and *Exodus* respectively, both insisting that

Trumbo's name appear in the credits; the American Legion picketed the films, but nobody cared much, and the reign of HUAC's ignorant crooks seemed to be over.

Another of the blacklisted screenwriters was Albert Maltz, who had scripted a wartime documentary in 1942, *Moscow Strikes Back*, which won an Oscar, and was nominated himself for his work on a 1945 flag-waver, *The Pride of the Marines*. He also wrote the screenplay for Sinatra's short film about tolerance, *The House I Live In*, which won a special Oscar in 1945. Opposition to HUAC and everything it stood for must have sounded good to Sinatra. In 1960 he decided to produce and direct a film of *The Execution of Private Slovik*, by William Bradford Huie, about the only soldier executed for desertion by the United States Army since the Civil War. He hired Maltz to write the screenplay, because Maltz would have made a good job of it; helping to consign the blacklist to history would have been a plus. But instead of waiting until the picture was shot to become a hero, Sinatra lost his way and finally made what I would describe as one of the biggest mistakes of his career.

Maltz was anxious; he knew that Sinatra was playing at politics, supporting Kennedy, but he wanted the blacklist ended by discrediting it as soon as possible, so he asked Sinatra if they couldn't make an announcement. Any suggestion that Sinatra needed to wait on the Kennedys or anybody else was like a red rag to a bull; the news got out in an article in the *New York Times* in March 1960, and all hell broke loose. It was the Hearst press all over again: the *New York Mirror* described Maltz as "an unrepentant enemy of his country"; the *Los Angeles Examiner* accused Sinatra of "making available a story wide open for the Communist line."

All-American hero John Wayne said, "I wonder how Sinatra's crony, Senator John Kennedy, feels about him hiring such a man?" Henry Fonda, James Stewart and many others had served their time in uniform; Gene Autry lost his title as King of the Cowboys to Roy Rogers while he was flying supply aircraft in Burma; but John Wayne did everything he could to avoid losing any career momentum, pretending to win the war single-handed onscreen and spending the rest of his life wrapped in the flag. He was proud of having driven Carl Foreman out of Hollywood (Foreman had also refused to answer HUAC's questions) because he disliked Foreman's film *High Noon*: a movie about a real hero made Wayne too uncomfortable.

Sinatra defended himself, using advertisements in the Hollywood trade papers. Hank Sanicola, Nick Sevano and lawyer Mickey Rudin were running a production company that had TV specials lined up sponsored by General Motors, who were threatening to pull out. They begged Sinatra to change his mind: He shrugged and said, "There'll be other specials." Sevano kept pleading until Sinatra got sore and fired him, and the production company broke up. But then the cardinals (not the baseball team, but the old men in funny hats) told Joe Kennedy that the furor was going to hurt JFK with Catholic voters, and the biggest problem JFK faced was the fact that he was a Catholic: No Catholic had ever been elected president. It only took one phone call to solve the problem. "It's Maltz or us," said old Joe Kennedy, and Sinatra caved in to the Kennedy glitz. He published a statement that was almost sarcastic:

I had thought that the major consideration was whether or not the resulting script would be in the best interests of the United States. Since my conversations with Mr. Maltz had indicated that he has an affirmative, pro-American approach to the story, and since I felt fully capable as producer of enforcing such standards, I have defended my hiring of Mr. Maltz.

But the American public has indicated it feels the morality of hiring Albert Maltz is the more crucial matter, and I will accept this majority opinion.

He paid off Maltz and gave up *Private Slovik*. (The story was made into a TV movie a dozen years later, starring Martin Sheen, with a different writer.) Sinatra had had a good idea for a movie and a scriptwriter that might have been one in the eye for the elderly Roosevelt-haters who were still running the newspaper business, but he took his cue from an elderly bootlegger who happened to be a candidate's father; and he knew he had made a mistake. A few days later he got drunk, almost started a fight with John Wayne, and did start a fracas in a Los Angeles parking lot;

some goon beat up a parking attendant, and yet another suit against Sinatra's temper had to be settled out of court. His temper was all he had left. He had sold out for nothing.

The American working class as a whole always despised communism, which was never a domestic threat in the United States, but the politicians and the John Waynes capitalized on it. After Franklin Roosevelt's death the political parties locked themselves into a historical trap of each having to be more anti-communist than the other, so that during his presidential campaign Kennedy invented a phony "missile gap" between the U.S.A. and the Soviet Union, touching off a grossly expensive and dangerous arms race; and before long he was sending advisers to Vietnam. But at least he wasn't embarrassed by his Hollywood friend hiring a blacklisted scriptwriter.

Sinatra campaigned for John Kennedy; at old Joe's suggestion he asked his gangster friends to help steal the election, and he continued passing his cast-off women JFK's way. Sinatra then remodeled the Palm Springs place at vast expense, figuring it would turn out to be JFK's favorite hideout; but his own tasteless horsing-around put paid to that. He had passed a brunette called Judith Campbell both to John Fitzgerald Kennedy and to top mobster Sam Giancana, and FBI chief J. Edgar Hoover knew it. Hoover and Bobby Kennedy, who was now Attorney General of the United States, did not have much use for each other, but Hoover passed the information about Campbell to Bobby, and when President Kennedy came to California in March 1962, he stayed at Bing Crosby's house instead. Sinatra was devastated, and blamed Peter Lawford, for reasons known only to himself; meanwhile the Mob grew disillusioned with Sinatra, who did not have enough influence to get the feds off their back after all. The 1950s had been a fantastic decade for Sinatra, and there would be more good music and more partying to come, but the real glory had peaked. The kid from Hoboken was full of passion, but, away from the songs, the passion was just foolish fury.

Chapter Six

The King of Showbiz

Frank Sinatra's comeback had been one of the most spectacular in the history of show business. His Capitol albums nearly all turned out to be classics of their kind, because his respect for musicians and for good songs was absolute. He had known since he was a teenager that his route to fame and fortune would depend first of all on his singing, and then he found within himself an ability to interpret his kind of songs which not even he perhaps fully understood; but the peak in the overall quality of his recorded work was now past. By 1960, Sinatra seemed to be winning all the games: the Westbrook Peglers and the Lee Mortimers were almost forgotten, and his pal John Kennedy was elected President of the United States. The studio system was collapsing and Hollywood, the world's dream factory, was Sinatra's playpen. What would he do with it? Like America, he floundered; but he floundered with energy and determination.

His Reprise record label was immediately successful. Sinatra had met Mo Ostin while he was trying to buy Verve from Norman Granz; MGM got Verve, but Sinatra hired Ostin, one of the most successful record men of all time, who subsequently oversaw Reprise for more than thirty years. Driving past the Capitol Tower with Ostin, Sinatra said, "I helped build that. Now let's build one of my own." The first five Reprise releases in 1961 included a Sinatra album; an instrumental set by Ben Webster, the great ex-Duke Ellington tenor saxophonist (*The Warm Moods*, with Johnny Richards and his orchestra); and *Mavis!* by Mavis Rivers, a highly rated New Zealand–born jazz-oriented singer who had made several albums on Capitol, including one with Riddle. On her Reprise debut Rivers was accompanied by eleven of the best West Coast jazzmen, the Marty Paich Dek-Tette, as was Sammy Davis, Jr., on *The Wham of Sam!*, and the fifth release was a comedy album, *It Is Now Post Time*, by Joe E. Lewis, the comic Sinatra had portrayed in *The Joker Is Wild*.

Other artists soon joining Reprise were Dean Martin, deep-voiced blues singer Jimmy Witherspoon, and the Hi-Los, the jazz-influenced vocal quartet, fresh from chart albums on Columbia. Comedy albums were very big in those days, when people still remembered how to listen to words without pictures, and were cheap to make; Mort Sahl as well as Joe E. Brown recorded for Reprise. Some people in the industry had thought that Sinatra was indulging himself with his own imprint, but by the end of the first year it was clear that Reprise was capturing a large piece of the mainstream, or what would become MOR music, the middle of the road. Record distribution in the U.S.A. had long had its shady side, and it no doubt helped to have friends in certain places (a federal wiretap caught mobsters including Sam Giancana talking about a debt of $14,000 that Reprise owed to somebody or other), but there can be no doubt about the success of Reprise's marketing and distribution.

As a label boss Sinatra was true to himself, first of all in freeing Reprise artists from the treatment he had himself received from the record industry: they retained ownership of their master recordings and owned shares in the company, they had complete control over their recording sessions, and their contracts were not exclusive: they could record for other labels if they wanted to. During the 1960s Bing Crosby and Rosemary Clooney recorded for Reprise, and there were three more albums by Mavis Rivers. From 1963 several Duke Ellington albums appeared on Reprise, not the peak of that great career to be sure, but including the love-ly *Afro-bossa*. During the decade eight of Sammy Davis, Jr.'s

Reprise albums reached the *Billboard* chart. Only one of Dean Martin's Capitol albums had charted, but during the 1960s an incredible twenty Martin albums on Reprise made it. Arranger and conductor Don Costa, soon recording with Sinatra, discovered folk-pop singer and guitarist Trini Lopez performing in a Hollywood nightclub; his "If I Had a Hammer" was the first big hit single on Reprise, in 1963, and fourteen Lopez albums charted during the decade.

There had been expensive competition with Capitol, caused first of all by Sinatra himself, insisting on recording for his new label and his old one at the same time. Capitol objected to the title of one of Sinatra's first Reprise sets: *Swing Along With Me*, they successfully argued, was too close to *Come Swing With Me*, just released on Capitol, so the title of the Reprise album was changed to *Sinatra Swings*. Then Capitol started selling all Sinatra's albums on that label at reduced prices, and after *Look to Your Heart* in 1959, *All the Way* and *Sinatra Sings of Love and Things* in 1961 and 1962 were more compilations of Capitol tracks. He was now competing with packages of his old recordings on two other labels; but, even so, Reprise was so profitable that in 1963, needing to divest himself of casino interests in Nevada, Sinatra sold two-thirds of it to Warner Brothers for a price said to be $3.5 million, far more than Sinatra had been willing to pay for Verve a few years earlier.

Warner Brothers was already successful with TV and film music, and comedy (Bob Newhart, the Smothers Brothers). Now Jack Warner acquired Sinatra's holdings in Nevada and got Sinatra as a member of the board, as well as his services in several films, and now that he had given up other interests and was concentrating on entertaining, Sinatra got what he had wanted at Capitol: his own label, with somebody else putting up the money. Sinatra also obtained one-third of Warner Brothers Records, and Warner got Mo Ostin. Warner Reprise went on to become WEA (Warner-Elektra-Atlantic) one of the top three or four conglomerates in the international record business, partly because Ostin looked after his artists and let them do what they did best, signing up the best of the new era: Joni Mitchell, Emmylou Harris, Ry Cooder, Neil Young, the Grateful Dead, and many more made albums in the Sinatra tradition: not many reached number one, but they are all still selling today.

Reprise itself was defiantly mainstream during most of the 1960s. Sinatra's daughter Nancy made a dozen flop singles before she finally convinced Ostin to let her record something rockish: her partnership with songwriter and guitarist Lee Hazelwood finally made a star out of her with "These Boots Are Made for Walkin'," a number one in 1966, and eight of her albums charted. (She couldn't swing a tune in a bucket, but the jukebox liked her voice; somebody wrote that she looked like a pizza waitress, and so did a lot of other young women in that decade.) But the biggest star on Reprise was the boss, who had the mainstream sewn up almost by himself. He made a phenomenal six albums in 1960–61, two for Capitol and four for Reprise, which all went top ten in *Billboard* on release; a compilation album in 1991 became Sinatra's thirty-eighth *Billboard* chart album on Reprise, and the first was *Ring-A-Ding Ding!*

The ever faithful-Cahn and Van Heusen wrote a title song on Sinatra's catchphrase, meant to be vaguely salacious. (He had already blurted it out on his recording of "I Won't Dance," one of the less successful tracks on *A Swingin' Affair* in 1956, where it was evidently meant to refer to sexual excitement, followed by the line "I feel so absolutely spunked out on the floor.") The lyric on "Ring-A-Ding Ding!" was on the lines of "Makin' Whoopee" and "The Tender Trap": the swinging bachelor gets nabbed by the girl, which is what sexual excitement can lead to. Harold Arlen's "Let's Fall In Love" uses one of a saloon singer's best tricks, starting with the bridge and then the verse (or introduction), which probably hadn't been heard since 1933, so that when he gets to the familiar chorus, our recognition of it is a reward for listening. "The Coffee Song" is also a highlight of the album, more fun than his 1946 recording on Columbia. Sinatra had embarked on a period of hiring arrangers for one-off projects: Axel Stordahl for *Point of No Return*, and now Johnny Mandel for *Ring-A-Ding Ding!*, a jazz musician who had worked with Mel Tormé, Hoagy Carmichael and Dick Haymes, and who was also blazing a path as a film composer (starting with *I Want to Live!* in 1958, a hit film which got Su.s.a.n Hayward an Oscar). Mandel farmed out bits of arrangements to others, but the album had a secure overall identity, studded with solo bits by superb sidemen, and the theme of ring-a-dinging carried on throughout by orchestral chimes, triangles and xylophone. *Ring-A-Ding Ding!* made a sprightly beginning to Sinatra's career on his own label, and the next was *Sinatra Swings*, with Billy May, made at more or less the same time as the last album with May, *Come Swing With Me!* on Capitol. Once again everybody had a lot of fun, this time with a mix of standards, remakes, rescuings of weepies-turned-jokies ("The Curse of an Aching Heart") and two tongue-in-cheek spectaculars, "Granada" and "Moonlight on the Ganges," which probably employed every percussionist in Hollywood.

Sinatra's third album on Reprise was *I Remember Tommy*, a tribute to Dorsey, whose death in 1956 had been a shock (mixing heavy eating and drinking with a sleeping pill, he'd choked to death in his sleep, a surprisingly common accident among highly strung show-business folk). Sinatra knew that a tribute album would be a good commercial idea; he reached back through the years for Sy Oliver to arrange it, and there were advance orders for 200,000 copies: word had got out and everybody was waiting for it. Thirty-five years later it never fails to disappoint. With this album it is suddenly clear that Sinatra was not as young as he used to be.

The words to "I'm Getting Sentimental Over You," which Sinatra had never recorded before, are not up to much, but we know that Dorsey's theme is only an opener; then disaster strikes with the second track, Burke and Van Heusen's "Imagination." The original 1940 recording opened with the full band, but without Dorsey's brass blasting out as Oliver's do here; they sound like they're playing a gig in a nursing home for half-deaf Swing Era fans leaning on their Zimmer frames. The gentle two-beat lilt of the original is gone, as though the bassist has to play four-to-the-bar or he'll turn into a pumpkin; but the worst part is Sinatra's vocal: instead of phrasing the song in a musical way as he did on the original, and which is the skill that made him famous, he drives the words down on the beat as though he hates the song. "It's Always You" is dreadful in exactly the same way. "East of the Sun" is taken at much the same tempo as the original, but it is now used to toss the song off without any style to speak of. "Take Me" is embarrassingly operatic: of all the songs from the Dorsey period, that was one they should have passed up; yet in general the ballads are the least objectionable tracks on the album. One of the best, "In the Blue of Evening," was not released until the CD edition.

Eight tracks were first recorded in March 1961, and rejected; the sessions had to start again in May. The rejected tracks sounded too close to the Dorsey originals, with a small string section (most of the original had had no strings at all); Sinatra was now over forty-five years old, probably doing too much recording and nervous about not sounding good, wanting more strings in back of him. "In the Blue of Evening" is the only track from March which was not remade, and it is clear that something was terribly wrong with the whole idea, beginning with the fact that Sinatra was effectively the producer of all his later records, and he needed some input from a cooler head. The tragedy is that the tribute idea was a sincere one. After Dorsey was dead, Sinatra could not stop talking about his erstwhile father figure; there are instances from the late 1950s onwards of him staying up all night with anyone who was willing to hear the old stories.

What went wrong with the album can only be fully understood with our hindsight. To begin with, the Swing Era could not be re-created by the original participants. There are those who think that rock 'n' roll swept away mainstream music, but it's the other way around: rock could not have happened unless the Swing Era had been *over*, in the cultural sense. It would be easier to re-create the era today with a bunch of good young well-rehearsed musicians than it was with middle-aged men in 1962. Whatever combination of circumstances made Oliver such an innovating arranger in 1940 no longer existed twenty years later, and as good a musician as he was, he was not the kind of artist who kept developing all his life. Nelson Riddle's work with Sinatra in the mid-1950s was successful partly because it could not have been written in 1940; Riddle was to some extent celebrating the past, but was looking back with affection, not trying to enter a time machine. (Billy May is an exception that proves the point: he could always sound like the Swing Era, but he was not trying to re-create anything, either; his object was to have fun, throwing in tuneable drums, slurping saxes or whatever he liked.)

James Fenton wrote in the *New York Review of Books* in 1996 on the subject of embalmed culture:

> There are paintings of famous moments in famous performances— Edmund Kean as Richard the Third, on the night before the Battle of Bosworth—and these paintings are always instantly recognizable as being depictions of theater rather than depictions of events. What comes across the centuries is the falseness of the gesture, whereas the whole reason for painting the scene was not for its falseness but for its truth. This was the moment when Kean froze the blood.
>
> In film, too, when a director wishes to suggest that we are now watching a play, he will introduce a kind of lighting from beneath, the falseness of which will suggest footlights. But it was never the intention of the inventors of footlights to introduce a false, an "alienating" effect onto the stage. Everyone knew that they were dealing in an illusion, but nobody felt this implied that the whole project was a deception. It is when it is *reproduced* that theater seems so false.

So it was when Sinatra tried to re-create his years of glory, from the *Song and Dance* album of 1950 through the later years. What critic Stanley Dance dubbed "mainstream music" was Swing Era veterans, like the Basie band, playing what they'd played all along, not a recording studio ghosting a band that never existed. The arrangements of the Swing Era are beautiful, many of them, but there was little that was original or innovative about the retro arrangements of two decades later; they imitated the half-remembered formula of *jeek-jeek-a-jeek* trumpets to please the middle-aged fans, which brings up another facet of retro music: The fans were easily pleased.

Charlie Barnet was one of the best leaders of the Swing Era, and no mean arranger himself; he tells the story in his autobiography (written with Dance), *Those Swinging Years*, of a series of tour dates in Texas in the mid-1950s. Barnet went to Dallas and rehearsed in the basement of a music store with a band of the best local musicians, but on the first out-of-town date none of the musicians showed up. They had wanted to play Barnet's charts, but not go on tour, so they all sent substitutes:

> The completely unrehearsed band was awful. After some thirty minutes of playing, or whatever it was they were doing, I called an early break and repaired to the band room, where I downed a third of a bottle of scotch.... When I got back to the bandstand, here comes the committee, to give me hell. Instead, they said, "Mr Barnet, we're so happy you brought the original band. We heard you on the air from the Palladium a few nights ago, and everything is just great." That only went to prove my theory about the public being tone deaf and being unable to distinguish between good and bad.

During the Swing Era the bandleaders wanted to enjoy their own music, so they saw to it that the music was good, and everybody enjoyed it; the knowledgeable fans were ecstatic, and the rest got a bit of musical education. But when the power passed from the leaders to the record companies, and more recently to the accountants who run the record companies, most people couldn't tell the difference, and nobody's ears learned a thing.

There is even an element of hubris, and something symbiotic about the direction of American culture, in the recorded sound of Sinatra's reprising-the-past albums: *I Remember Tommy* has an absurdly wide stereo soundstage, and actually sounds better if you listen to it in mono (except most amplifiers nowadays probably don't have mono buttons). The effect is garish, like seeing the star on a huge screen, as though the technology will compensate for the fact that the music is not the real thing. The absolute integrity of the Capitol recordings with Riddle of 1953–56 was left behind in more ways than one as the record industry as a whole began to suffer from overdoses of technology.

Another aspect of this watershed in Sinatra's career is that he was now so rich and famous that he could do nothing wrong. There are not all that many artists whose work is vital right up into old age, like Haydn, Thomas Mann, Picasso; many reach their greatest fame only as they are passing their peak, or even after it, like Pavarotti, Maria Callas, or Duke Ellington. (It is unfashionable to say so, but although Ellington often made beautiful music in his later years, there was no more innovation or artistic progress after a certain point, which is why 1940–42 is still regarded as his peak.)

Similarly, when Sinatra was one of the most famous people in the world, not only did the quality of his recorded work begin to fall off, but he made several embarrassingly bad films: *Ocean's Eleven, Sergeants Three, Four for Texas* and *Robin and the Seven Hoods* were all released 1960–64. *Four for Texas* was a ludicrously unfunny comedy western, flabbily directed, casually acted and instantly dated, in which Sinatra and Dean Martin played themselves. *Robin and the Seven Hoods* started out as an interesting idea, a musical setting of the Robin Hood legend in Chicago during Prohibition days; Sammy Cahn thought they had got Gene Kelly to direct and Saul Chaplin to produce, but they had got Kelly to produce and Chaplin to supervise the music, and both soon dropped out. Cahn wrote what he regarded as one of his best-ever Sinatra songs, "I Like to Lead When I Dance," and Sinatra loved it, but then didn't bother to perform it in the film. During this period Sinatra also made *The Devil at Four O'Clock*, co-starring Spencer Tracy, a melodrama that was too long, and *The Manchurian Candidate*, which is utterly remarkable, but, as in the recording studio, he seemed to be losing the ability to tell a good idea from a bad one.

There were better albums along with the less good. The last of six sets recorded in just two years was *Sinatra With Strings*, arranged and conducted by Don Costa. Costa was a self-taught producer, arranger, conductor and record-company executive; he made a star out of sixteen-year-old Paul Anka and his ballads of teenaged angst in 1957 on ABC-Paramount Records, and then moved to United Artists, where his recording of the film theme "Never on Sunday" is said to have sold ten million copies around the world. *Sinatra With Strings* was his first and most successful project with Sinatra. Cahn thought that Costa was a substitute for Stordahl, and certainly the "deep strings" style of the lushness seems to fill that gap. The twelve ballads were all familiar ones, including "Misty," the Erroll Garner song which was then becoming one of the most recorded songs in the world, and a famous version of "Star Dust," on which Sinatra sings only the introduction, and never gets to the chorus at all. (Hoagy Carmichael was irritated, saying, "I wrote a whole song, not just a verse." Yet the song as he originally wrote it was not the familiar smoochy ballad, but a sprightly mid-tempo instrumental for jazz band; and some think the verse or introduction was invented by Bix Beiderbecke.) There are too many bravura endings on the album, further evidence of Sinatra's moving away from the intimacy which was his great strength; yet curiously a remake of "All or Nothing at All" is a more vulnerable statement, with less bravura than the original; and a new version of "Night and Day," though still less famous than the one with Riddle, is superb; slower than in 1956, and his only studio recording of the song that includes the introduction.

Next came *All Alone*, with Gordon Jenkins, recorded in early 1962. All the tunes were in 3/4 time, and "Come Waltz With Me" was written by Cahn and Van Heusen, but didn't fit and was sensibly left off the album (though their movie theme "Indiscreet" was included, the album's weakest track). "Are You Lonesome Tonight" is a front-porch ballad from 1926, with which Elvis Presley had had a big hit single in 1960. There are no fewer than five songs by Irving Berlin, including his first heartfelt sentimental ballad, "When I Lost You," written in 1912 when his first wife died after only five months of marriage. On the title track and the last track, "The Song Is Ended" (both Berlin songs), an ethereal woman's voice (Loulie Jean Norman) sings a few phrases, sealing the nostalgia which seems to drench the album. Jenkins's arrangements are apposite, and Sinatra got in the mood, singing well behind the beat on every track, interpreting the songs with understated emotion, and on certain phrases allowing his voice to sound a bit worn, as though full of grief. The album was a success on its own terms, but did less well than any of his others in this period, reaching only number twenty-five in the *Billboard* chart.

Meanwhile, "Everybody's Twistin'" was recorded for a single with Neal Hefti, who had been hired as a producer at Reprise, where he made albums with Dean Martin and Alice Faye as well as Sinatra. The song was actually "Truckin'," written by Rube Bloom and Ted Koehler in 1935, with a nervous beat and altered lyrics; it was the kind of novelty that Mitch Miller might have thought of. Hefti made the most of it, but it didn't exactly mop up the pop chart. He was an experienced veteran of the Swing Era who later also became a composer of film scores; he had written a much loved album in 1956 for Count Basie (*The Atomic Mr. Basie*), and Hefti had led a good band himself in the early 1950s, but gave it up when he saw how times had changed. He later recalled that he could be fined by the musicians' union if he allowed himself to be interviewed at a radio station where no musicians were employed, while Local 802 in New York City would no longer allow out-of-town bands to play at the Paramount Theater, where all the greatest bands had once played. Thus the union had done its best to strangle what was left of the Swing Era; apart from Basie, only a few ghost bands and Frank Sinatra kept trying to breathe life into the corpse.

Sinatra and Swingin' Brass was written by Hefti and recorded in April; both it and *All Alone* were released in the autumn that year, but the Hefti album was released first and barely made the top twenty; perhaps the market was becoming saturated with Sinatra albums. *Swingin' Brass* had no more emphasis on the brass than on any other section of the band, but there were no strings; it was yet another retro Swing Era set, and unobjectionable on those terms, though again Sinatra's phrasing is sometimes choppy, and he sounds tired, as though some of the tracks called for too high a key. "Goody Goody" is a silly jingle of a song that Helen Ward didn't like when it was a hit for her with Benny Goodman in 1936; its identification with the Swing Era was hackneyed. Sinatra was trying too hard to recapture his youth. But Hefti had not completely lost his touch; among the album's best tracks are Cole Porter's "I Get a Kick Out of You" and Ellington's "I'm Beginning to See the Light." (Ben Webster plays some breaks on the latter, though the engineer has him so far off to the left that he's almost in another studio.) "Love Is Just Around the Corner" gets an amusing arrangement, and "Ain't She Sweet," one of Oliver's best charts for Jimmie Lunceford, is almost recaptured. *Swingin' Brass* is one of Sinatra's most successful "jazz" albums, but that's not saying a lot.

A month after President Kennedy had humiliated Sinatra by

staying at Bing Crosby's house instead of Palm Springs, in April 1962, Sinatra embarked on a world tour at his own expense, raising money for children's hospitals. Allegedly, President Kennedy had asked him to do it for the State Department, but he had just bought his own jet plane and wanted to sponsor the trip himself. Sinatra's image needed some maintaining at this point, yet there was very little publicity in the U.S.A. at the time about the tour. He visited Mexico City, Hong Kong, Israel, Greece, Italy, France, England, and Monaco, doing a total of thirty concerts and presenting large checks to local charities.

He traveled with a sextet of his regulars, including Bill Miller on piano, Al Viola on guitar, and Irv Cottler on drums. Many of Sinatra's fans always wanted to hear him in the more casual context of a jazz-oriented small group, but whether he did not want to expose himself that way or his ego could not resist the prestige of larger and more expensive forces, he never recorded commercially with a small group after the era of the Page Cavanaugh Trio at Columbia (which included Viola). English record producer Don Norman once proposed a small-group recording project, and Sinatra's office looked into it, but nothing happened. During the 1950s Sinatra had performed regularly with a similar group led by Red Norvo, always one of his favorite musicians; he traveled with that group to Australia in 1959, where a concert was recorded and subsequently bootlegged; on the 1962 tour Emil Richards played vibes, and concerts in London on June 1, and in Paris on June 5 were recorded: the first has been issued on JR for the worldwide Sinatra Societies, the second was bootlegged in 1992 and finally issued by Reprise. These concerts are especially precious to Sinatra fans, and the one from Paris is a good example of the saloon singer pleasing an audience in a setting that should have been his element. He even sounded younger than on his recent studio albums; that his phrasing is sometimes idiosyncratic and his jokes corny is part of the charm. Tossing off "Goody Goody" as an opener for a live concert of thirty or so songs was allowable, especially followed by a version of "Imagination" that is much better than the one on *I Remember Tommy*. "Ol' Man River" was accompanied only by Miller, and "Night and Day" was a duet with Viola, completely different from any of the other versions he recorded during his career.

Back in London in mid-June he made an album with Robert Farnon called *Great Songs from Great Britain*. Farnon began playing trumpet in Percy Faith's radio orchestra in Canada, and went to Europe during the war as leader of the band of the Canadian armed forces. (George Melachrino led the equivalent British band, Glenn Miller the American one, and to this day there are those who say that Farnon's was the best.) Subsequently Farnon has composed and recorded hundreds of short pieces for broadcast music libraries, as well as a dozen or so film scores; he has backed Tony Bennett, Sarah Vaughan, Lena Horne, Eileen Farrell, Joe Williams and many others on albums, and his own compositions include the lovely tone poem "À la Claire Fontaine," which critic Gene Lees (also Canadian-born) has described as Canada's "Finlandia." But best of all, Farnon made a series of instrumental albums for Decca in England in the early 1950s, orchestral versions of great pop songs, which have been used as teaching aids in music schools as an example of how to do it.

Sinatra's London recording sessions of June 1962 are still fondly remembered by those who were there; he is usually the soul of graciousness when he is surrounded by good musicians, and there were so many guests that even the control room was crowded, but Sinatra didn't mind. He was disappointed with the resulting album, though, which was briefly available in Britain, and not issued in the U.S.A. for thirty years. Nearing the end of his world tour he was tired and felt that his voice had suffered; in fact each track on the album is very well done, but the tempi are almost all very slow, and the overall effect of the album is soporific. Furthermore, some of the songs are simply not first rate. "We'll Meet Again" needs to be trundled out only for documentaries about the war, and some of the others are, as the British say, much of a muchness. Sinatra particularly disliked "Roses of Picardy," which was not released at all for decades; his voice is weak on that one, but the combination of his feeling and Farnon's arrangement turn a weak song into what some say is the best track of the lot. Others considered standout tracks are "If I Had You" (relatively uptempo) and "A Nightingale Sang in Berkeley Square." At any rate, the album remained the most sought-after collector's item in Sinatra's discography for many years.

Back in California, Hefti wrote Sinatra's next project, *Sinatra–Basie*, but the album that put Sinatra back in the top ten again was a big disappointment. "I've waited twenty years for this moment," he famously said at the beginning of the sessions, and he should have kept waiting. It is another example, like *I Remember Tommy*, of the big star doing something that is bound to make a few bucks, even though everybody involved sounds like they're just going through the motions. Not that the band doesn't play well: Basie's professionals of the period couldn't play any other way; Basie had the patent on four-to-the-bar swing (especially with Freddie Green laying down the best rhythm guitar in the business), and, far from recapturing the Swing Era, was the only band still successfully carrying it on. But the arrangements are not exactly inspired by the material; the best thing on the album is the rhythm section, and the tempi are so similar throughout that even that becomes a bore. Sinatra sounds, as he often does on the retro swing albums, as though he'd just wandered off the street into a toyshop. He sings well enough, though again he sounds as though the keys are too high, and we are reminded again that there is more to it than shoving a singer in front of a band. He pulls apart the lyric on the very first track as though he wonders why he's singing the song ("Don't you know each cloud contains [*long* pause] pennies from Heaven"). We don't need to hear "The Tender Trap" played by Basie. We don't need to hear "Looking at the World Through Rose-Colored Glasses" played by anybody. We don't need to listen to this album; but the idea of Sinatra and Basie together was a commercial hit.

Yet he could still pull a trick out of the hat. The very next album, made in early 1963, was different from anything he had done since some of his sides with Stordahl at Columbia. *The Concert Sinatra* isn't perfect; it's only thirty-two minutes long, with eight tracks; except for Kurt Weill's "Lost in the Stars," all the songs are by Rodgers and Hart, Rodgers and Hammerstein or Hammerstein and Jerome Kern, and I don't need to hear *anybody* sing "You'll Never Walk Alone." As befits show tunes, nearly all the arrangements have bravura endings (at least they are written by Nelson Riddle). Although "Ol' Man River" is very moving, and the recording balance throughout is good, and Sinatra sounds himself again, singing in a comfortable register, "Bewitched" is the last song that should have a bravura ending. Perhaps it is an album that few would want to listen to very often, yet here we have something tantalizing.

Part of the reason Sinatra's retro Swing Era albums don't work very well is that he should have matured into a dramatic singer, working as the singing actor he really was, rather than as a band singer. He served his apprenticeship as a band singer, but he needed a Harry James or a Tommy Dorsey to look after him; *The Concert Sinatra* is a hackneyed set in some ways, yet he sings better and sounds younger there than he does in the so-called "jazz" albums.

Listening to a lot of different kinds of music, the question arises: why haven't legit singers ever been able to learn from pop singers, and vice versa? Some opera singers can act: Norman Welsby, playing the King in Henze's *The Bassarids* at the English National Opera in 1974, was electrifying; but good singing actors in opera are the exception rather than the rule: they often seem locked into convention to the extent of counting the number of oscillations in each vibrato, as though they are afraid to act. On original-cast show albums it's the other way around: Ezio Pinza in *South Pacific* in 1947 brought his glorious bass voice from the Metropolitan Opera; but too many performers on Broadway sound like amateurs who can hardly sing at all. If only Sinatra, with his dramatic instinct and his powerful voice, could have inspired a new school of singing actors; if instead of chasing showbiz glory and spending money like a drunken sailor, he had commissioned original music drama, say for television. But he wouldn't have had the patience, and probably lacked the confidence for something so utterly risky. Yet he had played the Stage Manager in Thornton Wilder's *Our Town* on television in 1955, for which Cahn and Van Heusen wrote songs (that's where "Love and Marriage" came from); and *The Concert Sinatra* ended with his fourth recording of "Soliloquy" (counting two versions at Columbia and an unfinished attempt at Capitol). It is over eight minutes of music drama, and maybe that was the limit of his attention span; yet he kept coming back to "Soliloquy," which is about a man about to become a father: he believed in "traditional values," even if he couldn't practice them.

As we shall see, when he did commission some original work, the result was a disaster; but we can wonder about what might have been. Also in 1963, Sinatra produced four albums re-creating Broadway shows: *Finian's Rainbow, Guys and Dolls, Kiss Me Kate*, and *South Pacific* were collectively known as the Reprise Repertory Theater, with Sinatra, Davis, Martin, Crosby, Clooney, Jo Stafford and many others taking part, including the McGuire Sisters (one of whom was Sam Giancana's mistress). These albums are virtually the only ones on which Sinatra allowed his name to appear as producer, but they remained obscure. Sinatra might have played opposite Barbra Streisand in the film version of *Funny Girl*, but the producer wanted Omar Sharif, a fine actor "but no musical animal," said composer Jule Styne. It was one of the biggest disappointments of Styne's life (but of course Sinatra blamed it on Styne). In 1964 at MGM, *Say It With Music* would have celebrated Irving Berlin's career, with the ingenious idea of doing it backwards, ending up in the ragtime era; the film would have been produced by Arthur Freed and directed by Vincente Minnelli, and would have starred Sinatra and Julie Andrews. MGM pulled the plug because it was going to be too expensive. It might have cost half of what Sinatra was earning in a year, or half of what you have to pay just one of today's superstars to do a film, but it was too much. Freed retired, Minnelli left MGM and the studio never made another musical. And as for television, there too money was the only thing that counted. The U.S.A. had handed broadcasting to commercial interests in its earliest days; Britain's BBC could do anything it wanted because it *ought* to be done, while American culture was abandoned to the mentality of the balance sheet.

Meanwhile, one thing Sinatra's life did not lack was drama. During this unsettled period in his life and career came *The Manchurian Candidate*, which has become a classic of a kind, the second film he had made on the theme of the assassination of a president, and one of those accidental films, rubbish on the face of it, which are still compulsively watchable many years later. Greil Marcus's essay on the film (collected in *The Dustbin of History*, 1955) claims that it "may be the most exciting and disturbing American movie from *Citizen Kane* to the *Godfather* pictures":

There's a special thrill that comes over you when you recognize an author working over his head...and in *The Manchurian Candidate* everyone, from [director] Frankenheimer to Sinatra to the unnamed actor who flies across the stage in the midst of the carnage at the end of the film, seems like an author. ...

When you look at this 1962 black-and-white Hollywood movie made up of bits and pieces of Hitchcock and Orson Welles, out of *Psycho* and *Citizen Kane*, out of a lot of clean steals, workmanlike thievery, a second-class director using whatever he can get his hands on, what's so overwhelming is a sense of what the movie does that movies can no longer do.

Written by George Axelrod, adapting a thriller by Richard Condon, *The Manchurian Candidate* is nonsense based on communist "brainwashing" of American prisoners during the Korean war, but the film transcends its origin. The twists in the plot and the details in the finished film all seem inevitable in retrospect, as though some sort of once-truth had been captured. Laurence Harvey plays a character who is programmed to commit murder; Angela Lansbury was nominated for an Oscar in her role as his mother, an American fascist who is in league with the Chinese communists, and whose husband is about to be elected vice president, then president; Sinatra plays a sort of ineffectual hero who figures it all out at the very end, when the plot is resolved and the bad guys are all dead. But he can never reveal what he knows, because no one will ever believe him.

The Korean war had made Americans uneasy; they did not feel comfortable waging war for what seemed to be ideological reasons. The plot of the film is nonsense, but what it is really about is paranoia, and the fact that fascism and communism are really two sides of the same coin; as the title of Marcus's essay suggested, it is "A Dream of the Cold War." It is also about patriotism, and about politicians who are not what they seem to be, and about our own complicity in the Cold War. According to Condon, the film was made only after President Kennedy approved it: The president of United Artists was prominent in the Democratic party and didn't like the idea of the film, but JFK was a fan of Condon's novels. Then in November 1963 John Kennedy was murdered in

Dallas, and the ironies proliferate as fast as we can count them. At Sinatra's request, Chicago crime boss Sam Giancana had used his influence to deliver the trade union vote in the West Virginia primary, so that Kennedy got the Democratic nomination; and then Giancana probably helped Chicago mayor Richard J. Daley steal Illinois at the national election itself. Giancana didn't care who was president, but hoped to get the federal government off his back, and the Kennedy White House double-crossed him: Bobby Kennedy pursued the Mob with a vengeance. Giancana was a psychopathic murderer who ended up hating the Kennedys, and was himself murdered by the Mob. (Both the Chicago and the Florida crime bosses were murdered in the mid-1970s, probably on the orders of the New Orleans crime boss. Why?) We will probably never know whether the Mob was involved in the assassination.

The point here is not to endorse any conspiracy theory, but the biggest irony for our purposes is that Sinatra did not know what kind of a world he was living in, or what part he should have been playing. First he should have followed his nose as an artist and made a film with Albert Maltz, keeping showbiz separate from politics. Instead he swapped bimbos with Giancana and Kennedy, playing into the hands of J. Edgar Hoover, who was spying on everybody, while the FBI, the CIA and the Mob were all planning such infamous activities that it was almost inevitable that the double-crossing crackpots would cause a tragedy, whether they planned it or not. Sinatra's floundering in areas where he did not belong had helped to destabilize it all; and meanwhile he had made a film about a political assassination which should have been second-rate and somehow turned out to be a kind of parable of the times.

When Kennedy was shot, Sinatra was shattered, secluding himself in his grief; for three days, Nancy Jr. wrote in 1995, he stayed in his bedroom in Palm Springs, the only room in the compound that was unchanged since Kennedy had visited there. *The Manchurian Candidate* was not immediately withdrawn from circulation, contrary to popular belief; after the assassination, in fact, it was shown on television. But then it was withdrawn, and not rereleased until 1988. Marcus recites the assassinations and near-assassinations of our time, from Medgar Evers through

Ronald Reagan, and concludes, "There must have been a feeling, as the film was withdrawn, as year after year it, too, stayed hidden, that our real history, our history as we live it out every day, the fundamental premises of all our work and leisure, love and death, might be a kind of awful secret we will never understand." There was certainly a lot that Frank Sinatra never understood. During this period he was hanging out with and hero-worshipping mobsters like Sam Giancana, who hated his precious Kennedys, and who thought nothing of kidnap and murder; then the culture of violence and easy money struck close to home.

Frank Sinatra, Jr., had embarked on a career as a singer, a clone of his father, and he certainly couldn't have had a better teacher. In 1963 Frank Sr. scolded him backstage after a set, saying, "Don't ever let me catch you singing like that again, without enthusiasm. You're nothing if you aren't excited by what you're doing." Sixteen days after John Kennedy was shot, Frank Jr. had been singing in Lake Tahoe with a Tommy Dorsey ghost band, and was kidnapped for ransom. Still grieving for his dead brother, Robert Kennedy put 248 agents on the kidnapping. A ransom of $240,000 was paid, and Frank Sr. went to a pickup point, but Frank Jr. wasn't there; it must have been the lowest point in his life. Frank Jr. was eventually found stumbling along a highway barefoot, and the kidnappers were caught within a few days. Taking a cue from the gossip industry, they claimed in court that they had been hired to do it as a publicity stunt, and Frank Sr. famously said, "This family needs publicity like it needs peritonitis." The kidnappers went to the slammer for a long time, Frank Jr.'s singing career never recovered, and Frank Sr. continued hanging out with mobsters.

That was the worst experience any Sinatra kid ever had, but bearing that name was never easy. Jilly Rizzo, a New York restaurateur who became Sinatra's right-hand man and was close to the whole family, used to say with a sad grin, "We can't go dere." He meant that being famous the way a Sinatra was famous did not confer freedom. When Nancy was a teenager, if she went to a party where marijuana was being smoked, she had to leave, because she knew that if there was any trouble the headlines would link "Sinatra" and "drugs." Nancy married singer Tommy Sands in September 1960; Sands is said to have wanted to move to New York to avoid becoming one of the Clan's mascots, but the marriage lasted less than four years.

The parade of Frank Sinatra's albums and movies continued. After *The Manchurian Candidate*, and not counting the Rat Pack films and several where he played cameos, usually as himself, Sinatra made twelve more feature films, all now fodder for late-night TV. *Come Blow Your Horn* was based on a Neil Simon play; *None But the Brave* and *Von Ryan's Express* were World War II adventure yarns, the former with a part for Sands; *Marriage on the Rocks* was a romantic comedy with a part for Nancy Jr. (they were shooting it when Tommy left her). *Assault on a Queen* was a caper movie involving the ocean liner *Queen Mary*, with music by Duke Ellington; *The Naked Runner* was a spy picture; *Dirty Dingus Magee* was a burlesque western; *Contract on Cherry Street* was a TV movie, and *The First Deadly Sin*, Sinatra's last starring feature, in 1980, was a disappointing cop movie.

Journalist Pete Hamill once wrote, "A Sinatra film never reached down into the darkness the way the songs did. He never cheated on the songs." Along the way, in 1967–68, there were three other cop/private-eye movies, to which Sinatra seemed to bring something of himself. In *Tony Rome* he played an aging, cynical and world-weary character with something of Bogart in it, solving an old-fashioned murder mystery; the script had a touch of the amorality of the 1960s. In *The Detective* he carried a badge through a good script, with Robert Duvall one of the supporting players; then *Lady in Cement* was another Tony Rome story, but the return to the Bogart-type thriller had already run out of steam: this time the script just wasn't good enough. Despite Sinatra's obvious potential as an actor, he did not develop a true film star's instinct for what he was doing; most of the films turned out to be, as Pauline Kael described *The Naked Runner*, "a good movie to read by if there were light in the theater."

During the filming of *None But the Brave* in Hawaii in May 1964, Sinatra and a few others went swimming in the surf; Sinatra and Ruth Koch, the wife of executive producer Howard Koch, were swept out to sea, became exhausted, and almost drowned. For thirty years the story has been that brawny actor Brad Dexter saved their lives, swimming out to their rescue and keeping them

Meanwhile, Frank's nemesis at Columbia Records was producer Mitch Miller, shown here meeting Frank at La Guardia Airport in 1951. Frank's hits had dried up, but it wasn't Miller's fault; he had no taste and helped to 'dumb down' the record business, but what neither he nor Frank knew was that singles were becoming passé: Frank Sinatra was born to make albums. *(Frank Driggs Collection)*

Above Frank's career had slipped so far that it had nowhere to go but up in 1952 when Ava helped him get the part that made him a film star, in *From Here To Eternity*. Montgomery Clift (left) was a great actor, a hard drinker and also a hard worker; Frank learned a lot from him, and his portrayal of the doomed wise guy Angelo Maggio won an Oscar the following year for best supporting actor. (*Kobal Collection*)

Below In another of his best pictures, *The Man With The Golden Arm* (1955), Frank played a gambler who was also a heroin addict. His portrayal of withdrawal from drugs was electrifying at the time, perhaps because, as a self-confessed manic depressive, he could try to imagine what it was like to be in that hell. (*Frank Driggs Collection*)

Arranger Nelson Riddle was assigned to work with Frank by Capitol producer Voyle Gilmore. Riddle also worked with Nat Cole, Ella Fitzgerald, Peggy Lee, Sara Vaughan, Judy Garland and many more; and all of his work was first rate, but when Riddle wrote for Frank Sinatra, it was as though a twentieth-century Mozart had written the song, orchestrated it and chosen the singer. Riddle got a lot of credit, but not much of the money.
(*Michael Ochs Archives/Redferns*)

Billy May also worked with Frank at Capitol and later on Frank's own Reprise label. May wrote wonderful arrangements for Charlie Barnet in 1939-40, then worked for Glenn Miller; in the 50s he became an *éminence grise* at Capitol, the only swing-era bandleader to have hit albums in the 50s, also conducting pop sessions including those of satirist Stan Freberg. He had a musicianly sense of humour; everything he did was fun.
(*Michael Ochs Archives/Redferns*)

Above When Frank first signed with Capitol Records in Hollywood in March 1953, they were the only label that would have him, and the contract was for only one year. But history was about to be made. With ups and downs behind him, he was a better singer than ever; in the mid-50s he was the *only* singer whose every album was a hit, and they are all still selling (*London Features*).

Below By the end of the decade Frank was the king of show business and could do as he pleased, not necessarily a good thing. *Ocean's Eleven* (1960) was one of his caper movies featuring his pals, and shot in the Sands Hotel, where they were also doing a show every night. It all seemed like fun at the time, but the films have dated badly. Left to right, the Rat Pack and guests: Richard Conte, Sammy Davis Jr, Frank, Buddy Lester, Dean Martin, Joey Bishop, Peter Lawford and Henry Silva. (*Ronald Grant Archive*)

Frank always liked to have an audience. Even in the recording studio or at a rehearsal, friends and fans kept him honest; it was as a singer that he knew he couldn't fool anybody. Preparing a show in 1960, perhaps in Las Vegas, a few of his more attractive acquaintances are in evidence. 'I loved them all,' he told journalist Pete Hamill. 'I really did.' (*Redferns*)

Right Frank recorded with Count Basie in the studio in 1962 and 1964, and live in Las Vegas in 1966, but the results did neither of them any credit: who needed to hear the Basie band play 'Hello, Dolly'? The 60s were a confusing decade for America, and Frank was nothing if not an American; apart from anything else, we were running out of Sinatra songs. (*London Features*)

Below From left to right in 1970: Frank, Nancy Jr, Big Nancy, Tina and Frank Jr. Frank married Mia Farrow in 1966, but it didn't last long; perhaps his long periods of bachelorhood partly reflected the fact that his first family always commanded his loyalty. It was never easy being a Sinatra kid, but whatever Dad may have been up to, he was always available. (*London Features*)

This page & overleaf
A lifelong Democrat, Frank attended a fund-raiser for John Kennedy in July 1960 *(left)*. By 1972 American politics seemed to have disappeared into a black hole, and Frank consorted with losers and crooks like Spiro Agnew and Richard Nixon (below, with Pat Nixon at the 'Western White House' in San Clemente). Frank had retired in 1971, but he came back in 1973 and became one of the most successful concert artists of all time *(overleaf)*, bringing his unmistakable nut-brown voice back to the people who had been there since the beginning: the live audience. Near the end of one of the most publicly scrutinized lives of the century, he could still fill any venue in the world when he was seventy-nine years old.
(Corbis/Bettman/UPI, Corbis/Bettman/ UPI, London Features)

afloat until more help arrived on surfboards. Dexter and Sinatra became close for a while; Dexter had a part in *Von Ryan's Express*, and became a vice president of Sinatra Enterprises in charge of production. Dexter told Kitty Kelley many years later that he tried to interest Sinatra in better movie material, which was a matter of trying to get Sinatra Enterprises to acquire properties. Sinatra was interested in *Harper*, but his lawyer Mickey Rudin didn't like the deal, and Sinatra turned down *A Clockwork Orange*, which he didn't understand. (*Harper* became a better-than-average private-eye film starring Paul Newman, Stanley Kubrick made *A Clockwork Orange*, and both pictures earned a lot of money.) Finally Dexter came up with *The Naked Runner*, the spy film in which Sinatra was to play an unwitting assassin.

Some of the film was shot in England, where Sinatra had a temper tantrum about a helicopter ride: the weather, the air traffic over southern England, and the daily business of Britain's armed services should have been subordinate to Sinatra's comfort. Dexter had to coax him into going back to work. The next location was to be in Denmark, after Sinatra went back to California to dabble in politics, campaigning for a third term for Governor Pat Brown (who was beaten by Ronald Reagan). Sinatra decided not to go to Denmark, and Dexter was ordered to bring all the footage back to California. Dexter complained that he had production commitments in England; he and the director, Sidney Furie, no doubt fed up with Sinatra, rewrote the script and edited the film so as to finish the picture without him. Thus Sinatra had agreed to make a film as a shareholder in Warner Brothers, and then ensured that it had to be cobbled together after he'd short-changed everybody with his juvenile behavior. No wonder it turned out to be the kind of film that made Pauline Kael wish for a book to read. Dexter delivered the finished picture to Jack Warner, and never received the rest of his fee as producer. Dexter had tried to help rescue Sinatra's film-acting career, and once told someone "I'd kill for him." In Nancy Sinatra's first book (*Frank Sinatra: My Father*, 1985), she tells the story of the near-drowning in Hawaii in 1964 and mentions Dexter's part in it, but then Dexter told Kitty Kelley stories about Sinatra's manic-depressive behavior (for Kelley's book, *His Way*, 1986), and in her next book

(*Frank Sinatra: An American Legend*, 1995), Nancy tells the story without mentioning the name of the man who saved her father's life.

Actually, Dexter's days as a Sinatra intimate had already been numbered; he had made an earlier mistake. When Sinatra asked him whether he should marry Mia Farrow, who was then starring in a television soap opera, and who was less than half his age, Dexter told him to go ahead and marry her if he wanted to, but he didn't think it was a good idea, and Sinatra had one of his countless tantrums. He married Mia in July 1966 and tried to get her to quit show business; when she refused to walk off the set of *Rosemary's Baby*, one of the biggest hit films of the decade, the marriage crumbled. It was the best role she ever had, but then she already knew what it was like to sleep with the Devil.

When the marriage was over, Sinatra's valet of many years, George Jacobs, met Mia in a nightclub and danced with her; and of course this was reported in some gossip column, and Sinatra fired Jacobs. Jacobs later talked to Kitty Kelley too, of course; he had nursed Sinatra through a suicide attempt, he said; he had helped him get over Ava, waited on Sinatra's gangster friends, made John Kennedy laugh so hard he fell in the pool, had a plate of spaghetti shoved in his face by Sinatra, drove Sinatra's women to their abortionists and all the rest of it, and his reward for many years of loyal abuse-taking was summary dismissal, and without any explanation. For Sinatra could not fire Jacobs himself any more than he could fire Dexter. That's what Mickey Rudin was for.

And through all the melodrama the work continued, albeit of decreasing value. There were an incredible twenty more Reprise albums between *The Concert Sinatra* in 1963 and his temporary retirement in 1971. There were good things on almost every album, but nearly all of them were spoiled by a kind of self-indulgence: cabaret singers from Bobby Short onwards are still mining the century's obscure but worthwhile songs, but the man who had once chosen the standards for us no longer tried hard enough; clearly his albums would have sold well and made a profit even if they had been better ones, yet he aimed too low. *Sinatra's Sinatra* was entirely remakes, including "Young-at-Heart," which he hadn't particularly liked in the first place, and the dreary "Second Time Around"; *Days of Wine and Roses, Moon River and Other Academy Award Winners* had the kind of tunes that come out of the ceiling at the airport, including "Three Coins in the Fountain," "Love Is a Many-Splendored Thing," and the two Henry Mancini songs (but it was interesting to compare Sinatra's "Secret Love" to Doris Day's virginal original); and *Moonlight Sinatra* was what the concept album had now come to: twelve songs with the word "moon" in the title. At least these three albums were all with Nelson Riddle, who made as much as could be made of them. *America, I Hear You Singing* was made with Fred Waring and His Pennsylvanians, a mishmash of Christmas songs, patriotic songs (including a remake of "The House I Live In") and two tracks with guest Bing Crosby. Maybe there was something Sinatra admired about Fred Waring, who had made jazz-influenced records in the 1920s, was enormously successful on radio in the 1930s, and ended up essentially a choral conductor, having grown mellow as his fans grew older and distracted from music by his business interests. In 1966 Waring said, "We don't sing music, we sing songs," which could be translated as "Nice songs, shame about the music."

Softly as I Leave You marked the end of an era: the first Sinatra album to have three different arrangers, and the CD doesn't even bother to tell you who arranged what. The opening track, "Emily," is a sickly-sweet movie song (from *The Americanization of Emily*, which was coincidentally another book by William Bradford Huie), while "Here's to the Losers" is more fun, but there isn't one really first-class song on the album, so while the singing is good, it doesn't matter. *It Might as Well Be Swing* was another album with the Basie band, this time arranged by Quincy Jones; it included "Hello Dolly," hardly material of Sinatra quality, and a country song, "I Can't Stop Loving You." (I try to imagine a Sinatra country album: he might have mopped up Nashville if he'd tried, but not with the Basie band; and he was probably not capable of choosing the right songs.) *My Kind of Broadway* was a compilation album, including the "Hello Dolly" with Basie; not Sinatra's kind of Broadway, but a marketing job. Speaking of marketing jobs, *A Man and His Music* was a two-LP compilation, with most of the tracks edited and *narrated* by Sinatra. It went top-ten and won a Grammy as Album of the Year in 1966, but by then the market had changed utterly: everybody was buying lots of albums, and anything might float to the top, and by then it should have been clear that the reason Sinatra was still king of showbiz was by default. It was too soon to offer the title to Mick Jagger, and there had been a lost generation between the two, except for Elvis Presley, whose hit albums during this period were the soundtracks of movies that were even worse than Sinatra's.

An album which *Billboard* called *Frank Sinatra* (aka *The World We Knew*, after the first track, a Bert Kaempfert song) was a compilation that included the dreadful (Oscar-winning) movie song "Born Free," as well as a number-one hit single, a duet with Nancy on "Somethin' Stupid," a dumb song with a *kling-kling-kling* beat. *A Man Alone and Other Songs of Rod McKuen* is some kind of nadir: from the man who once chose our standards for us, a set of "songs" by the most banal McPoet who ever schmoozed Hollywood. This was 1969, and Sinatra was so eager to be loved that he had now sunk as far as he could into the mass market; he had managed to make some of the best and some of the worst vinyl LPs ever pressed. But it is hard to choose a nadir, really. *That's Life* includes the stereotype title track, which became a Sinatra anthem, as well as "Winchester Cathedral," one of the dumber pop songs of the Swinging Sixties. *Strangers in the Night* was a number-one album on the strength of the nasty title song, arranged by Ernie Freeman and produced by Jimmy Bowen, who'd started as a Texas rocker in the same recording studio as Buddy Holly, and later became a successful producer of country music at MCA; "Strangers" is another Kaempfert song, and Sinatra openly professed to dislike it, so why did he sing it? The single won four Grammies; probably the industry was grateful to Sinatra for his capitulation to kitsch. But the rest of the album is arranged by Nelson Riddle, and has some good things on it that completely overshadow the title track, especially "Summer Wind," and a completely new treatment of "All or Nothing at All," Sinatra's third recording of the song. *Sinatra at the Sands* is a two-LP set with Basie released in mid-1966, almost the only live set Sinatra ever authorized; fans regard it as better than either of the studio sets with Basie.

Francis A. and Edward K. is an album with Duke Ellington, arranged by Billy May, and at first you think it's going to be saved by the sound of the band, especially as the first track is the best: "Follow Me," from Lerner and Leowe's *Camelot*, swinging at a slow tempo, and obviously heartfelt. (Was that Cootie Williams? There's Paul Gonsalves.) But Ellington did not like sharing the spotlight, his men were not good readers, and they had not bothered learning the arrangements, which were not very inspired anyway. (To be fair to May, no one could write for the Ellington band, which hated to play arrangements from outside.) They had to pull it together in the studio, with lead players added (Al Porcino in the trumpets) and three pianists in the end: Ellington, Jimmy Jones and Milt Raksin. Ellington's amanuensis, Billy Strayhorn, virtually the band's co-leader, might have played piano and done the arrangements, and the band would have played them happily; but Strays, the beloved Swee'Pea, had died of cancer earlier that year. The result was a shambles, one of the nadirs of both careers. Even the songs were badly chosen: the worst is "Sunny," a dreary country-pop dirge of the period. Most of the album was very slow and the last track absurdly fast; even the engineering was awful, as though echo could cover up the sloppiness of the idea.

Cycles, recorded in late 1968 with Costa, was a set of ten of the decade's folk-rock songs, and a good example of a later Sinatra album that could have worked but didn't. It is interesting to hear him sing Joni Mitchell's "Both Sides Now" and Bobby Russell's "Little Green Apples"; if anyone could have bridged the gap between the songwriting of two or more generations, it might have been Sinatra, but those two tracks are the best ones on the album. Sinatra was simply not the sort of artist who could let his hair down. There is a clue in Sinatra's version of John Hartford's "Gentle on my Mind"; lyricist Gene Lees put his finger on it in 1969:

At the end, he "corrects" Hartford's grammar: he sings, "the rivers flowing *gently* on my mind," and it kills the mood. Hartford's use of "gentle" as an adverb is an Americanism, parallel to "Drive Slow" which bothers none of us anymore. We are in the process of dropping a lot of adverbial endings on this continent, and the

English language in another fifty years is going to be radically different than it is now. As Chaucer used a lot of "low" English only to have it become standard English, Hartford uses the people's English of our time, and Sinatra makes a serious error in tampering with it. As a matter of fact, he doesn't do the song at all well. He tries to make it swing in the manner of jazz, and country-and-western music swings in quite another way. By punching out the time, he kills the swing and diminishes the depth of the song....

This goes straight to the heart of why Sinatra was never going to make a success of this kind of material. He was a jazz-oriented artist, the songwriters he loved best were influenced by jazz, and jazz had come indoors and got respectable: in the 1960s it was being regularly played in concert halls. To be sure, the best of it always includes freedom of interpretation, but the musical values are sophisticated ones. There have been a lot of good songs written in country music and country rock, but the values are entirely different: they call for a kind of resignation, a capitulation to timelessness, and Sinatra, as an artist or as a man, could never be resigned to anything. His kind of passion would not allow it.

And most of the songs on *Cycles* are badly chosen. "Rain in My Heart" (the album's opener) is absurdly overwrought, while "By the Time I Get to Phoenix" is too laid-back: Sinatra got stoned on Jack Daniels, not the other stuff. Yet if he was going to make an album of this sort of material, the biggest hits of the type had to be chosen rather than songs that might have been better suited to him, and again a lack of judgement is evident from someone who once seemed never to fail. He doesn't sound fully engaged; the photo on the cover of the album is apparently supposed to portray him in a thoughtful mode, but the way he's holding the bridge of his nose he looks like he needs an aspirin. Finally, the songs are overarranged and too prettified; Costa was a talented man without genius, trying to do too many things, and the album jangles with too much soft-rock rhythm section, as though to make things easy for the middle-aged.

My Way in 1969 is perhaps the strangest tragedy of all these late albums, because he is in such fine voice and sounds like he's giving it all he's got. But there are only ten songs, and they do not make a coherent album. On Jimmy Webb's "Didn't We," the Jacques Brel–Rod McKuen "If You Go Away," and especially on "A Day in the Life of a Fool" (Luiz Bonfa's "Manha de Carnaval" with English words), once again he makes the songs better than they are. But on Lennon and McCartney's "Yesterday" he seems to have trouble with the word "yesterday" all the way through, and Paul Simon's "Mrs Robinson" is a bad joke, overarranged by Costa, and Sinatra forcing himself to utter lyrics like "wo wo wo" and "hey hey hey." The album was memorable chiefly for a sleeper: "My Way" was a French song with English words by Paul Anka, and reached the top thirty as a single, eventually included on at least five Sinatra albums; it would assume more importance in the following decade.

The best of nearly forty albums on Reprise are undoubtedly two very different ones: *September of My Years*, an unusual admission of the passage of time, and *Francis Albert Sinatra and Antonio Carlos Jobim*. These two are treasurable, almost up to the level of the best Capitol sets, making comparison with the rest of the Reprise output all the more stark.

September was made mostly in April 1965, just before he got involved with Mia Farrow, and a year before the final descent into "Strangers in the Night." Arranged and conducted by Gordon Jenkins, it is nearly Sinatra's last and certainly his most personal concept album; in fact it is the logical conclusion to all the "loneliness" concept albums; the would-be, has-been lover can see the end of the road in the distance, and is looking back with affectionate amusement, as well as regret. The first (title) track is one of Cahn and Van Heusen's best, the gentle modulations coming as mildly pleasant surprises rather than being telegraphed. (It is also the best-sounding track on the album, recorded all by itself in May, with a different engineer; the rest of the album desperately needs remixing to match it as closely as possible: Sinatra's voice is too far forward and the tinniness of the background doesn't do anything for Jenkins's fiddles.) There are two songs by Jenkins, a handful of standards (Alec Wilder, Arlen and Harburg, Rodgers and Hammerstein); and the rest were all surprises.

"The Man in the Looking Glass," by Bart Howard, who wrote "Fly Me to the Moon," is completely disarming. Sinatra got in the news when he had a hair transplant and at one point he allegedly paid a woman $400 a week to look after his forty toupees (his hair loss is the reason he wore so many hats on the record covers). But now he sang "I knew that dopey guy / When he didn't know how to tie his tie / He stood right there / And he had hair / Galore." The same fellow "seems so much wiser now / Less lonely, but then / Could be he's only pretending / Again." But the album's centerpiece is "It Was a Very Good Year," written by Ervin Drake, who wrote Billie Holiday's "Good Morning Heartache," and was also one of those who wrote words for instrumentals to make them more saleable: "Castle Rock," "Perdido," "Tico Tico." Here he outdid himself and received one of Jenkins's best symphonic-style arrangements; in fact the opening oboe tune, reprised at the end, sounds like it could have been snatched from Sibelius. "It Was a Very Good Year" has been attacked by feminists as implying a catalog of conquests, with its "small-town girls," "city girls" and "blue-blooded girls of independent means (We'd ride in limousines / Their chauffeurs would drive / When I was thirty-five)." But the work of art exists independently of what we know about Sinatra; and in any case what we know about him is that he had believed in love, just as most of the women did, even if he ultimately couldn't stand to be in the same room with it. The song is about memories of love, not sex; it is about happiness that ran through his fingers like sand. The longest track on the album, it is also an example of the singing actor at the heart of Sinatra's work: you can't dance to it; you can only listen. The last perfect concept album ends perfectly, with another piece of dramatic magic, Weill's "September Song," including both verses of introduction. Sinatra would soon be fifty years old, and he never made a more revealing document.

September of My Years is the only Sinatra album on Reprise that did not disappoint on first hearing except for the one with Jobim, made in early 1967, arranged and conducted by Claus Ogerman. Sinatra abandons himself to the bossa-nova beat, one of the nicest things to happen to postwar pop, and the result sounds like memories of love and jazz heard through the prism of the tropics. Seven tunes were Jobim's; the other three were two standards lending themselves to the treatment, and another recording of "Baubles, Bangles and Beads," infinitely preferable to the earlier one with Billy May. The gentle Jobim joins in vocally on four tracks. Gene Lees wrote the lovely English words to "Corcovado," which then became "Quiet Nights of Quiet Stars," and Lees published a memoir of his friend Jobim in his *Jazzletter* in 1995. Talent and genius are not the same thing, Lees reminds us, and in the same way that we can tell a Gershwin song within a few bars,

> if you examine the song "Dindi," you'll find that it's not terribly unusual, harmonically or melodically. The problem is that it *is* unusual, and I can't tell you why. It has a distinct but ineffable quality; it is one of the most beautiful songs I know.
>
> The gift of writing melody is a mysterious one. Not every educated musician has it; Nelson Riddle and Gil Evans didn't. Nor does lack of education preclude it: Irving Berlin had no musical education whatsoever, and Harry Warren didn't have much, but each of them had an inexhaustible gift of melody.

Lees goes on to describe the uniqueness of the bossa-nova rhythm, which came from the samba, and was something new that Jobim and others were doing in Brazil in the 1950s. (For example, the songs were notated in 2/4 rather than the 4/4 of American ballads, but when they were brought to the U.S.A., northern publishers had them renotated in 4/4.) It is a gentle yet inexorable beat, timeless and evocative; it was a fad in the U.S.A. for a while, yet it was more than a fad: it has never really gone away, and retains its timeless beauty. "Dindi" was one of the songs on the first Sinatra-Jobim album, which was recorded halfway through the marriage to Farrow. Lees wrote about "Dindi" in 1967: "It is filled with longing. It aches. Somewhere within him Frank Sinatra aches. Fine. That's the way it's always been: The audience's pleasure derives from the artist's pain."

The Sinatra-Jobim album was something special, and they recorded ten more tracks together, in early 1969, arranged by Eumir Deodato and conducted by Morris Stoloff, but the second album was never released properly. One of the tunes was "Off Key," the English version of the lovely "Desafinado" ("Out of Tune"), which of course was not off-key at all, but a response to early Brazilian critics of bossa nova, who didn't understand it. Nine of the tracks have been scattered across compilation albums (seven of them on one side of *Sinatra and Company* in 1971), and "Off Key" has never been released at all. As they say in New Jersey, Go figure.

Sinatra never seems to have been interested in doing "songbook" albums, perhaps because Ella Fitzgerald did it first; Sinatra may have been another, like Ellington, who didn't like to share the spotlight. On the basis of what he did with the songs of Cole Porter, Irving Berlin and others, to say nothing of Jobim, we may wish that he had done songbooks; but apart from the Jobim (a masterpiece) and the Rod McKuen (dreck), virtually the only such album Sinatra ever released was a compilation of Van Heusen songs on CD, because most of them were associated with Sinatra and some were Oscar-winners: another marketing job. (And it is interesting that some of the best songs on the album were written by Van Heusen and Johnny Burke, rather than with Sammy Cahn.)

And then came the worst boondoggle of all, or the biggest tragedy, depending on how you look at it. *Watertown* was not a bad idea: a middle-aged man in a small town watches his wife leaving him. Maybe she's bored, maybe he's taken her for granted, but he doesn't know why she's leaving; all he knows is that a part of his life is over. It is virtually the only time Sinatra commissioned anything like dramatic music or a song cycle for himself, and the project was bungled badly.

Goodfellas (1990) is one of the all-time best gangster movies, written and directed by Martin Scorsese. It has a scene in a neighborhood nightclub where the thugs and their women are being entertained by one of those Italian-American singers who had brash hit records in the late 1950s–early 1960s, and it is perfectly judged: the banality of the entertainment is matched by the banality of the people, the men all pointing their suits at each other and the women all looking like retired pizza waitresses. The singer in the film is Dion Belmont or somebody like that; in fact maybe it's Frankie Valli. Frankie Valli and the Four Seasons (named after a bowling alley in New Jersey) had over forty hit singles starting in 1956, many of them co-written by Bob Gaudio (a former member of the Royal Teens, as in "Who wears short shorts") and Bob Crewe, who'd come from Swan Records, one of those labels like Cameo and Parkway that came from nowhere to have so many hit singles in that era that they helped trigger a congressional investigation into payola. Apparently Frankie Valli had bragged to Frankie Sinatra that the reason they had so many hits was that Gaudio had written them; and Bob Gaudio was hired to co-write, co-arrange and produce *Watertown*.

It was going to be done for television, but an album was all that resulted. The backing tracks were recorded in July 1969 in New York, and overdubbed by Sinatra later in Los Angeles. According to John Ridgway's *Sinatrafile*, the recording sessions used over thirty musicians including strings, but they sound like a cabaret bar-band, with a thumping electric bass and banal rhythms throughout. The writing for strings may as well have been an off-the-shelf synth program, except that hadn't been invented yet; the first song has a choo-choo sound in it as the wife leaves, a device that thankfully wasn't available for Schubert's song cycles. Nearly all the ten songs are faded out at the end, a first for a Sinatra album, and the sure sign of an arranger who can't think of anything to do.

Watertown is so hard to listen to that one wonders if something might have been done with the songs; Gaudio had had a number of years practicing as a writer, after all, and Nelson Riddle might have made something of some of the songs, we'd like to think. But there was not enough inspiration on this team. The fact is that Gaudio was one of those who helped turn rock 'n' roll into what we now call "pop music," elbowing other musics out of the marketplace. Rock was supposed to be a gloriously raucous and uninhibited pig's ear, at its best retaining its country-music heritage as a superb vehicle for a troubador's story-songs; but no matter how many hacks try to make a silk purse out of it, that's never going to work. The tunes on *Watertown* are simple and repetitious rock-aballads, and the words are banal; not even Sinatra can make the word "tragedy" rhyme properly with "in the tea." At the end of the last song, the singer thinks his wife is coming back, but apparently she doesn't get off the train. Maybe she's in New York listening to Bobby Short.

Gene Lees, who attended one of the recording sessions for the first album with Jobim in 1967, was glad that Sinatra refused to record with headphones on. People who recorded with Tommy Dorsey in 1940 know that the headphones belong on the engineers, not the musicians; they also know that the singer sings in the same room at the same time with the band. Why did Sinatra agree to overdub *Watertown*? Why did he surrender to this rubbish two years after the Jobim album? Sinatra sounds terrible on *Watertown*; his diction sticks out because it is wasted on the material. The truth is that, although he chose good songs in the 1940s and mostly stuck with them through the 1950s, he always wanted to sing *contemporary* songs, and the craft of songwriting was falling on hard times. I think he tried to get into Gaudio's stuff, but couldn't manage the plaintive, self-serving whine that this kind of music requires; if he was trying to sound like Frankie Valli, he failed. Having divorced Mia, he should not have tried to dabble in the music of her era.

Sinatra had campaigned for Hubert Humphrey in the 1968 presidential election, in his last act as a Democrat from Hoboken. (Humphrey lost to Richard Nixon, who Sinatra seemed to despise.) In early 1969, Marty Sinatra finally succumbed to complications of the asthma that had bothered him all his life. Marty's medical problems overwhelmed him, and nothing could be done; Dr. Michael De Bakey in Houston, Texas, was deeply moved: "I saw the way he kissed his father." In April 1970 *Watertown* was released, and didn't even make the top one hundred albums in *Billboard*; in November the film *Dirty Dingus Magee* opened, and was generally agreed to be one of Sinatra's worst movies. On his birthday in December something good finally happened: his Little Nancy got married again, this time happily (until Hugh Lambert died of cancer in 1985). During this period, as we'll see in the next chapter, he washed himself up in Las Vegas. There were a few more benefits and TV specials; in January 1971 Sinatra opened a Medical Education Center in Palm Springs, named after his father; and in March, he announced his retirement from public life. In June, at yet another benefit, he made his farewell performance; the last song performed was an intimate saloon song, "Angel Eyes," and on the last line, "Excuse me, while I disappear," the spotlight went out.

And Sinatra was gone. But not for long. He tried to relax in the desert, he looked after his bank accounts, and he made new friends among the social and political glitterati, but of course he could not stay away from performing, even while the world changed around him. In the following decades he would become more famous than ever as a concert artist, a new king of show business, and the fact that he could not stay away from that spotlight is an endearing quality. It is not given to many of us to know what we do best.

Chapter Seven

The American Aristocracy

F rank Sinatra's oldest friends from Hoboken have testified that he was a skinny little kid and couldn't possibly have been in as many fights as he claimed; his upbringing had really been quite comfortable, thanks to his mother's ability to manipulate the local society to her liking. He must have got his combativeness from her. On the plus side was his instinctive feeling for the underdog; he hated racism, anti-Semitism or injustice of any kind, and to be fair, maybe he got some of that from his mother too. But his hatred of injustice was in the abstract. When it came to individual underdogs, they were either his friends or his enemies, and woe to them if they stepped out of line; neither strangers nor close friends were immune.

He threw hamburgers at the wall; he sometimes had members of the public beaten up if they had the temerity to approach him for the purpose of hero-worship; on one occasion he punched a bartender at a party because a drink didn't come fast enough. The stories are legion. Sammy Davis, Jr., was supposed to co-star along with Peter Lawford in *Never So Few* in 1960, but had been candid on the radio about Sinatra's behavior: "I love Frank, but there are many things he does that there is no excuse for. I don't care if you are the most talented man in the world. It does not give you the right to step on people and treat them rotten." Davis was replaced by Steve McQueen, and it was some time and a lot of groveling before Davis was allowed back into the presence. The Rat Pack constantly played childish practical jokes on one another, but outside his circle of acolytes Sinatra demonstrated only lack of humor. He was the despair of his publicity people, who knew that he could have charmed the pants off the press anytime he wanted; but he preferred to lose his temper. The man who wanted to be the coolest animal who ever walked too often lost his cool.

The greatest artists in history have understood that imagination can sustain us if reality does not: contemplation can be as valuable as experience; art can transcend the life. It is possible to get too close to some kinds of experiences, and be shattered by them; that is where some of our proverbs come from: Familiarity breeds contempt; Absence makes the heart grow fonder. For most of us there is a middle ground between promiscuity and denial; but notwithstanding the quality of Frank Sinatra's best work, he has fallen down as an artist because his personal motivation has always been instant gratification. Once again, in this respect he was a bellwether: "Seize the day!" has become a common mode of behavior during his lifetime; nobody wants to wait for anything. It is also a typical American belief that there is or should be no difference between the private behavior and the public life, and here is where Sinatra has exhibited the most confusion, demanding high standards of others while often behaving badly himself. The only time he seemed to be in complete control of himself was when he was behind the microphone.

He always tried to insist that both his private and his public lives were his own business. A sometime girlfriend, actress Gloria Rhoads, was writing a biography of another actress who had also dated Sinatra, and submitted her manuscript to Sinatra's people for approval; they forbade her to write anything at all about him, threatening to see to it that she never worked in Hollywood again, and sure enough, she said, she never did. In the early 1980s Sinatra tried for a year to prevent Kitty Kelley from writing a book about him. Not only was public curiosity about a star of his magnitude bound to be intense, but some of his displays of bad manners and temper tantrums were very public, which meant that anybody had a perfect right to write about them, but he could never understand that. Trevor Howard, his co-star in *Von Ryan's Express*, said that Sinatra's goons would go into a taverna, take all the records off the jukebox and fill it with Sinatra's: he had to try to order the world into a mirror. If only half the stories about him are true, Sinatra had a serious behavior problem. Yet lots of people are spoiled, selfish and bad-mannered, and not many are also superstars. As somebody once said of tenor saxophonist Stan Getz, "He's a nice bunch of guys."

Sinatra followed a pattern established in childhood of buying his friends presents; he passed out gold bracelets and watches like box-top premiums, and even gave away cars and pianos. Some of this was guilt (he allegedly sent a piano to Judy Garland after he had stood her up). Most of this was primitive psychological gestures, virtually tribal in its meaning: his friends gave him gaudy junk, too; when he and Barbara Marx auctioned off a lot of their stuff at Christie's at the end of 1995, the auction catalog included any number of jewel-encrusted boxes, a fancy microphone cover and even a diamond-studded shoehorn. But although he bought friends that way, he was embarrassed to accept gifts. Shirley MacLaine gave him a cigarette lighter of which he was quite fond, using it for many years, but when she gave it to him, he just slipped it into his pocket, finding it impossible to express any gratitude. When Brad Dexter had saved Sinatra's life, the best he could manage was, "My family thanks you."

And there was another kind of generosity which was deep and genuine, and embarrassed him even more. When comedian Rags Ragland died suddenly, his partner Phil Silvers was utterly grief-stricken; Sinatra dropped what he was doing, flew to Silvers's side and did the club act with him, knowing all of Ragland's lines by heart (Sinatra and Silvers had done the routines together on the USO tour). And much of Sinatra's generosity was less public than that. When another old girlfriend was dying of leukemia, he paid all her hospital bills. When Sammy Davis, Jr., lost an eye in a car crash, when Bela Lugosi was hospitalized for drug addiction, when Charlie Morrison, owner of the Mocambo nightclub in Hollywood, died suddenly leaving debts and no insurance, these people and their families benefited from Sinatra's gifts not just of money but of his time. The excellent actor Lee J. Cobb had testified before the House Un-American Activities Committee, and had few friends in Hollywood when he had a severe heart attack in 1955; he was broke and depressed, and thought his career was over. Cobb barely knew Sinatra, though they had met on the set of *Miracle of the Bells* in 1949; but Sinatra came to see him every day in the hospital, bringing him books and other presents; he put Cobb in a rest home for six weeks, then in his own home in Palm Springs, then in an apartment in Los Angeles, paying his bills until he was on his feet. Cobb lived another twenty years and had more success as an actor (he played Sinatra's father in *Come Blow Your Horn* in 1963).

All this happened in the 1950s, when Sinatra's image was that of a bad-mannered playboy; but his spontaneous generosity was kept secret for a long time, because he knew that his motives would be suspect. Many years later, he hadn't stopped: when his old rival Bob Eberly was in hospital with lung cancer in 1981, he offered to have him transferred to the best clinic and to pay all his medical bills. Sinatra had absolute faith in Dr. De Bakey in Houston, and sent him a few patients: "When [Joe Louis] had his stroke, Frank sent him to me. I'm not sure he'd want people to know this, but he said: 'Take care of him and just send me the bills.'... None of the people who made money off Joe Louis when he was fighting were there for him. Only Frank." Sinatra's kindness to people who could do nothing for him had little to do with the favors his mother had done for people in Hoboken. He had started out in 1915 very nearly born dead; he came from nowhere to be the sensation of the 1940s, and then knew what it was like to go back down to the bottom. He knew that he owed something, somebody, somewhere, for his power and his stardom, and for his ability to reveal his vulnerability in a song, which is where the power ultimately came from; he had a duty to give something back. Much of his generosity, such as his twelve or fifteen benefits a year for various causes, was a kind of karmic obeisance to the gods who had once brought him so low that he lost weight he could not afford to lose, lost his voice, and even attempted suicide.

He also knew, must have known at some level, that a great

many of his personal and professional problems were his own fault. "Women," he once said to Pete Hamill. "I don't know what the hell to make of them." The first thing about women is that they are other people, like other men, and you have to allow other people to exist, but there was something missing in Sinatra's psychological makeup. Each of us is supposed to learn in childhood that we are not the center of the universe; one's freedom ends where the other person's nose begins. If we allow other people their space, demanding neither too much nor too little, sometimes they understand and appreciate it, and that is the best we can hope for; sometimes they want more than you can give them, or they will not allow you to be nice to them at all, or they want to treat you like dirt, especially if you're a big shot like Frank Sinatra. And Sinatra, with his weird upbringing, his crazy mother and his quiet father, could not even try to get the balance right.

Yet another part of getting along with others is tact, which often means telling white lies. This was a skill that Sinatra did not have, and his honesty may have had the effect of a bull in a china shop, but it was very real. Again and again his Hollywood friends, Kirk Douglas, Cary Grant, Gregory Peck and the others, say variants of the same thing: You never came away from a conversation with Sinatra wondering, "What did he mean by that?" He was capable of lying endlessly to the authorities, but that was part of the game: cops, governments, taxmen, all want to take advantage of you or tell you what to do, which is to be avoided. Person-to-person was another matter, and Sinatra's face-to-face honesty was strong stuff. His opinion of newspaper people is almost unprintable, and in the 1970s it was intolerably vulgar and sexist as well, but the gossip columnists he had known were liars, and metaphorically they were whores, printing anything about anybody that would sell papers, and even taking tips from crackpots like Harry Anslinger and J. Edgar Hoover. There may be many who did not like Sinatra's manners, but only a fool would have preferred the honesty of the tabloid journalist to his. Then there was the problem of being so famous: Elvis Presley could not cope at all with fame on that scale, and cocooned himself, never seen in public; he would charter an aircraft, or rent a theater or an amusement park for the night, keeping everybody out except for his entourage.

Sinatra knew that he could not walk down the street like anybody else, but he was a gregarious man who wanted to go to a nightclub or a restaurant or attend an opening, where he might have expected to run into people much like himself without being hassled. If his own public high spirits were often those of a spoiled working-class nouveau riche from Hoboken, well, that is what he was.

Yet he had a mysterious charm that usually allowed him to get away with it. He was capable of exquisite manners when the occasion demanded it, and his brutal honesty was also part of his power. On one occasion, after a spectacular display of Sinatra's temper, somebody asked Jimmy Van Heusen why he put up with it, and Van Heusen replied, "Because he sings my songs. I'm a whore for my music." But there was more to it than that. Sinatra's peculiar power over a great many people was that of one of nature's aristocrats. Like a great many of the most fascinating people in history, both good and bad, he had the ability to wield power over others by simply assuming it. This is an inexplicable quality, and comparatively few people are immune to it.

In earlier times, the kings, princes and popes who possessed Sinatra's kind of power were responsible for much of the world's great art, because they commissioned and patronized the poets, composers, painters, sculptors and architects. But they were well educated, and had political skills, while Sinatra's judgement was limited to his own sphere, having not much taste outside it (and he lived in an era when the bottom line was fame and riches rather than political power, increasingly not worth having anyway). Sinatra also had the problem that he was himself the artist. He put everything he had into that, and invaded people's lives with his art, from the years with Tommy Dorsey, when he helped his generation to define their own feelings, to the concerts of nearly fifty years later, when those same people came to listen, and their children and even their grandchildren came to hear what the magic was about. Sinatra's temperament and power over others meant that he could do as he pleased in the rest of his life, but his lack of political skills (such as patience and judgement) meant that of his fifty or sixty films and the equivalent of seventy or eighty albums, only half a dozen films and a dozen or two albums remain timeless. Yet that is enough to ensure artistic immortality, such as it is today.

And the life of a tyrant is lonely. Sinatra could neither let others get too close nor keep them away. Nick Sevano, Brad Dexter, George Jacobs, even Hank Sanicola—sooner or later, no matter how loyal they were, the time would come when most of the people who worked for him or with him had been around too long, and he owed them too much. (Somebody once said that no man is a hero to his valet, and to Sinatra they were all valets.) In the 1960s he had serious romances with actress Dorothy Provine and dancer Juliet Prowse; then he tried marriage again, with Mia Farrow, but he would always expect a woman to give up everything else. In particular, she should give up her career and stay in the kitchen, as Nancy Barbato had once done. But he could not go back to Nancy, either, because he had treated her disgracefully once, and he knew that he would do it again. She had known him when he was a teenager; she had given herself to him wholly, forever; he could trust her more than anyone else, but he could not let anyone get that close again. Loneliness is part of the human condition, the one lesson that Sinatra learned better than most people ever learn it. He could go halfway around the world to see Ava, but she eventually gave up on men, on her career, on everything, and as she got older she drank too much, and he could not bear to watch that, either. Yet he would not have traded anything, not even happiness, to be anything other than he was; he described himself as a manic-depressive, and in his life as in his art there was, to quote Arnold Shaw again, the constant counterpoint of toughness and tenderness. Henry Pleasants, concentrating on Sinatra's art, wrote that "fastidious taste, a different upbringing or a successful psychoanalysis would have destroyed him as an artist."

It is easy to be generous when you are rich, and Sinatra knew that, too. There were times when he could say the right thing in public. When the film industry gave him the Jean Hersholt Humanitarian Award in 1971, an honorary Oscar, he said,

If your name is John Doe, and you work night and day doing things for your helpless neighbors, what you get for your effort is tired. So Mr. and Mrs. Doe, and all of you who give of yourselves to those who carry too big a burden to make it on their own, I want you to reach out and take your share of this, because if I have earned it, so, too, have you.

Above all, Sinatra was an American.

Thomas Jefferson and James Madison, as well as the French observer Alexis de Tocqueville, could see at the beginning that the principal American problem was going to be the tyranny of the majority. De Tocqueville also remarked that the liberty to say or do what you want is accompanied by extraordinary social pressure to conform. In a new nation swamped by waves of immigration and with no traditions of its own, borrowing this from England, that from Germany and the rest from somewhere else, the rules would have to be made up as we went along, and would always rest on a fragile attitude of community rather than on centuries of tradition. There would always be somebody trying to tell somebody else how to behave, and this above all Frank Sinatra could not tolerate.

American manners and standards of behavior had been dominated by the influence of the old East Coast families, who in turn took their cues from the British upper classes. In a book called *The English House*, German architect Hermann Muthesius wrote about life among the style-setters:

> From the very fact that the members of the household regularly meet for dinner in evening dress...the act of taking nourishment is sublimated by a pleasing presentation of what is offered. And this is where England can take credit for having created a fine tradition which has become the model for the world at large...summoned to the table, usually by three muffled notes of a gong, the company in its ceremonial attire moves toward the dining-room two by two....

Our peasant ancestors ate hunkered around the fireplace where the food was cooked; then Muthesius was writing in 1904 about a house which also contained a small army of servants, and in which the children were served separately, in the nursery. Although the evening dress was eschewed, one of the ways in which we aped the mores of our betters was in everyone sitting down to eat at the same time. (In the early 1930s in Hoboken,

Dolly Sinatra's plastic flowers were a similar attempt at class.) Yet increasingly the families of the 1950s served their meals out of the saucepans, because there were no servants to wash the serving dishes; and nowadays we often eat hunkered around the colder glow of the television screen. Standards have slipped.

The manners of the New York society knowingly described in the novels of Edith Wharton were ultimately the reason for the morals clauses in the Hollywood contracts, and the rule in the TV sitcoms that Ozzie and Harriet had to sleep in separate beds. But by the 1950s that world was fraying around the edges, for several reasons. Everybody knew that the public behavior of the rich and famous covered up a lot of fundamentally bad manners (that's what F. Scott Fitzgerald's *The Great Gatsby* was all about); the sheer nastiness of gossip columnists and self-interested politicians became increasingly evident, while two world wars had raised questions about the very nature of civilization itself; Alfred Kinsey's research into sexual behavior exploded the myths of our morality in that area. And increasing prosperity seemed to make the traditions less important: as the working class joined the middle class (with mortgages, two-car garages and a TV set in every room) there were more demands on everyone's time: many families had two wage-earners. And to the extent that manners carried less class distinction, they had lost some of their point.

The 1950s seemed to reach an apotheosis of mass culture and social cohesion, when everybody knew their place and gave lip service to the same shibboleths, but this was an illusion. The need for "dating do's and don'ts" was accepted by teenagers even while, at the drive-in movies, the windows of their cars were fogged up with their passion. And that was only the first stage of cultural revolution: soon there would be even more freedom (or license) in a nation that paradoxically seemed to be frightened of the freedom it already had. For thirty years after the Second World War the U.S.A. was the richest and most powerful nation on earth, and the largest and most prosperous generation of Americans had less and less in the way of tradition to hang on to.

Sinatra must have been familiar with the music of Ozzie Nelson's dance band in the late 1930s, and its vocalist Harriet

Hilliard; no doubt he later snorted at the artifice in their harmless TV sitcom. Yet there was a reason for that artifice: we need some attitudes, some standards against which to measure ourselves. What one can say about Frank Sinatra is that he was consistent in his confusion, trying to deal with the world without compromise, taking cues from no one; he often did it badly, but he did it his way, and many people admired that because they were just as confused as he was. Sinatra needed to struggle against any constraint yet also wanted to cling to orderly ways, to the extent of compulsively straightening the ashtrays on the table. Mia Farrow had something of the image of a free spirit, a "hippie chick"; it was during his marriage to her that he got drunk one evening in a private club and began insulting Harlan Ellison, a scriptwriter. Sinatra had never met Ellison, but took exception to his casual dress, subsequently forcing changes to the club's rules because he didn't want to have to look at anyone not wearing a tie. He was going to hold back the 1960s all by himself, even if he had himself been responsible for kicking over some of the fences, and even if his wife wouldn't obey him.

His obsessiveness, his bad temper, and his awful relationships with women were simply clues to the fact that no matter how big a star he was, he could never get enough attention. He was a spoiled brat. It was the combination of bad temper and powerful charm that made him dangerous, and the danger added to his appeal for many; yet by the end of the 1950s he was no longer trying to kick over the establishment, but to join it and even to dominate it. And even in this he was ahead of his time: the U.S.A. today is a nation of victims who all want to have their own way, a selfish society that whines a lot. As Michael O'Brien wrote recently in the *Times Literary Supplement*:

Much in American culture is passionate, ugly, violent, committed. Americans like it that way; it is part of their sense of self. They do not want to be Denmark writ large. The Scarsdale housewife with a gun in her bag, the Southerner with a Confederate flag on his lawn, the Jew in Brooklyn wishing death to Palestinians, the Minnesota feminist reviling men as potential rapists, the black professor chanting anti-Semitism—these are not candidates for membership in urbanely voluntary affiliations. These are angry people, who want to keep and share their anger. American culture teaches them that emotion is good, enthusiasm validating, and release a gift.

Sinatra became a star because he was a great pop singer, and subsequently remained one of the most famous people in the world partly because he could behave badly and get away with it. He was nothing if not a dude; despite his own apparent contradictions, his public and private behavior really did seem to be the same. His life can be seen as a paradigm of the American experiment: if he seems to have had an emotionally deprived childhood, similarly the great question of modern times is whether or not we can govern ourselves without a state religion, the divine right of kings, or centuries of tradition to keep in check our tyranny over each other. If our old social cohesions are dissolving, we will have to discover new ones; that struggle has given rise to a lot of bad behavior, and even a new American language, described by film critic David Thompson (in 1994, in *The New Republic*). It is the squeak of the Rat Pack. Thompson calls it "tough mouth," or neo-gangsterese.

> It is theatrical, modulated, with aspirations to a kind of don't-interrupt-me eloquence...not just the disclosure of cynicism or depravity but the feeling that someone is getting away with talking like a movie gangster. It's dream talk, such as few of us manage in life. The listener has either to take it, to swallow it or to smack the speaker in the face....
>
> This kind of talk is all around us. The air is barbed, whether it's our kids wiping us out with "dude" one-liners from Ninja turtles, or our politicians pushing their eight-word slogans through the CNN grinder. Very often it comes from male voices who have a hard time getting a woman's point of view. You can hear it in rap, in Scorsese's street films, in Mamet and Quentin Tarantino....
>
> ...The Mob cherished movies. They could see that, whatever their moral endings, pictures like *Scarface* and *Public Enemy* were helping the public understand the gangster's point of view, his take on free enterprise. Little boys in the street liked to sneer, strut and

stagger in the gutter like Cagney. Dude-ism was born. The gangsters were flattered to socialize with Hollywood elites; and actors got off on real-life models.

Gore Vidal said about the Puritans that they did not leave England for the American colonies because they were being persecuted, but so they could persecute other people. The U.S.A. is both a place where anything goes and a place obsessed with morals, but there is one American minority group which has never had any illusions or doubts, and which has always known exactly what it was doing. In James Elroy's novel *American Tabloid* (1995), about fictionalized events leading up to the JFK assassination, the characters are FBI and CIA agents, hired killers, politicians, Howard Hughes, J. Edgar Hoover and so forth; but the only people who are not double-crossing each other are the gangsters. (And in the novel they are also the funniest, because they understand the other characters better than the others understand themselves.) A nation with a strong puritan streak but also devoted to the pursuit of pleasure, and which measures status in terms of personal wealth and power, is going to give rise to a class of businessmen who are going to buy or sell anything they want, no matter what rules they have to break; by simultaneously ignoring the majority and pandering to it, gangsters have been the true American aristocrats of the twentieth century. And some of the most prominent members of this peculiarly American aristocracy were to be counted among Sinatra's friends and associates. If Sinatra was not a prince, he knew who the princes were; he understood them, and they understood him.

While I have been writing this book, the one question my friends have been asking is, "Was Frank a member of the Mafia?" But the Mob doesn't have a membership list. Gangsters don't carry cards. No secretary sent Sam Giancana an annual reminder to pay his dues. Giancana was a full-time gangster; Sinatra had grown up with gangsters, and became a singer who sometimes needed a favor; still other people were more or less straight lawyers or businessmen who helped gangsters bend the rules, or helped them get out of trouble, and it was all just business. For decades J. Edgar Hoover pretended that there was no such thing as organized crime, because he couldn't find a membership list. The Mob no doubt appreciated having such a man as head of the nation's premier law-enforcement agency, but meanwhile anyone who ever ate spaghetti in a Brooklyn restaurant, bought a cinema ticket or put a coin in a jukebox was as much a member of the Mob as Frank Sinatra. We were all Americans, and the business of America is business.

When America's first experiment with Prohibition was over, the Mob needed a place to put its new wealth, and was already moving into entertainment and other industries. Bugsy Siegel had relocated to the West Coast in the 1930s, and soon mingled with the Hollywood smart set; in the following decade, Frank Sinatra and Phil Silvers hero-worshiped him. Siegel thought of building a sports palace in Los Angeles, but then he realized that Las Vegas was the place to make the American dream visible, and built the Flamingo Hotel there. Gambling was legal in Nevada, and entertainers were used to lure the suckers; there were almost no controls, and for decades the Mob skimmed the revenue and paid no taxes. While Elvis Presley performed in Vegas, his manager, Tom Parker, lived in one of the hotels and gambled half of Presley's money away; Sinatra and all his chums were big draws in Las Vegas, and for many years Sinatra took his pocket money from the tables: he got chips free for the asking, cashed them in when he won and walked away when he lost.

The American love affair with the Mob had not ended with George Raft and Jimmy Cagney. Joe Kennedy was not the last to recognize his own kind on the other side of the law, and John Kennedy probably got an extra thrill out of balling a gangster's chick. The evidence of our fascination is shot through our popular culture. Francis Ford Coppola's series of *Godfather* films (1972–80) are recognized as American classics; Sergio Leone's *Once Upon a Time in America* (1984) was beautifully made, and much of the early part of it looks like Sinatra's Hoboken. Barry Levinson portrayed *Bugsy* with style (1991), but Martin Scorsese is one of our most valuable observers: he made *Goodfellas* (1990), went back to Edith Wharton's old New York, drenched in manners, for *The Age of Innocence* (1993), and then to Las Vegas for *Casino* (1996). The worst gangster picture has some truth in it, because when we look at gangsters we are seeing ourselves: our contradictions, our world-weariness, our hollow souls "in the loop."

Of course Sinatra was in the loop. So what? Long before Las Vegas the Mob had moved into American watering holes, and when Sinatra's career had bottomed out around 1950, Moe Dalitz booked him into the Desert Inn. Skinny D'Amato ran the 500 Club in Atlantic City, Willie Moretti the Riviera in Fort Lee, New Jersey; Joe Fischetti and Sam Giancana could hire anybody they wanted in Chicago, and other guys had the Fontainebleau in Miami: if the Mob couldn't own the places outright they had front men to do it for them. (We knew that.) With enemies like gossip columnists and his own big mouth, Sinatra needed friends; and later, when he was back on top, he repaid the favors. At the Villa Venice in suburban Chicago in the autumn of 1962, Sinatra and all his pals performed for nothing so that the Mob could fleece the punters (who were willing: that the gambling was illegal was part of the fun). He recorded radio jingles for a Chicago car dealer who was a friend of the Mob, and took his fee in Pontiacs. The Westchester Premier Theater in Tarrytown, New York, was opened in 1976 and made millions with the help of Sinatra and his buddies; the Mob kept all the money and allowed the facility to go bankrupt within a year. (Sinatra was also photographed with a group of Mob bigshots, including Carlo Gambino.) So what? One hand washes the other, and there's always a developer to remake a site when the Mob is through with it.

When Sinatra wanted to settle with Tommy Dorsey in 1943, he probably phoned a few of his friends to see what they could do. But the Mob doesn't very often make offers that you can't refuse; if you can't do them this favor now, you can do them another later. Sinatra was leaving one of the most successful acts in the business to go solo; nobody knew he would turn into a gold mine. The Mob had its tentacles into the booking agencies and the entertainment unions; maybe they helped broker a deal that made everybody happy, but they would have been foolish to shove a pistol in Dorsey's mouth. A decade later Sinatra was at the bottom; he didn't look bankable, and the Mob wasn't going to tell Harry Cohn who to put in *From Here to Eternity*. Cohn allegedly wore

Johnny Roselli's friendship ring, and Frank Cosello allegedly made phone calls to Hollywood, but the muscle, if there was any, was not going to be conclusive; filmmaking was left to the filmmakers because lousy pictures don't make money. Besides, it was good for Sinatra to grovel a little; he had caused most of his own problems, and not too many years later Sam Giancana would be warning the others to beware what they said in front of Sinatra because he had a big mouth. When Sinatra launched Reprise Records, maybe the muscle in record distribution saw to it that plenty of records were available on time, and that singles made it to the jukeboxes and were played on the radio; but it was Sinatra and Mo Ostin who saw to it that the artists were happy and that the pressings were of good quality. It was all good business. Let us imagine, for a moment, that one of the most dismal Sinatra albums was made because the Mob wanted to do somebody a favor: this would have been an exception to prove the rule. There's not much money in a flop album.

There can be few show-business folk who have not crossed the paths of gangsters of one kind or another. In a filmed interview, Duke Ellington was asked about the people who ran the Cotton Club in the late 1920s, where he first became nationally famous; he replied with a sly smile: "Gangsters? . . . . You're talking about my *friends*!" Each entertainer handled the situation in his or her own way. Tony Bennett is a gentleman and a devout Catholic; his career had faltered when he was no longer making hit singles for Mitch Miller, perhaps because he preferred not to play certain places rather than become indebted to the wrong kind of people. Sinatra praised Bennett's singing in *Life* magazine in 1965, and his career picked up again; today he is more popular than ever, and has always been grateful to Sinatra, but he never had any trouble keeping his own hands clean.

Dean Martin had a different kind of integrity. Louis Buchalter, alias Louis Lepke, was the owner of the Club Alabam in New York City, where Martin worked in the 1940s before he teamed with Jerry Lewis. Lepke was a Mob hit man, wanted for murder; when he was finally awaiting execution, his wife was running the club in his absence. Martin was still young and unknown, but the family had given him work and he stuck by them, sitting with them during the execution and loyal to them afterwards. That was the kind of manners the Mob understood. They never gave Martin any trouble, but he never asked them for anything, either.

One of Shirley MacLaine's stories concerns Martin. Ed Torres ran the Riviera in Las Vegas, and thought he was Dean Martin's boss. Martin owned a stake in the hotel and kept a suite there with his wardrobe in it; on one occasion he arrived a day early with Mort Viner (his agent as well as MacLaine's), and discovered that Torres had been renting the suite while Martin wasn't there. MacLaine tells the story:

> Mort and Dean said nothing. Dean played his engagement, and on the last night Mort played rough. He paid off a bellboy to collect Eddie Torres' clothes and put them in the middle of the floor in Dean's suite. Just before Dean left the hotel, Mort set fire to Eddie's clothes and then rang the fire marshal and said that he smelled smoke on that floor. Eddie gave up his need to control Dean.

Martin never took any nonsense from Frank Sinatra, either. They were close friends for decades, but in the early years when Sinatra offered to help with Martin's career, Martin wanted to make it on his own. Later, during the Rat Pack period, if Martin didn't feel like partying he went home and watched television. Sinatra could have learned what real cool was from Martin. But when Sinatra was at his peak, and with so much money growing on trees, who cared whether a valise full of hundred-dollar bills belonged to Sinatra or to somebody else? ("There's plenty more where that came from," he was heard to say.) There were coincidences over the years when people Sinatra didn't like got hurt or threatened. Buddy Rich got mugged when Sinatra was sore at him. Comedian Jackie Mason joked about Sinatra and Mia Farrow; so did Johnny Carson, but Carson was lovable, one of the biggest stars in show business and Sinatra's pal, while Mason was a comic for grownups, a former rabbi: even when his wisecracks were innocuous, they seemed close to the knuckle because Mason didn't laugh at his own jokes. And Sinatra was not a grownup. Bullets were fired into Mason's hotel room; he was assaulted and his nose was broken. A food-industry executive, Frederick R. Weisman, was having a drink with a friend in a room where Sinatra and his pals were making so much noise nobody could think; Sinatra's goons took exception to being shushed and Weisman ended up in a coma. Sinatra's friends of the period said that during the wait for news from the hospital was the only time they ever saw him frightened; but as soon as Weisman was on the mend his family received threatening phone calls, and they refused to press charges.

Some of the stories can be verified, but there are too many of them. If hoodlums did Sinatra's bidding every time he got sore at somebody, they had to be awfully stupid hoodlums, because too many times Sinatra's big mouth and foul temper coincided. And it is precisely for that reason that the stories will follow him to his grave. Some of the best stories are suspect because gangsters, too, like to brag and exaggerate, especially if they live long enough to retire; but the story about Willie Moretti shoving a pistol in Dorsey's mouth isn't even firsthand. It's just a rumor. Mickey Cohen had become a West Coast boss after Bugsy Siegel had been terminated, and later told a story that rings true: In the late 1940s, when Cohen knew his house was being watched night and day, Sinatra insisted on coming there to ask Cohen to stop Johnny Stompanato from seeing Ava Gardner. Cohen was disgusted, and told Sinatra to go back to his wife and kids; but the point of the story is that Sinatra's personal life was more important to him than the fact that Cohen's house was being watched. This was not a man who could be trusted. He told Pete Hamill that if he ever allowed someone to write his biography, there would be a lot that could not be revealed; no man capable of discretion would have said such a thing to a journalist.

The gangsters were thugs, of course; most of them, like Sinatra, subscribed to traditional values while they treated women like dirt. But like Sinatra, they didn't pretend to be anything they were not. Johnny Stompanato was one of the worst; he was present in the kitchen at Billy Berg's Hollywood club on New Year's Eve in 1948 when somebody got stabbed and Billie Holiday and her boyfriend John Levy were arrested. (Stompanato bought the farm in 1958, when Lana Turner's daughter had enough of his violence and stabbed him to death.) Stompanato and Levy were minor hoodlums, wanna-be gangsters, but sometimes the worst people got to the top, and one of those was Sam Giancana.

Giancana began as a driver for Al Capone, and eventually inherited Capone's Chicago-based business empire. After Albert Anastasia was murdered in his barber chair in Manhattan in 1957, there had to be a conclave of the Mob to find out what was going on, and it was foolishly decided to hold it in the tiny town of Apalachin in New York State. A local state trooper was puzzled at the number of black limousines buzzing around, decided to set up a road block, and sixty of the nation's biggest bosses were arrested. It was very embarrassing, but they all got off, claiming that they had all come to visit Joseph Barbara because he had a heart condition, and anyway there was no law against having a meeting. The Justice Department estimated that up to fifty more kingpins had got away, and Joseph Valachi, the first important insider to turn witness, claimed that Sam Giancana was one of them. Valachi was disgusted.

I'll tell you the reaction of all us soldiers when we heard about the raid. If soldiers got arrested in a meet like that, you can imagine what the bosses would have done. There they are, running through the woods like rabbits, throwing away money so they won't be caught with a lot of cash, and some of them throwing away guns. So who are they kidding when they say we got to respect them?

But short, balding Sam Giancana was respected. He had been arrested more than seventy times, served some time in prison, and was suspected of having ordered more than two hundred murders, and he wore Frank Sinatra's friendship ring. The irony is that the friendship between Sinatra and Giancana may have done as much as anything to convince the Nevada authorities to start cracking down on the Mob.

Sinatra hung out at the Cal-Neva Lodge in Lake Tahoe as early as 1951, for it was there that he took some sleeping pills and had to be rescued by George Jacobs. (Whether this was a suicide attempt or not, he had to have his stomach pumped.) In 1960 Sinatra and his friends became the owners of Cal-Neva, with Giancana as a secret partner, who figured on taking his money out after a while, because the trouble with Cal-Neva was that it was only open from June until September. But Sinatra and his pals wanted to make it a year-round operation. They enlarged the casino, built more hotel rooms and constructed a showroom for entertainment. They needed to borrow money for this, and Giancana was overheard by federal wiretappers complaining about not being able to borrow from a Teamsters union's pension fund; the heat was on Teamsters leader Jimmy Hoffa at the time, and like any other businessman, sometimes he had to be careful to whom he lent other people's money.

Some of the biggest stars played the Celebrity Room at Cal-Neva, while slightly lesser acts (like Trini Lopez, under contract to Reprise) would play the Cabaret Lounge. In mid-1962 Sinatra officially owned more than a third of the place, and a year later he owned half of it; Hank Sanicola had a third and Sanford Waterman had a piece. Skinny D'Amato kept an eye on Giancana's investment, and it all should have been perfect, but trouble followed Sinatra everywhere. An employee was shot on the front steps. A few days before Marilyn Monroe died in Los Angeles of an overdose, she had her stomach pumped at Cal-Neva. A deputy sheriff stopped by to pick up his wife, who worked there as a waitress; Sinatra tried to throw him out and got thumped; the deputy was suspended from his job, and a couple of weeks later his car was forced off the road. (He was killed and his wife badly injured. She decided not to go back to work at Cal-Neva.)

But the worst problem was Giancana. Shirley MacLaine tells of an incident in Mexico City, when Giancana twisted her arm behind her back, Sammy Davis, Jr., broke it up, and Giancana punched Davis in the stomach. Giancana wasn't even supposed to be at Cal-Neva, but he got in fights there, too. He knew that he was under constant surveillance; in fact, he took the FBI to court for harassment and won a victory of sorts: the FBI was fined $500 and told to stay at least one hole behind Giancana on the golf course. Yet he and Sinatra couldn't stay away from each other. Ava Gardner and Mia Farrow couldn't stand Sinatra's Mob friends (and the Mob didn't like them either, because they didn't behave like wives were supposed to behave); but Giancana and men like him were more important to Sinatra than his women. Nancy Sinatra's story is that Giancana was visiting his girlfriend, one of the singing McGuire Sisters, when they were working at Cal-Neva, and that her father didn't know he was there; but Giancana and Sinatra were seen together at Palm Springs, in Hawaii, in New York and in Nevada, and it was against the law for Sam Giancana to set foot in Nevada.

The state's Gaming Control Board had a booklet distributed to law enforcement officers with pictures and details of eleven gangsters who were not allowed in the state, Giancana prominent among them; but he had to be Sinatra's honored guest whenever he felt like hanging out. True, half of the resort was in Nevada and half in California; Sinatra joked to his audience that "this is the only place in America where you can walk across the lobby and get locked up for violating the Mann Act." That was an obsolescent law against transporting a woman across state lines for immoral purposes, but it was not a joke: it got Chuck Berry a trumped-up racist jail sentence because of a teenaged hat-check girl who had a record for prostitution; and Cal-Neva was crawling with federal agents because of an alleged prostitution ring there that used girls from California. But nothing could stop Sinatra from sucking up to Giancana.

Italian, Irish and Jewish mobsters had a lot in common: they were all members of minority groups, their families recent immigrants, and they all hated Irish cops. Sinatra resented U.S. Attorney General Bobby Kennedy for several reasons (that's why he decided to campaign for Hubert Humphrey in 1968, after Bobby entered the race), but also because his gangster friends hated him. Sinatra would never hear a word against John Kennedy, but the Mob hated all the Kennedys, and also hated Fidel Castro, because Havana had once been their playground; and meanwhile, such was the confusion in America in those years that one branch of federal power was stalking Giancana while the other half may have been hiring the Mob to rub out Castro, and a little later Sinatra's hero John Kennedy got rubbed out instead. Yet Sinatra couldn't help groveling at the seat of perceived power: Shut out of the White House, he needed the adulation of the gangsters even more.

Finally the state of Nevada could not ignore all the flagrant violations that were going on, and the reports they were getting from the FBI, so Ed Olsen, the Chairman of the Nevada Gaming Commission, insisted on interviewing Sinatra, who of course was as insulting as possible, using the banal, don't-fuck-with-me variety of tough-mouth. (This allegedly astonished even Giancana, who knew when to keep his mouth shut.) Even so, Olsen tried to go easy on Sinatra, knowing that Sinatra would only lie to him anyway; but then at the Lodge Sinatra attempted to bribe two audit agents from the Commission. This was not a serious attempt at bribery, only a childish attempt to insult the agents, but they reported it, and Olsen was forced to seek a revocation of Sinatra's license at Cal-Neva (and at the Sands in Las Vegas, where Sinatra had a holding of 9 percent). And finally Hank Sanicola had had enough. He had his own money invested in Cal-Neva and he didn't want to lose it, so he wanted out, unless he could get assurances from Sinatra that Giancana would never set foot there again. "Out of Cal-Neva, out of everything," Sinatra decreed; short of cash, he gave Sanicola music-publishing holdings worth far more than the stake in Cal-Neva, and they parted for good. It was Sanicola who had convinced Sinatra to keep going when he was with the Harry James band, depressed that the band wasn't doing well and he wasn't becoming a star quickly enough; Sanicola had stuck by him through everything, but gangsters were more important.

During this period, President Kennedy toured the state of Nevada, and put in a good word for Sinatra with Governor Grant Sawyer, who also reported phone calls from people who promised big contributions to his next election campaign; and Mickey Rudin hired a Las Vegas attorney (who later became the first federal judge to be convicted of tax evasion) to defend Sinatra. But when they realized how much evidence the state had, they gave up, and Sinatra announced that he was getting out of the gaming industry to concentrate on entertainment. That is when Jack Warner came to the rescue, leasing Sinatra's Nevada holdings from him, selling him one-third of Warner Brothers Records and buying two-thirds of Reprise, making a movie deal and giving Sinatra the title of "assistant to the president" of the company, to help save his face. Such was Sinatra's public identification with the Mob that a rumor arose that the Mob was taking over Warner Brothers, which Warner angrily denied.

Yet there is another version of the story which is just as plausible: that the record and film deal was already going down, and

Warner told Sinatra that the deal was off if he kept squabbling with the state of Nevada. Giancana was Sinatra's friend, and he did not want anyone telling him who he could consort with; but one way or another he was forced to choose between show business and the gaming industry. He was also always interested in working with juvenile delinquents, and is supposed to have told a group of boys about crime, "It's a mug's game. For half the brains and guts it takes to stay alive and out of jail in the rackets, you can be a big shot, sleep safe at night, and have twice as much." Sinatra may have chosen some of his friends badly, but they were his friends, not mine, and he was loyal to them until he lost his playpen.

During Sinatra's marriage to Mia Farrow his bad temper seemed to reach new depths. She had already been a big star on television, a medium Sinatra never mastered; and Farrow famously cut off her very long blonde hair just as Sinatra's fiftieth birthday was dominating the showbiz news: perhaps her tender years did not preclude an instinct for publicity of her own. He still performed at the Sands in Las Vegas, but no longer had a stake in it. By then it was owned by Howard Hughes, and when he signed a new contract with the Sands, he made it a condition that Hughes would buy Jack Warner's lease in Cal-Neva. But Hughes wasn't cooperating; and when the Sands cut off Sinatra's credit because he was losing heavily at the tables, he started tearing the place up, and ended by being punched in the face by Carl Cohen, the executive in charge of the casino. Cohen weighed about 250 pounds, and Sinatra had to have two teeth repaired; this was at the time of the 1967 Arab-Israeli war, and a Las Vegas comedian cracked, "I *told* Frank not to fight with a Jew in the desert!" (In her recent book, Nancy Sinatra credited her father with making the joke.)

Jack Entratter was another executive at the Sands, who had been manager of the Copacabana and helpful to Sinatra during the low point in his career. Elaine Brown was a guest in Sinatra's home in 1965; she recorded an incident (in her book *A Taste of Power: A Black Woman's Story*) when Sinatra threw a heavy brass bowl full of cigarettes at Entratter, causing blood to trickle down his forehead, and then made Entratter pick up all the cigarettes. Despite everything, they had been pals for twenty years, but after the trouble at the Sands Sinatra never spoke to Entratter again.

He signed a contract with Caesar's Palace, and later, in 1970, the flow of pocket money from the tables there stopped too, because an IRS agent was watching. Sanford Waterman, one of the former investors in Cal-Neva, had become the Caesar's casino manager, and the last thing he needed was trouble with the Internal Revenue Service; businessmen and tax collectors can agree on where the lines have to be drawn, but not Sinatra. When his credit was stopped he began winding up for a tantrum, and Waterman pulled a pistol on him. Waterman had to be questioned about the incident, but this time even the sheriff showed signs of being fed-up, and Sinatra had to pretend not to care if he ever worked in Las Vegas again. This does not sound like the fate of a card-carrying member of the Outfit.

His third marriage had quickly flopped, his latest album and his latest film had flopped, and then he had washed himself up in Las Vegas. No wonder Sinatra retired. He certainly had enough money; in 1969 he is said to have sold his holdings in Warner Brothers, including Reprise, for more than $22 million. His retirement, though temporary, marked quite a few changes in his life and career, but the cushy days of the Mob in Las Vegas were running out anyway. Within another decade or so the Nevada Gaming Control Board's procedures and accounting began to take effect, because (if for no other reason) the Mob was taking too much money out. Las Vegas had become one of the most famous towns in the world, and if Nevada was going to be famous for a glitzy toilet, at least the citizens wanted a decent return on the deal. By the mid-1980s the regulations and rigorous checks meant that the Mob had to deal with both bureaucracy and sharehold-ers, and they apparently gave up. In that decade, too, the casinos shed a lot of talent, switching to tape recordings and synthesizers: at least the Mob had employed musicians. In the 1990s the last remaining wing of Bugsy Siegel's Flamingo was pulled down, along with the Dunes, once a notorious Mob hangout; and today Las Vegas has been made safe for families, a theme park in the desert whose murder rate is no higher than that of Washington, D.C.

For decades most of the entertainers had been in the loop in one way or another; the Mob needed them and paid well. Only Sinatra was so childishly in thrall that he lost Cal-Neva, the best plaything he ever had, and from then on he was associated in the public mind with the Mob. He was investigated and subpoenaed on various occasions; sometimes he simply said, "I don't know," or was suspected of lying, and often the various law enforcement agencies weren't cooperating closely enough, so that evidence such as the federal wiretaps was not available. In 1969 Dolly moved to Palm Springs, because Marty had died, and partly because Sinatra could not set foot in New Jersey: there was a subpoena to be served by a state commission investigating rackets, and Sinatra sued the commission, going all the way to the Supreme Court, on the grounds that the subpoena was unconstitutional. He lost, and was then being threatened with extradition from California; he gave in, and testified in Trenton in February 1970. The commission asked a lot of silly questions about the Cosa Nostra and the Mafia, of which there are no membership lists. They had nothing on Sinatra; his lack of respect for their competence was justified.

Often enough it was a case of politicians making names for themselves, just as in the old days of the gossip columnists. Sinatra had made himself such a big shot among the gangsters that they tossed his name around even when there was nothing in it. The New Jersey commission asked him about Angelo "Gyp" DeCarlo, who had bragged over the phone to another mobster that he was going to get money from Sinatra, but no connection could be proven. After Sinatra had become friendly with Republican politicians, DeCarlo was serving twelve years for extortion, and President Nixon commuted his sentence in December 1972. There were more whispers, but DeCarlo died of cancer in 1973; there seems no reason why he should not have died in prison, but also no reason why Nixon's commutation of his sentence had not been a simpleminded humanitarian gesture. In July 1972 Sinatra was threatened with yet another subpoena, and testified voluntarily before a congressional committee investigating racketeering in sports; there were rumors about a racetrack in Massachusetts that Sinatra was supposed to have invested in, and again it came to nothing. His letter to the *New York Times* that month was more than a little self-righteous, but Sinatra had divested himself of his gaming interests, and made the valid point that he had been forced to testify about nothing during an election year, saying "If this sort of thing could happen to me, it could happen to anyone, including those who cannot defend themselves properly."

After Sinatra's retirement was over, Sanford Waterman was in trouble with the law and no longer a manager at Caesar's Palace, and Sinatra worked there again. In 1981 Sinatra applied for a Nevada gaming license as a "key employee," which he did not need to perform there; the necessary investigation cost him half a million dollars, but he got his license back, which was important to him: he thought he had cleared his name. But the stories about Sinatra will never lie down, even the ones that aren't true; he often said that he was persecuted because his name ended in a vowel, and maybe he actually believed that himself. By then an era was over. Sam Giancana had been murdered in 1976; his empire had come crashing down, and he had been living in Mexico. The Mob connection with plans to assassinate Fidel Castro was being investigated, and maybe Giancana was getting ready to sing; for whatever reason, even the Mob had had enough of him.

The American experiment is as confused as ever. The old East Coast establishment that gave rise to presidents as recent as George Bush can probably no longer get elected, and the bloom is certainly off the Kennedy dynasty. Today's movie stars are famous only for opening restaurants, and all the best mobsters are dead; America may have to learn to get along without any aristocracy at all. But then again, maybe not.

In April 1996, there was a news item about George Seminara, author of *Mug Shots*, a collection of police photographs of famous people who had been arrested. Thinking that Sinatra had been arrested in Las Vegas after one of his more violent temper tantrums, and reasoning that there must have been a mug shot, Seminara was trying to find it. He received a call from the office of lawyer Bruce Culter: "We understand you're looking for information on Mr. Sinatra. Mr. Sinatra would greatly appreciate it if you would cease and desist." Culter was the lawyer for John Gotti, the New York City neighborhood hero and alleged mobster who was sent to prison in the early 1990s. Mr. Seminara decided to desist.

Chapter Eight

The Splendid Arrogance

Stand-up comics used to make jokes about Sinatra's come-backs, but he hadn't really gone anywhere in the early 1950s: when he looked like he was down and out, he was still earning more money than most of the comics ever did. And there was only the one retirement in 1971–73, until age finally caught up with him twenty years later. He recorded two duets with Nancy in November 1970, and did no more recording for over two years.

He had always been a Sunday painter; now he spent a lot of time in his studio in Palm Springs, and presumably had more time to play with his model trains, a hobby he had acquired from Tommy Dorsey. He looked after his business interests, and he admitted to being bored. His old friends Mike Romanoff and publisher Bennett Cerf died in 1971, which no doubt reminded him of his own mortality. He sang at a fund-raiser for the Italian-American Civil Rights League; and he returned to politics, making friends among a new class of amateur gangsters. Republicans.

Lyndon Johnson should have been the greatest president in American history, but his hubris had brought him down. To quote Kitty Kelley on Sinatra and Johnson:

Both men needed to be the focus of other men's eyes, and they dominated their own worlds by the sheer force of their personalities. Both were unscrupulous, admirable, treacherous, devoted, and mean. Both were adored by their mothers...the thirty-sixth President of the United States and the country's most popular singer were so alike that they circled each other warily. Both were naturally attracted to the ebullient Humphrey, who flattered each of them unashamedly.

Hubert Humphrey, Johnson's vice president, was an old-fashioned liberal from the era of Franklin Roosevelt, a supporter of civil rights since his days as mayor of Minneapolis. It was partly Humphrey's insistence on a civil-rights plank in the Democratic Party's platform in 1948 that split the party that year. (The only reason Harry Truman beat Thomas E. Dewey was that Republicans were so confident they didn't bother to vote.) This was Sinatra's kind of politician, and furthermore Humphrey was a lovable man. Johnson wasn't running again in 1968, but Bobby Kennedy was, so Sinatra had campaigned for Humphrey. His daughters and his estranged wife hated the Vietnam War; all the liberals in Hollywood were supporting Kennedy or Eugene McCarthy for the Democratic nomination, and it was one of the most tempestuous years in the history of American politics. Bobby Kennedy was murdered during the campaign; Humphrey was nominated at the convention in Chicago, while Mayor Daley's cops rioted outside, the heads of anti-war demonstrators attacking their clubs. The nation was split by Vietnam, perceived to be Lyndon Johnson's war, while Humphrey was too decent a man for politics and could not repudiate the war. (One campaign button read, "Hubert Humphrey: Boy did you turn out to be a schmuck.") Richard Nixon, the man from whom nobody wanted to buy a used car, made his own comeback, winning a very close election, and Sinatra, like the rest of the country, began to turn to the right. Liberalism was seen to be tottering, and we all wanted to be on the winning side.

In 1966 Sinatra had interrupted shooting of a film in England to campaign in California for Pat Brown for governor against Ronald Reagan, and all his friends knew that he couldn't stand

Reagan, a washed-up actor of whom he observed accurately, "The trouble with Reagan is that no one would give him a job." In 1970 Sinatra shocked everyone by supporting Reagan for another term as governor instead of Jesse Unruh, the extremely competent speaker of the state legislature. Unruh had been a Bobby Kennedy supporter in 1968, and was brokenhearted at Kennedy's murder; he did very little for the national Humphrey campaign, which had rankled Sinatra. The only thing Sinatra seemed to understand was loyalty, yet in the America of the 1970s he discarded his own life-long political identity. The truth was that the Democrats were tired and demoralized after the disaster of the Johnson presidency and the Vietnam War, and Sinatra had always been a hawk anyway when it came to foreign policy; he probably thought that if the Vietnamese couldn't do as they were told they deserved to have bombs dropped on them. Like a lot of people, he was frightened by the divisions in the country, and voted to paper over the cracks.

Sinatra's support for Franklin Roosevelt had been considered daring in the 1940s, but his political affiliations would be boring nowadays, when every squirt in Hollywood volunteers his or her political opinions and Barbra Streisand's endorsement is probably a liability. What is interesting is the way Sinatra mirrored what was going on in the country as a whole. He suddenly seemed not to have held any real political opinions at all, throwing everything overboard and grasping at straws; yet the whole nation was drifting. Hollywood has always been overwhelmingly left/liberal, and once again Sinatra was a more typical American than he seemed to be at the time.

Spiro Agnew, a politician from Maryland, had been selected as Nixon's running mate in 1968 because he was perceived at the time as moderate, from the liberal wing of the party. But there was trouble from the beginning. During the campaign he said in Detroit, "If you've seen one city slum you've seen them all." As vice president, in New Orleans the following year, he thought that "a spirit of national masochism prevails, encouraged by an effete corps of impudent snobs who characterize themselves as intellectuals." As Nixon and Agnew presided over the decline of the American economy Agnew complained about "the nattering nabobs of negativism." Sinatra liked all this, and Agnew became an intimate, spending holidays at the Sinatra compound in Palm Springs, where the food and drink were available free around the clock, and where Agnew played tennis and other games with Barbara, Zeppo Marx's erstwhile wife.

As late as 1970 Sinatra still didn't like Nixon, but then the Agnews and the Reagans became regular guests in Palm Springs. While agreeing with Agnew about the "hopeless, hysterical hypochondriacs of history," Frank Sinatra (of all people) worried publicly about amorality. When Nixon was thinking of dumping Agnew from the ticket at the following election, Sinatra raised money and campaigned for him, singing "The Lady Is a Tramp" with new words: "The Gentleman is a Champ." Agnew was neither. In 1972 Sinatra campaigned for Nixon and Agnew because he thought Agnew should become ppresident in 1976; when it was discovered that Agnew had been taking bribes from contractors in Maryland since 1967, Sinatra's lawyer, Mickey Rudin, began planning his defense, but Agnew was forced to resign the vice presidency in October 1973, and disappeared from history.

Nixon and Sinatra understood each other: they both valued personal loyalty above all else. Sinatra sang for the Italian Prime Minister at the White House in April 1973; there were protests at a man with his known associations performing in the White House, but Nixon paid no attention, toughing that out just as he was hoping to tough out Watergate. Sinatra sang, "The House I Live In" while Nixon beamed; it apparently didn't bother Sinatra that Nixon had begun his career as a young congressman on the House Un-American Activities Committee when it was smearing him in the late 1940s. And finally, during the Nixon and Reagan years, Sinatra achieved the status of White House insider, which was what he'd wanted all along. Jack Kennedy, for all his faults, at least had some style and wit; Sinatra now joined the court of one president who eventually had to resign in disgrace and another who took advice from astrologers.

Bruce Bliven wrote a good piece called "The Voice and the Kids" in *The New Republic* in 1944, which included this: "He earns a million a year, and yet he talks their language; he is just a kid from Hoboken who got the breaks. In everything he says and does, he aligns himself with the youngsters and against the adult world. It is always 'we' and never 'you.'" But it was with his own generation that Sinatra aligned himself, and he was still doing that when he switched (with his generation) away from the Democrats to Nixon and Reagan.

Apparently Nixon also urged Sinatra to go back to work as an entertainer. There was one short recording session at the end of April 1973 which was aborted; and then in June he began making the album that was called *Ol' Blue Eyes Is Back*. This was produced by Don Costa, who arranged some of the tracks; most of it was arranged and all of it conducted by Gordon Jenkins. It is good to hear that nut-brown voice again on the first track, "You Will Be My Music," one of the least bad songs on the album, and certainly heartfelt; the next three songs are so dumb that Sinatra clearly doesn't know what to make of the banal soft-rock melodies, and nearly every track on the album has that dismal soft-rock beat, ubiquitous in elevator music, effectively eight beats in a bar for people who don't know where the beat is, or for drummers who need something to do to keep them awake on the gig. "Dream Away" is a film song, a Hollywood hack's stab at folk-rock. The two best songs on the album are Stephen Sondheim's "Send In the Clowns" (if you like it; some people hate it) and "There Used to Be a Ballpark," one of three songs by Joe Raposo (the other two are awful; Raposo also wrote "This Way to Sesame Street"). Both should have been dramatic set-pieces and right for Sinatra, but both are too slow and lugubrious, the Sondheim at least eschewing the twinkling soft-rock rhythm section.

Some Nice Things I've Missed the following year was similar, but a lame concept: they were songs that had been hits while he'd been retired. "Bad, Bad Leroy Brown" was a genuine folk-pop song, a hit in 1973 by Jim Croce, and ludicrously wrong for Sinatra; covering other people's hits was something Sinatra had never done before, and in the 1970s it meant imitating Neil Diamond or Elton John. There was no point. On Sinatra's best albums, Nelson Riddle had provided a setting for a Sinatra vocal, pointing at harmonies but rarely underlining anything; but the folk-pop stuff Sinatra was covering on these albums wouldn't have been worth that kind of treatment. He seems to have felt that

Costa would provide a way into the ears of the younger generation, and Costa was highly skilled at what he did, but paradoxically the reason that none of Costa's later work with Sinatra was as good as *Sinatra With Strings* of 1962 is that the material wasn't right to start with. It comes as a shock to remember that *Ol' Blue Eyes Is Back* and *Some Nice Things I've Missed* were almost all the studio albums of the 1970s; in retrospect it is as though the real Sinatra never came back at all.

But this begs the question: Who was the real Sinatra? All he had wanted to do was be Bing Crosby, and in this he succeeded beyond even his expectations; we even have to admire the sincerity with which he approached some of the soft-rock stuff. But he does not appear to have had much judgement or ambition beyond the three- or four-minute length of the 78 rpm sides he started out with, and we have to ask whether his interpretative ability was a separate thing from the quality of the songs themselves. It's true that he reached back to rescue songs from old movies and shows that might otherwise have been forgotten, especially in the 1940s on Columbia, but it is also true that he made a lot of records, and the largest number of songs he recorded in those years were more or less contemporary. He had grown up listening to the radio, and it is not unlikely that he simply wanted to record contemporary songs, to be in touch with the current generation, even after the quality of the songwriting had changed dramatically.

The reason Jimmy Van Heusen and Sammy Cahn wrote so many songs for him in the 1950s and 1960s was that they were at least bringing with them the values and the working methods of the golden age; Van Heusen used a piano rather than a guitar, and he used both the white and the black keys. But Sinatra's choice of contemporary material for his albums in the mid-1970s forces speculation about his judgement. It is entirely possible that his ability to interpret a song, and often to make a song sound better than it deserved, was always more a function of his exposure of his own vulnerability in the act of singing, rather than coming from the quality of the song itself. He took his art seriously and gave it full measure, and that self-expression no doubt compensated for a lot of things in his life, which would be one reason why he could not retire. But he had started out when the golden age of

American songwriting was still fresh, and his later choice of unsuitable material is startling. There was also a measure of danger in his interpretations: At his best, the way he made a song come alive, often convincing us (at least while we were listening) that his version was the only one we needed, was like a challenge; and he could not accomplish this with the Hollywood-cowboy soft-rock of the 1970s. On his post-retirement albums Sinatra appeared to have outlasted his art.

But it was an entirely different story on the road. After his retirement Sinatra became a concert artist, and he damned near succeeded in reviving the Swing Era after all. Those of us who did not bother to go see him live because his albums were such stinkers missed the point, and missed more than that. Sinatra had started out performing live onstage, in an era that was still a mixture of films, vaudeville and the Swing Era; then he performed in nightclubs where he did at least three shows a night because there wasn't room for everybody who wanted to get in; then he worked in Las Vegas, where those who couldn't pay for an overpriced hotel room were excluded. For most of this time he was extremely busy making films and albums every year; yet for three decades Sinatra had continued to need a live audience, so that he could somehow contrive to sing to each member of it. And then in the last stage of his career, despite a few lousy albums, he remained the biggest live act in the world. In less than a month in 1975 he performed in eleven American cities; in a two-week period he sang in nine European capitals, and later the same year in Israel; at the end of the year his press office said that in 105 days he had given 140 performances to more than half a million fans. It is possible that more people saw him in the flesh in those last two decades than had seen him in his entire previous career.

By the 1970s one of the biggest problems facing live music was where to play. Since the war people had stayed home to watch television, so that the smaller venues closed down, so that more people stayed home to watch television; and anyway the economics of the business were such that the biggest acts could not afford to play smaller venues. By the time he had tried and failed to retire, the only places Sinatra could play and make it pay were huge auditoriums and sports stadiums, the sort of places the big rock acts played, and nobody knew whether or not it could be done. Jerry Weintraub, a promoter who had worked with the rock acts and knew all the stadiums, started planning Sinatra's new concert career, and it was immediately successful.

In fact it began with a bang. In July 1974 he went to Australia again, and had his biggest run-in with the Australian press, when a chauffeur was supposed to deliver him to a rehearsal hall, and instead let him off where a gaggle of journalists were waiting. There was a melee, Sinatra was subsequently insulting from the stage at a concert, and the politicians got into the act. Sinatra couldn't get his plane refueled; labor leader Robert Hawke said he could leave only if he could walk on water, unless he apologized. Australians are not the kind of people to have the wool pulled over their eyes; according to drummer Irv Cottler, there were people marching in the streets in Sydney waving placards: "We want Sinatra! Down with the press!" But none of that was reported at the time. Robert Hawke later became Bob Hawke, a comic-strip prime minister, famous for his alcoholism and his ability to weep in public; Australia is a place where the winds of freedom still blow, where the sense of the ridiculous still lives, and where nobody wants to take any nonsense from anybody, and Sinatra's willingness to allow his goat to be gotten made headlines all over the world. He later said, "I used to blow whole countries. Now I blow continents." But it didn't matter, because there was no doubt about his artistic success. The Sydney *Daily Mirror* reflected the sort of reviews Sinatra's concerts would get for many years to come:

Too much booze, too many smokes, too many long, long nights have taken the glow from his voice, but no one gave a damn....For Sinatra still has the phrasing which cannot be surpassed, the timing, the splendid arrogance of remarkable talent.

In October that year a tour of nine East Coast cities, with Woody Herman's band of the period, called the Young Thundering Herd, ended with several concerts at Madison Square Garden, where Sinatra had watched many a fight in his youth. He joked from the stage, "As they say in Australia, 'Ol' Big Mouth is back.'" It was Jerry Weintraub's idea to record the whole thing for television, and in December *The Main Event Live* was released, an album put together from the highlights. It was the best Sinatra album for years (even to a more convincing version of "Bad, Bad Leroy Brown"), evidence that Sinatra was now at his best live; even so, the reviews of the album were mixed. The concerts at the Garden had to be interrupted constantly by a TV crew, and people who were on the tour said that the rest of it was even better, without the interruptions. The mystery is why more of the live concerts of the 1970s and 1980s have never been issued commercially, but tapes exist of some of them.

The big venues worked, but the Woody Herman band could not be a permanent solution to the other problem, which was finding musicians. The people Sinatra had been used to working with in the recording studios were getting old themselves, had plenty of studio work, and didn't want to go on the road. He always had a hard time in Las Vegas, which is probably why there were not more live albums issued from that period; the musicians in Vegas were often frustrated jazz musicians, sore at themselves for having ended up there and too world-weary to give what they were capable of; when he played there Sinatra had to bring key men from Hollywood at great expense. When he began his post-retirement concert career, he had Miller, Viola and Cottler, who'd done the world tour with him in 1962; Emil Richards was still around on vibes for a while; Sinatra's longtime bassist Ralph Pena had been killed in a car crash, replaced by Gene Cherico; section leaders often included Billy Byers on trombone, Marvin Stamm on trumpet and Bud Shank on alto sax (who all went to Australia in 1974), and Charlie Turner was another featured trumpeter. Miller quit for a while in the late 1970s, and Viola retired, around 1980, replaced by Tony Mottola, an old Sinatra acquaintance who hadn't played for several years and had to be persuaded to unretire. But Cottler was Sinatra's backbone on the road for thirty-five years.

During the 1940s, Swing Era veteran Johnny Blowers had become a studio musician and was Sinatra's drummer of choice; by the mid-1950s, working for Norman Granz at Verve and on most of Nelson Riddle's sessions at Capitol, the wonderful Alvin

Stoller had played with Billie Holiday, Art Tatum, Sinatra and many others; but then Irv Cottler, another veteran who'd played his first pro gig in 1938, became Sinatra's favorite drummer of all time. Stoller was probably the better jazz musician, but Sinatra was not, in the final analysis, a jazz singer, and anyway live music is different from studio work, demanding in a different way. When Sinatra started over as a concert artist in 1973–74, Cottler joined full time, giving up studio work entirely because the music had gone to hell anyway, and he was a rock in the drum chair: he put the tempo where he knew Sinatra wanted it, and Sinatra could know that it would stay there.

Even with the key men, putting together the rest of an orchestra on location was a headache. An unofficial New York band would be put together by a contractor, playing all the concerts in the East and many of the overseas ones; the New York musicians were not necessarily better players than the West Coast ones, but they were more professional, not such wise guys: postwar California had become Lotus Land to the extent that by the 1970s the musicians found it too much trouble to play together in ensembles, and everybody wanted to be a leader. Wherever the bulk of an orchestra was drawn from for each tour or concert, a pattern was established: the key men would rehearse with the locals; in the early years Sinatra would turn up for a final rehearsal, and the playing of the locals invariably improved as soon as he appeared. Later, after the routine was well established, Sinatra would appear only for the concert itself.

Pianist and conductor Vince Falcone had given up a good job managing a chain of music stores to play in Las Vegas, and hated it; but he first worked with Sinatra in 1973 at Caesar's Palace, and in 1978 joined full-time as conductor, or playing piano when Bill Miller was conducting. Falcone knew the music inside-out, and turned out to be a born conductor. Though Sinatra found him in Vegas, he was from New York State originally, and was one of those who appreciated the professionalism of the New York band; he had some important coaching from Gordon Jenkins, mainly not to take his eye off Sinatra, so that he was as reliable as Cottler was at the drums. Sinatra was looking after himself, and would quit smoking and drinking before a concert; Falcone remembered going with him to see Pavarotti at home for advice on how to keep his pipes burnished. (Sinatra also went to see Robert Merrill, the Metropolitan Opera baritone; he mentioned this somewhere, and Merrill, who had never been a teacher, was bemused to have people calling him for voice lessons.)

There were occasional halfhearted or private recording sessions from which nothing was issued; an album with Riddle was started in 1977 called *Here's to the Ladies* ("Linda," "Laura," "Nancy," etc.) but it was never finished. Sinatra kept trying to find new songs to record, and there were good songs around. Admittedly, the 1970s seemed like a desert when it came to saloon songs, but Cy Coleman had been writing with Carolyn Leigh since 1957; Alec Wilder was still around in the 1970s, and the words were still being written to his tunes; and cabaret singers are still reviving good old songs in the 1990s. The good songs that Sinatra had not already recorded, most of them, would have sounded obscure to the audiences of the 1970s and 1980s, but that hadn't stopped him recording anything he liked in the 1940s, and anyway the last two decades of Sinatra's career proved that people would have stood in line to hear him recite the phone book. But the man who had created markets and practically invented the twelve-inch long-playing album seemed to have forgotten how to do it, and kept looking for contemporary songs that already had a commercial track record, which in the 1970s meant shlock. But in his concerts the classic Sinatra material amounted to more than half of the repertoire, sometimes in the good old arrangements, sometimes in new ones which were fun to hear; and the contemporary stuff, which kept changing anyway, was easier to take in that context. It wasn't all fun and games: everybody liked Don Costa personally, but a lot of Sinatra's people didn't like the soft-rock stuff, especially Cottler. Yet Sinatra had an edge. In the last few years of her life Billie Holiday was reduced to singing the same dozen or so songs, partly because her health was so poor, and she had trouble learning new songs anyway; but Sinatra had already recorded hundreds of the best songs of the century, and was still in good voice. The magic still worked onstage, and the late 1970s and early 1980s were in some ways the best years of Sinatra's life.

But the recordings were dodgy. In 1980 came *Trilogy: Past, Present and Future*, a three-LP set that reached the top twenty in the *Billboard* chart. Conceived and presented as an idea by Sonny Burke, Sinatra's favorite producer during the 1970s, *Trilogy* was almost his last gasp as a recording artist, and an utterly peculiar souvenir.

Past was arranged and conducted by Billy May and recorded in Hollywood. It was a triumphant success, better than the Capitol and Reprise albums that tried to re-create the Swing Era, perhaps because more time had gone by: the songs are well chosen, the huge orchestra plays like a smaller group, and everybody is just having a ball, with no self-consciousness, no ego-tripping, no uncertainty. May outdid himself in the sheer integrity-with-flavor of the charts. Superbly recorded (the engineer was Lee Herschberg), *Past* sounds today like one of the better Sinatra concerts must have sounded. "The Song Is You" is a splendid opener, while "But Not for Me" and "I Had the Craziest Dream" recapture the feeling of the Dorsey years better than anything on *I Remember Tommy*: Sinatra sings in unison with a chorus, almost like he's standing at a microphone with the Pied Pipers, and the murmuring of a woodwind choir is also profoundly evocative. What makes these ten tracks so successful, in fact, is that we are reminded that a great band was a team, with everybody on the same side. "It Had to Be You" includes the verse, which makes consummate musical sense. "Let's Face the Music and Dance" picks up the tempo, and has a surprise at the end: no Billy May record would be complete without some wacky humor, and Sinatra was delighted to hear five notes of mariachi fanfare ending a song about paying the piper. "Street of Dreams" has a swinging medium tempo and is faded out at the end, suiting a sort of fairy-tale saloon song. "My Shining Hour" is the album's weakest track, because it's the weakest song (even if it is by Johnny Mercer and Harold Arlen): the chorus seems superfluous, the arrangement a bit overdone and the tempo too slow. Cole Porter's "All of You" is a quick swinger in more senses than one—it's less than two minutes long—and it solves a mystery for the listener: "All of You" was recorded two days earlier than "Let's Face the Music and Dance," but programmed later on the album; the mariachi fanfare drives you nuts at the end of "Music" because the fragment is hauntingly familiar; later you realize it's a phrase from "All of You." On "More Than You Know" Sinatra proves that he could still sing a slow one when the song was good enough; and "They All Laughed" is a fine closer, again in more ways than one: at the end, the whole band breaks into sarcastic haw-haw hilarity. It is as though we have been visiting the nicest part of Sinatra's neighborhood; this is what his world was supposed to be like.

Unfortunately, *Past* having done the best job of capturing Sinatra's world since the heyday of Nelson Riddle, the other parts of the trilogy are thrown into rather sad relief. It was thought at the time that a lot of people were buying a three-LP set just to get one of them.

Present was yet another wad of soft rock, recorded in New York, mostly arranged and conducted by Don Costa. "You and Me (We Wanted It All)," by Carole Bayer Sager and Peter Allen, is one of those banal 1970s cabaret songs with a twinkling guitar, a minimalist piano, and a melody line that never seems to stop descending; a couple of almost-clever rhymes in the lyrics only betray the rest of it. Billy Joel's "Just the Way You Are" gets an arrangement in the style of *Past*, which doesn't do enough to raise its boredom threshold. George Harrison's "Something" works better, because the arrangement and Sinatra's delivery turn it into a show tune, leaving you curious to hear the rest of the show; and in fact there is something familiar about the arrangement: the solo violin cannot be Felix Slatkin, because he died in 1963, but it comes as no surprise, perusing the small print in the CD booklet, to discover that "Something" was arranged by Nelson Riddle, and conducted by Vince Falcone, the only track on *Present* that had nothing to do with Costa. But Jimmy Webb's "MacArthur Park" is rubbish no matter who does what. "New York, New York," by Fred Ebb and John Kander, is the strongest track on the set, and in fact doesn't fit with the rest of it; the theme from Martin Scorsese's movie (which was beautifully observed, but flopped because it was too long and too earnest), the song was already becoming a staple of Sinatra's concerts, and as a single was his first top-forty hit in over ten years (and his last). "Summer Me, Winter Me" and "Song Sung Blue" are paeans to a generation that was effectively illiterate, jingles that would insult an intelligent child; Falcone and Cottler hated Neil Diamond's "Song Sung Blue," which was apparently a big hit single in 1972, for those who hadn't stopped listening to the radio by then.

Eileen Farrell is one of the few opera singers who can handle good pop songs, and has made two or three lovely albums of them with Robert Farnon; but singing a duet with Sinatra on Kris Kristofferson's "For the Good Times" she is completely wasted, and it is this track which convinces me that Sinatra never could have made an album of country songs. At its best, Kristofferson's world-weariness is valuable, but wholly different from Sinatra's: it is working-class rather than Hollywood. As a manic-depressive, Sinatra was either lonely or he was flying, either up or down, but the music of the American prairie requires the willingness to allow time to pass, and an entirely different kind of phrasing. "Love Me Tender" was a nineteenth-century campfire song with new words when we heard Elvis Presley sing it on television in 1960, and we knew that something terrible had happened to him; what the hell was Sinatra doing recording it nearly twenty years later? And so we come to the last track on *Present*: All the world's bishops, rabbis, and ayatollahs should have combined in a *fatwa* on whoever convinced Sinatra to record tosh like "That's What God Looks Like to Me."

Yet even worse was to come. *Future* is the last part of the trilogy, composed, arranged and conducted by Gordon Jenkins, and it is more than half an hour of tosh: With the Los Angeles Philharmonic, alto and soprano soloists, and a chorus, it begins with the orchestra tuning up (a bad sign), and goes on to celebrate sentiments about space travel, world peace and living in the desert without a single bar of memorable music. "The future will almost certainly be / Whatever you want it to be," it says here; the past is now an unbelievable place, where Sinatra made *Past* and *Future* in the same year; where Jenkins composed *Manhattan Towers* and went downhill from there. There can be few who have listened to *Future* all the way through, let alone more than once. This and *Watertown* is what Sinatra did in the way of commissioning original music drama, and we have to be grateful that he didn't do any more. The *Future* is inexplicable.

She Shot Me Down, the following year, was made in New York, and was at least a more interesting failure than most of the post-retirement sets. The nine songs included a Sondheim, a Gordon Jenkins and two co-written by Alec Wilder and pianist Loonis McGlohon, the kind of interesting obscurities Sinatra should have been seeking out. But he sounds uninvolved, as though he hadn't decided how to phrase them, and his pronunciation of certain words is as though the first run-through was issued by mistake, or as though he was finding it more difficult by 1981 to learn new songs. Most of the album was arranged by Gordon Jenkins, who was in failing health; it was his swan song, after the critical roasting he had got for his work on *Trilogy*. There's a lovely "Thanks for the Memory," and a medley Sinatra had been doing in concert, "The Gal That Got Away / It Never Entered My Mind," arranged by Costa from Riddle's charts and conducted by Falcone. And there's the title track, "Bang Bang (My Baby Shot Me Down)," by Sonny Bono (Cher had a hit on it in the early 1960s). I am reliably informed that Sinatra's "Bang Bang" is moving if you're stoned; it's not entirely out of place on an album of saloon songs.

In 1982 Sylvia Syms, an old friend from the great days of 52nd Street, made an album for Reprise. Allegedly, Sinatra and Syms were introduced in the early 1940s by Billie Holiday, who then took them both across the street to hear Mabel Mercer, who influenced everybody; and Sinatra and Syms became mutually admiring friends. After Syms had both legs broken in a car crash, she told Whitney Balliett, Sinatra sent her a pair of roller skates; when he next opened at Caesar's Palace, she sent him an antique silver ear trumpet. Once when she was a guest at his home in Palm Springs and the entourage went out to a lounge after dinner, Sinatra asked her to sing, but she could not bring herself to sing in front of him; his response, she said, was, "Sylvia, you're nuts." Syms had a million stories and some of them were suspect, but this one rings true: Sinatra was never slow to express admiration for another artist, and as fine a singer as Syms was, cabaret or supper-club singers in the 1970s seemed to be a disappearing breed. He conducted the orchestra on her Reprise album; the arrangements were by Don Costa, the last he ever wrote. But the Syms album has not been reissued on CD, because nobody in the shopping-mall record shops has ever heard of her.

In 1983 a duet album with Sinatra and Lena Horne was planned, a star-studded extravaganza, perhaps a three-disk set to follow *Trilogy*, but the planning bogged down, complicated by a temporary illness on Horne's part. Quincy Jones was going to be involved. The trumpeter and bandleader had become a vice president at Mercury Records in 1964, one of the first African-Americans to hold such a post in the record business, and had gone from strength to strength; he wrote the arrangements and conducted Count Basie's band on two Sinatra sets in 1964 and 1966; he had produced the album on Lena Horne's Tony-winning show *The Lady and Her Music* in 1981. Jones was always a highly regarded arranger, but had become an even more valuable producer, and finally quit arranging because the kind of music he'd started out in had pretty much disappeared anyway. He became one of the most famous producers in the world with Michael Jackson's *Thriller* in 1982, a number-one album for thirty-seven weeks in the U.S.A.; it is still the biggest-selling album in history.

Jones and Sinatra went on to make *L.A. Is My Lady* in New York in 1984. The title song, by Jones with Marilyn and Alan Bergman, was not written for Sinatra, but it was his idea to use it as a title track. The concept albums he and Riddle had invented never needed a title track, but ever since "Come Fly With Me," "Nice 'N' Easy," and the rest, this was the kind of concept he'd got used to, so they used a corny geographical hook, the irony being that "New York, New York" was recorded in Los Angeles, and "L.A. Is My Lady" in the other place. Otherwise it was a good album of songs he mostly hadn't recorded before, such as "Teach Me Tonight" (co-written by Sammy Cahn and Gene De Paul in 1953, with one of Cahn's best lyrics), "How Do You Keep the Music Playing" (by the Bergmans with Michel Legrand, a song that Tony Bennett had been doing in concert), and "Mack the Knife," which was becoming a staple of Sinatra's concerts. Jones farmed out the arrangements to Frank Foster, Sam Nestico, Torrie Zito and Joe Parnello; the album made the top sixty in *Billboard* on Jones's Qwest label (part of Warner Brothers), the first Sinatra album for over twenty years not on Reprise, and Sinatra's last album for a decade.

There can be no doubt that much of the credit for the excellence of Sinatra's best work should go to the arrangers, especially Nelson Riddle. Maybe this had something to do with the fact that Sinatra and Riddle were not on speaking terms for much of Sinatra's career. They made it up before Riddle died in 1985, but unlike Stordahl and Jenkins, Riddle never had his last hurrah; Sinatra could not even finish *Here's to the Ladies*, which should have been his last album with Riddle. When a benefit honoring Riddle was scheduled in 1978, Sinatra canceled, and when it was rescheduled for Sinatra's convenience, he canceled again.

Riddle was not a good conductor and not a composer, but as an arranger he knew his own worth, and never received his just due. The record industry honored Riddle for the albums he made just before his death with Linda Ronstadt, who has a beautiful voice when she is singing her folk-rock type of material, but had no idea what to do with Sinatra's type of song. Just as Sinatra and his cohorts could not re-create the Swing Era in the 1950s because they were too close to it, so Ronstadt had no chance of re-creating the 1950s, which is what she thought she was doing. "It's taken her a whole goddamn week to do four sides, and she thinks she's going fast!" exclaimed Riddle. The music business was not even willing to pay Riddle what he was worth at the end of his career; he had to take a percentage on the Ronstadt albums, but he got lucky: they were big hits, charting in *Billboard* and charting again when they were compiled in a box. (Popular music was becoming fragmented; the mainstream had got so bad that a lot of people were looking elsewhere: in 1977 there were only nine radio stations in American major markets playing standards; in 1984 there were 173.) An album had to sell a lot more copies to reach the top ten in 1985 than in 1955, and Riddle's estate probably made more money on the Ronstadt albums than on all the work he did with Sinatra.

Sinatra was doing some of the most interesting work of his life in concert in the late 1970s–early 1980s, despite the fact that his studio work of the period was disappointing. In concert he occasionally revisited his saloon-song persona, doing intimate things, for example, with just Mottola on guitar: "It's Sunday" is a lovely duet with Mottola recorded in 1984, issued on a single and later in the four-CD compilation of the Reprise years, and it is rumored that there was a ten-minute *Porgy and Bess* medley for just Sinatra and Falcone on piano. We can only hope that more of this work was recorded and will eventually see the light of day.

For someone who had led such a tempestuous life, Sinatra was managing his final decades more or less gracefully. After Spiro Agnew left the scene, Sinatra's steady woman friend had been Barbara Marx. He sometimes treated her as badly as he had treated most of his women, and the relationship was on-and-off, but she took it like a trouper, and he married her in July of 1976. A blue-eyed blonde, Barbara had been a chorus girl in Las Vegas, where she met her second husband, Zeppo Marx, to whom she was married for thirteen years. Nancy Sinatra has written that she was terribly disappointed that her father did not marry her mother again, and that Nancy Sr. still kept jars of his favorite spaghetti sauce in the refrigerator, but all that was wishful thinking; Barbara seems to have been exactly what Sinatra needed. While he was treating her like a toy that he could always do without, Barbara may have worried about her future, but she had a few things going for her. She was beautiful, but had no career to give up; she was glamorous, but supportive; she appeared submissive, but was not a fool. She no doubt spends half of each morning putting on her makeup, but that is the kind of woman Sinatra would want, especially as he was still climbing socially. They were married at the home of Walter H. Annenberg, whom Sinatra had known since the 1940s, and who had become old Joe Kennedy's successor as Ambassador to the Court of St. James in London during the Nixon administration.

The marriage took a few years to settle down. There were times when they swore at each other in public, and times when friends thought they'd split up, but Sinatra must have known that this was his last chance. For the most part, whatever Sinatra wanted to do was what Barbara wanted to do, yet she was not a total wimp; if he wanted to drink and gamble all night long in Las Vegas, she would fly home and go to bed. Sinatra always had plenty of servants, and all Barbara had to do was give orders and follow them. Jimmy Carter was in the White House in 1976, but it was only a matter of time before Sinatra's new friend Ronald

Reagan took over, and when the Sinatras began mixing at that level, Barbara was a definite asset. Interviewed by Jody Jacobs for the *Los Angeles Times* in 1983, Barbara had been helping with an important benefit in Las Vegas, looking after the decorations, the menu and the seating (a former president, two former ambassadors, a studio head, etc.), but not the entertainment. "There's room for only one star in this marriage," she said with a smile, and a smile like hers is worth a lot. In 1996 they had been married for twenty years.

Dolly Sinatra had long since decided that she disliked Nancy Barbato (but Nancy, to her credit, always treated Dolly properly). Dolly hated Barbara, for whatever reasons of her own, allegedly calling her a whore to her face. In January 1979, Sinatra was opening once again at Caesar's Palace, and had chartered an airplane to bring Dolly to the opening, and the plane flew into the side of a mountain near Palm Springs. Sinatra was devastated. Whatever anybody thought of Dolly, she had been the only benchmark he had all his life, her attitudes the only ones he had ever learned, the only ones he measured himself against. And Nancy Jr. gives Barbara credit for helping him through the loss, and helping him back to the Catholic Church for consolation.

Before his mother's death, Sinatra had planned to buy himself some kind of membership in the Knights of Malta, which seems to have been a scam perpetrated by his gangster friends. This might have pleased Dolly, but she never knew of it. Then in 1978 he had his marriage to Nancy Sr. annulled, so that he and Barbara could be married by a Catholic priest. Witnesses said that Barbara was not a Catholic and had to take instruction, but Nancy Jr. wrote that the whole thing was Barbara's idea. It is impossible to know what the family's feelings were, but Sinatra's obeisance to his mother's memory was certainly a slap in the face to the mother of his children. Some members of the public were outraged at what appeared to be Sinatra's influence in Rome, but in fact the Church had changed the rules: it was no longer necessary to apply to Rome, to shell out a lot of money in bribes, or even to get the Catholic spouse's permission.

In 1982 Sinatra mended an old fence, and Barbara probably deserves some credit for that, too. He went to see his godfather,

Frank Garrick, in Hoboken, after nearly fifty years. Garrick and Marty had remained friends, but Garrick had not seen his godson since having to fire him from his newspaper job all those years ago; he had not been invited to his godson's wedding to Nancy Barbato, nor even to the fiftieth anniversary party Sinatra threw for his parents in Hoboken. But now both Marty and Dolly were gone, and Garrick was the only connection with his origins Sinatra had left. He finally appeared on the doorstep of the humble Garrick home, with his secretary and Jilly Rizzo, his right-hand man. He said that he should have come to make his peace a long time ago, and Garrick agreed with that. From then on he kept in touch, sending gifts and concert tickets; on another visit he brought Barbara, and it was clear to Garrick that she had been a good influence on him. He'd changed, Garrick told Kitty Kelley. "In the beginning, he was just like his mom. A real pusher, and tough, tough, tough, but now he's like his old man. Real quiet and calm. That's Barbara that's done that. She's a real lady." We could be forgiven for wondering if Dolly had helped, by getting off her son's back at last.

And meanwhile Mr. and Mrs. Sinatra were glittering stars of the social whirl, receiving countless honors and seen at uncounted ritzy functions, constantly making the news in one way or another. Their favorite charities were for children. To mention a few highlights: in November 1983, Variety Clubs International threw a star-studded bash, taped for NBC-TV, announcing that Sinatra had raised enough money to build a wing on the Seattle Children's Orthopedic Hospital, called the Sinatra Family Children's Unit for the Chronically ill. Nelson Riddle led the orchestra, and Steve Lawrence and Vic Damone sang a medley called "Sinatra from A to Z"—from "All or Nothing at All" to "Zing! Went the Strings of My Heart." A few days later he threw his weight around at a casino in New Jersey, insisting that a blackjack dealer break the rules and the state law by dealing from an open deck; the incident was taped by security cameras and broadcast on network television. A few days after that, in early December, he was awarded the Kennedy Center Honor for Lifetime Achievement, along with actor James Stewart, choreographer Katherine Dunham, director Elia Kazan, and composer–music critic Virgil Thompson. The following year, in October 1984, after performing in a huge concert hall in Austria with Buddy Rich's band, paying all the expenses himself, the concert takings going to children's charities, he received the Medal of Honor for Science and Art in Vienna, Austria's highest civilian honor.

The following January he performed at both the vice presidential and presidential inaugurals, as well as producing Ronald Reagan's inaugural party, the most expensive in history, and which some critics thought was lacking in grace. It included someone called Ben Vereen performing in blackface. Sinatra had always indulged in ethnic jokes, which was typical of his generation and background: in Las Vegas he once joked that "the Polacks are deboning the colored people and using them for wetsuits." We used to tell Polack jokes in the car factory where I once worked, and in Britain I have heard all the same jokes, but in Britain they are Irish jokes, and I am told that on the Continent they are Belgian jokes. There were once hit songs called "All Coons Look Alike to Me," by a black songwriter, about a girl who is jilting her boyfriend for someone with more money; and "Sheenies in the Sand," by a Jewish vaudeville comic, about having a good time on Coney Island. There were any number of dialect songs and comedians in the so-called melting pot; as late as 1949 we had a Swedish-dialect novelty hit called "I Yust Go Nuts at Christmas," by Yogi Yorgesson. But the year after that, blackface died with Al Jolson, and today Americans are more polite to one another (despite one of the highest murder rates in the world). An entertainer in blackface in 1983 at a presidential inaugural was pretty bad judgement. One of the most acerbic columnists in America, Mike Royko, then of the *Chicago Sun-Times*, wrote, "It's possible that this performance offended some black viewers, but it probably made many of the rich Republicans in the audience yearn for the days when you could get good domestic help." So who ever accused Frank Sinatra of good judgement? He was an American of a certain age.

In May he received an honorary degree in engineering from the Stevens Institute of Technology in Hoboken, and on the same day his buddy Ronald Reagan gave him the Medal of Freedom at the White House. In September he sold out nine shows at Carnegie

Hall. His adoring daughter recorded what one critic wrote: "'Through subtleties of gesture and of voice—a shift of tone, a way of rushing or delaying the beat—Mr. Sinatra brought to his songs a sense of hard-fought inner drama that made them character studies as well as musical gems.'"

Inevitably, during the 1980s, the clock began slowly to run down. Vince Falcone left the Sinatra group at the end of 1983, having worked for him off and on for a decade; then bassist Gene Cherico left, and there never was another regular bass player. Trumpeter Charlie Turner and Mottola were the next to call it a day. Costa was a workaholic and in poor health; he died suddenly, on tour in South America, where he was a big star, only fifty-seven years old. By the end of the decade Gordon Jenkins, Nelson Riddle and producer Sonny Burke had all died; meanwhile, on the road, Joe Parnello took over the conducting for a couple of years, Falcone came back for a year or so, and in 1988 Frank Sinatra, Jr., took over.

Unlike his father, Frank Jr. was a formally trained musician; he was competent, but not inspiring, and Irv Cottler for one did not get along with him. In 1989 Cottler died, and Sinatra never had another regular drummer. Sol Gubin was just as good as Cottler, but he and Frank Jr. despised each other. Gubin was temperamental, but every musician has a temperament, and the conductor's job is to manage them: Duke Ellington managed an unruly bunch of geniuses for nearly fifty years, but Frank Jr. was no Ellington. He had led a band of his own in Las Vegas, and hired his friends as Frank Sr.'s old-timers left, and things continued rolling down the gentle, inevitable slope of passing time.

When Dolly's aircraft hit Mt. San Gorgonio in 1977, Dean Martin's son Dino, who wanted to be a pilot, said that the mountain was a hazard and ought to be moved. Ten years later, in March 1987, Dino's Air National Guard Phantom jet hit the same mountain, and Dean was never the same again. In March 1988 Sinatra, Martin and Sammy Davis began a reunion tour of twenty-nine cities, but Martin left the tour, and left show business, after a week. Liza Minnelli joined in April, the tour subsequently called "The Ultimate Event"; in April and May 1989 the trio went to Milan, London and Dublin.

In November 1989 Sinatra and Frank Jr. tried to mediate between the hotels in Las Vegas and the American Federation of Musicians, but failed because the hotels had made up their minds. There were no more union contracts and no more house bands in Las Vegas. Another era had ended.

Sinatra had said to Pete Hamill in 1974, "You think some people are smart, and they turn out dumb. You think they're straight, they turn out crooked." This was the period when his friends Spiro Agnew and Richard Nixon had to resign in disgrace. "You like people, and they die on you," he continued. "I go to too many goddamned funerals these days." In May 1990 Sammy Davis died of cancer. (During the 1950s Sinatra had bought Davis a house in Beverly Hills, so that he was one of the first African-Americans to live there; after Davis died, deeply in debt to the taxman, Sinatra reportedly gave the widow a million dollars so that she and her thirteen-year-old son could stay there.) Davis was followed within a few years by Jule Styne, Jimmy Van Heusen, Sammy Cahn and Swifty Lazar; and Jilly Rizzo, the former New York restaurateur who had not only been Sinatra's right-hand man for many years but a loyal friend to the entire family, was killed in a car crash. At the end of 1995 Dean Martin checked out.

Sinatra had often claimed that if a book about him were to be done he wanted to do it himself, so it would be done properly; as a publisher's editor in New York, Jackie Onassis tried to sign him up to do an autobiography, but nothing came of it. Sinatra cooperated with interviews for a charming book by Robin Douglas-Home published in England in 1962, but for the most part he hated books about himself. In 1976 came a self-serving book by Earl Wilson, a Broadway columnist who had been Sinatra's friend for many years; Sinatra hated the book and tried to sue Wilson. Then there were two lavishly illustrated books: *Sinatra: An American Classic*, a well-written book by John Rockwell, came from the Rolling Stone Press in 1984, and the next year, marking his seventieth birthday, came Nancy Jr.'s first book, *Frank Sinatra: My Father*, full of anecdotes. But the family regarded Kitty Kelley's *His Way* in 1986 as a disaster; in 600 pages it reported all of the punch-ups and business deals that were already a matter of public record, buttressed by copious interviewing. Sinatra had tried for a year to stop Kelley, and then seemed to give up, perhaps resigned at last to the fact that his life was public property. Tina Sinatra produced *Sinatra*, a five-part TV miniseries on her father's life, starring Broadway actor Philip Casnoff, first aired on CBS-TV in November 1992; it was accurate and honest as far as it went, but it was somehow wooden viewing, too slick and self-conscious. The most moving scenes were those about Marty's death.

In 1993 came *Duets*, Sinatra's first album in a decade. To everyone's surprise, it was issued on Capitol, who covered the costs and promised a lot of promotion; produced by Phil Ramone, a successful pop producer who'd begun as a recording engineer, it was a technical tour de force. Sinatra was reportedly confused in the studio at one point, unable to remember why he was recording some of the songs yet again. But suddenly, in July 1993, a session was set up like a live gig, with a hand-held wireless microphone for Sinatra: the band was in the groove, and nine takes were laid down in one night. On the CD he sounded good, but any amount of tweaking might have been done to the tapes; none of the other artists actually sang with him on the spot, but phoned in their parts on different dates, using a digital telephone line. And with the exception of Tony Bennett, none of them was suitable for a Sinatra album. The duetees besides Bennett were Bono (the fellow without a proper name from the rock group U2), Aretha Franklin, Barbra Streisand, Luther Vandross, Anita Baker, Carly Simon, Charles Aznavour, Liza Minnelli, Natalie Cole, Gloria Estefan, Julio Iglesias, and most useless of all, white-bread saxophonist Kenny G. The album was a cheesy, pointless farrago; it reached number two in the *Billboard* album chart, which made Sinatra very happy, but it is hard to say which was the worst track.

In March 1994 he was given a lifetime achievement award at the Grammy ceremonies in New York, and his acceptance speech was cut off for a TV commercial. A few days later he slowly collapsed while singing "My Way" in Richmond, Virginia; but he was just tired and overheated, and waved to the audience as he was carried off. There is an awful Italian bootleg called *Sings to the New Yorkers* on a phony "Capital" CD, said to be from the "RCMH NYC" (Radio City Music Hall) on April 24, 1994. Somebody must have had a digital tape recorder in the audience, and he should have bought a better seat: the orchestra is miles away and Sinatra sounds like he's off mike. The rhythm section is undistinguished, the drummer apparently hitting rim shots all the way through; Sinatra's warm vocal color is unmistakable, but the famous phrasing is often wobbly, and at the end of the last track, "I Get a Kick Out of You," he tries for a bravura ending and is horribly off-pitch. The audience was appreciative (the applause near the recordist is particularly well captured) and the sense of occasion is palpable.

In November 1994, *Duets II* was released, with Gladys Knight (and Stevie Wonder on harmonica), Jon Secada (a Cuban-born, Miami-based pop singer and songwriter), Luis Miguel (another similar), Patti Labelle, Linda Ronstadt, Antonio Carlos Jobim, Chrissie Hynde, Willie Nelson, Lena Horne, Jimmy Buffett, Lorrie Morgan, Neil Diamond, Frank Jr., and Steve Lawrence and Eydie Gorme. Most of the tracks are as bad as those on the first *Duets* album; the one with Jobim is surprisingly clumsy (an alcoholic, Jobim died soon afterwards). But the tracks with Gladys Knight, Lena Horne, and Steve and Eydie are really quite palatable, proving that it wasn't the idea that was so bad but the execution. The thinking behind both albums was to match him with the biggest names in their respective markets, since there weren't many left in Sinatra's category, but that just isn't true. Where are the duets with Marlene VerPlanck? Julius LaRosa? In Carnegie Hall in July 1995 there was a Sinatra celebration featuring Rosemary Clooney, who can still sing any of today's pop stars off the stage, as well as Maureen McGovern, Vic Damone, Margaret Whiting, Betty Comden and Adolph Green, and others; yet most of the names on the duet albums had to be big names in pop, rock, and country music. Sinatra had become an artifact, an icon, no longer belonging to himself; at the very end of his career he was the willing victim of the Hollywood values he had spent much of his career struggling against.

And yet, and yet. Maybe the important thing was never the records, but the audience; not posterity, or even prosperity, but the sea of upturned faces in front of him, to whom he could expose his heart without being threatened. In December 1994, a few days after his seventy-ninth birthday, he sang in Japan, but it was announced that there would be no more live shows. In February 1995 he sang six songs for a private audience on the last day of the Frank Sinatra Desert Classic golf tournament, and was said to be in superb form. But he had been reading the words to the songs from a prompter for some time, and was finding it more difficult even to do that. It must have been hard for him to give up, but the calendar is the enemy that will not be denied.

Also in February, it was announced that Sinatra's oil paintings of city scenes of New York were being copied onto a range of silk ties.

There had been a *Duets* TV show, again with the partners in different studios, but enlivened with film clips featuring Dean Martin, Sammy Davis, and Elvis; and there were more celebrations on American television to mark his eightieth birthday. In 1995 the Sinatras sold the compound in Palm Springs, complete with model trains, which he had owned since 1954; and at the end of the year, two weeks before the birthday, there was an auction at Christie's in New York of many of Frank and Barbara's possessions. There were not only bejeweled knick-knacks, but gorgeous works of art: scenes of New York by Leon Kroll, Max Kuehne, Ernest Lawson, Max Wiggins; views of Tuscany by William Merritt Chase. Some years earlier, Sinatra had sold off a few Impressionists to concentrate on collecting American art; but now the Sinatra century was closing down, and his collecting years were over.

Chapter Nine

The Sinatra Enigma: or,
He Is Us and We Are Him

Frank Sinatra began as a scared, lonely kid, emotionally deprived because his mother was too busy running her neighbors' lives to bring him up properly. But she managed to spoil him, and she also taught him both how to manipulate people and how not to behave: he learned from her negative example. He eventually had far more success than she ever did in acquiring power over others in order to cope with the loneliness, so that he ended up hobnobbing with presidents. Paradoxically he was successful because he was a great pop singer, perhaps the greatest of all.

This is superficially paradoxical because the apprentice gangster, the wheeler-dealer with the sometimes appalling manners and the tough mouth, basically accomplished it all by touching hearts.

The distinction between "popular" and "classical" music was less profound when Sinatra was starting out. Before the Second World War symphony orchestra concerts paid their own way, anybody could afford to buy an opera ticket, and the biggest stars at the Metropolitan Opera were happy to be paid perhaps 15 percent more than the others. In 1996 Luciano Pavarotti earned between $15 million and $18 million and all the orchestras and opera companies have to be subsidized, but it is still true in popular music that if you can't make a living at it you don't give up your day job, whether you want to play jazz piano, or rock drums, or write country songs in Nashville, or sing on the Broadway stage. Popular music is *commercial* music; and this determines much of its character: as we have become more prosperous the musical quality of mainstream pop has gone downhill because in order to make the big money it has to be aimed at the largest possible audience.

If Sinatra in his personal life was often vulgar in his taste, and if he commissioned no great works of art, nevertheless he achieved his enormous fame by showing us, at his best, how to sing good songs. If much of our popular culture at the end of Sinatra's century is violent, trashy and sexist, if our pop songs seem to have no tunes, it cannot be blamed on him, because he did his best to stem the tide. But he got to the top by struggling in a dog-eat-dog business.

To be successful in the popular-music business, you have to offer something that the public wants. Frank Sinatra has done that longer and more successfully than anybody else in history. Nobody else had come *close* to having hits with new albums for fifty years. I would nominate as his best single "Everything Happens to Me" (with Dorsey in 1941), and as his best album *Songs for Swingin' Lovers* (with Riddle in 1956), and these were but two Sinatras: the young, sweet voice and the hip, more mature playboy (both before stereo, but before and after Ava Gardner). Other Sinatra fans will have their own nominations (a charming British novelist, who I met at a party once, will be sore at me for dumping on *Watertown*). But the arguments are fun, because we can talk endlessly about songs and arrangements, and about what we get from each record; and about one thing we can agree: There has never been anybody else like Sinatra, and there never will be again.

But having hit records isn't all there is to it. Sinatra is not the first recording artist to become even more famous and rich after (in my opinion) he'd passed his peak; Pavarotti is another, and Elvis Presley a third. In order to establish anything like Sinatra's kind of longevity you have to hang on to your audience. Somebody described Presley's death at the age of forty-two as a good career move, and certainly his estate is worth more now than it was when he was alive. Jimmie Rodgers, Fats Waller, Hank Williams and Buddy Holly all died young: Williams is a legend today, over forty years after his death at the age of twenty-nine, but his best biographer, Colin Escott, feels that he had zero crossover ability, and would soon have been washed up in country music: "The market would not have changed to accommodate him. If he had tried to change to accommodate it, he would have lost the essence of his music in the process." Frank Sinatra did not have to die to become a legend; on the contrary, he grew more famous by living. His body of recorded work is bigger than anybody else's, and his earliest recordings were being reissued on CD and his concerts and radio airchecks bootlegged while he was still working.

All Sinatra had to do was carry on, apparently, but in fact he had to be in charge of his career. It is axiomatic today that in order to call the shots and keep most of the money in the music business, you have to start your own music publishing, set up your own label and effectively produce your own recordings, and it is also a good idea to raise your profile by becoming a movie star. Sinatra did all that when today's rockers were still sucking on rusks in their highchairs. He learned some of it from Dorsey, but he did it by having powerful friends, such as Manie Sacks at Columbia Records in the 1940s and Jack Warner later on; and by walking all over people to get what he wanted. His gangster friends helped, too, if only by hiring him to sing in their upholstered rooms when he seemed to be on the skids in the early 1950s.

So Sinatra could sing, and in business he could also punch above his own weight. There are endless stories about the tantrums, the bad behavior, and the gangster friends; and a billion words have been written about the music. But you can't have one Sinatra without the other.

The American novelist and critic Cynthia Ozick has written, "The great voices of Art never mean only Art; they also mean Life, they always mean Life." The zeitgeist, or time spirit, is the spirit or the attitude of a specific time or period: I would maintain that Frank Sinatra, in his clumsy, violent, often ugly way, has been the master of the zeitgeist of the twentieth century. He not only gained fame, wealth and power, but influenced the lives of countless millions with his art; thus he touched all the bases, accomplishing things that most people, in one way or another, would like to do, and he did it his way. But his way was according to the rules of the society in which he lived: it was just that some of the rules were written and some unwritten.

He or his associates committed assaults on bystanders. That is because he brought to his struggle the values of corrupt power: If you can't stand the heat, stay out of the kitchen; the way to acquire and hang on to power is to steamroller anyone in your way. In Sinatra's case he could have charmed the bystanders and the gossip columnists if he had tried, but he was far from the only man to grow up in the twentieth century who might lose his temper, or build up his own self-image by punching somebody. History is out of control; our politics and our politicians are banal and useless; the heroes of the masses are found in popular culture today because they appear to be winning the game, and the frisson of danger helps.

Sinatra liked gangsters, one observer said to journalist Pete Hamill: "He thinks they're funny." Gangsters *are* funny. Many of them come to sticky ends sooner or later for the same reason that in the meantime they can afford to laugh at anything: They have jumped over the fence to discover, as Bob Dylan has tried to tell us, that the only thing to understand is that there is nothing to understand. Each of us has to decide for him/herself whether or not there is such a thing as morality, and upon that decision will depend, in the end, whether or not we can learn to govern ourselves in a world without touchstones.

In the film *Ocean's Eleven* (1960), the Sinatra character says, "I didn't invent myself. I don't own the pattern. I can't change the way I am and anybody who says he can is a liar." This is, of course, a self-justifying speech; Hitler couldn't change the way he was, either. The problem is the size of today's world: it is both bigger and smaller than it was in the days when there were no world wars and no world-famous singers; we are no longer ants, our decisions being taken for us by the barons in their castles. We each have to decide what kind of people we want to be, and refusing to decide is itself a decision. On his own terms, Sinatra was no doubt a moral man, with his own standards of loyalty, keeping his word and so forth; but he has been a paradigm of our century because he has been neither more nor less confused (and touchy about it) than the rest of us. As individuals we may disapprove of his friendships, his womanizing, or his occasional violence; but as a society, when we look at Sinatra we see what we would like to see in the mirror: the guy who has it all, and can still effectively say, "Who, me?"

When he sang he was honest. If it takes only three minutes to sing a song, there were almost as many women as songs. He bedded an unusual number of women, and he no doubt treated some of them badly, but as far as we know they were willing; it seems possible that when he made love he was honest: he told Pete Hamill, "I loved them all. I really did." "Love means the pre-cognitive flow," wrote D. H. Lawrence. "It is the honest state before the apple." His sexual behavior was as compulsive as any other part of his life, but no matter how many apples he ate Sinatra could not find the love he should have had as a child, and so had to keep searching. That is what the songs are about; that is where the vulnerability found a home. All or nothing at all. I'm a fool to want you. You make me feel so young. In this area, too, he lived through a time of change.

Barbara G. Harrison wrote an article for *Viva* magazine in 1976 called "Oh, How We Worshiped the Gods of the Fifties". In the mid-1950s Harrison went to live in Greenwich Village, where there seemed to be a new kind of freedom: nowadays young people try to protect themselves, to appear to be insensitive, but forty years ago the idea was to be infinitely sensitive: key words were "aware," "evolving," and "becoming." Their heroes were Frank Sinatra, because he sang the way he did and because he had fought his way back from what had looked like the end of his career; and Marlon Brando, who also had more than a hint of danger about him; and the writers J. D. Salinger and Albert Camus, who appeared to be opposites. Salinger looked for ecstasy, while Camus struggled with despair, but both brought the same message: that man had to carry the weight of life alone, as Sinatra and Brando seemed to do.

In their love affairs with their poets and their jazz musicians, the young women of Greenwich Village argued about who suffered the most pain. Harrison later wrote:

It is only on rereading Salinger and Camus that I realize how necessary women were to them as foils. Preferably long-legged, cool, innocent young women with undiscriminating hearts.... We could accept any damned nonsense from a man, provided it was haloed by poetic *feeling*. If our men were struggling and in pain—not to put too fine a point on it, if they were losers—we brought them cups of consecrated chicken soup.

... We invested every fast-talking faithless womanizer we knew with noble qualities. We lived to be loved, possessed, conquered, and consumed.

But Harrison was ultimately amused by her younger self; she was more political twenty years later, but still had the same values, and she was still a Sinatra fan. ("Fifties women are incredibly loyal: they don't forget," she wrote.) Men and women still dance around one another, looking for love; the goalposts keep moving, but it's the same old game. Sinatra may have been doomed to permanent loneliness, but he lit the corners of dark rooms for those who had to keep searching.

Gene Lees has written that Sinatra could hire people to do everything for him except sing. He did that for us. His career is over, but what we have left of Frank Sinatra, the recordings, is the best part. The rest is the echo of our times.

Index

Other than in the entry under his name Frank Sinatra is referred to as S.

the Window," 112; "Do I Worry?," 54; "Dolores," 53; "Don't Ever Be Afraid to Go Home," 112; "Don't Like Goodbyes," 139; "Dream Away," 237; "Dum-Dot Song," 84; "East of the Sun," 49, 179–80; "Ebb Tide," 157; "Embraceable You," 101, 164; "Emily," 197; "Everybody's Twistin'," 184; "Everything Happens to Me," 54–5, 56–7, 62, 138, 260; "Fable of the Rose," 48; "Faithful," 112; "Falling in Love With Love," 86; "Fella With an Umbrella," 104; "Five Minutes More," 85, 108; "Foggy Day, A," 127; "Follow Me," 199; "Fools Rush In," 102, 164; "For the Good Times," 246; "For You," 54; "Free For All," 58–9; "From Here to Eternity," 131; "From the Bottom of My Heart," 31, 32; "From This Day Forward," 85; "From This Moment On," 141; "Full Moon and Empty Arms," 59; "Gal That Got Away, The," 247; "Gentle on My Mind," 199–200; "Ghost of a Chance," 162; "Ghost of a Chance (I Don't Stand a)," 83; "Gone With the Wind," 157; "Goodbye," 156–7; "Goodnight Irene," 109–10; "Goody Goody," 185, 186; "Granada," 179; "Guess I'll Hang My Tears Out to Dry," 82, 102, 157; "Hear My Song Violetta," 48; "Hello Dolly," 105, 197; "Here Comes the Night," 32; "Here's That Rainy Day," 162; "Here's to the Losers," 197; "High Hopes," 166; "Home on the Range," 85; "House I Live In, The," 197, 236; "How About You," 59, 61; "How Are Ya Fixed for Love," 162; "How Cute Can You Be," 85; "How Deep Is the Ocean," 164; "How Do You Keep the Music Playing," 248; "Hucklebuck,

The," 106; "I Begged Her," 76, 77; "I Believe," 87; "I Can't Get Started," 162–3; "I Can't Stop Loving You," 197; "I Concentrate on You," 85–6, 101; "I Could Write a Book," 112, 145; "I Couldn't Sleep a Wink Last Night," 75; "I Didn't Know What Time It Was," 146; "I Don't Know Why (I Just Do)," 83; "I Dream of You (More Than You Dream I Do)," 76; "I Fall in Love Too Easily," 76; "If I Didn't Care," 32–3, 34; "If I Had You," 86, 102, 142, 187; "If I Knew You Were Comin' I'd've Baked a Cake," 110, 112; "If It's the Last Thing I Do," 139; "If You Are But a Dream," 76; "If You Go Away," 201; "If You Stub Your Toe on the Moon," 86–7; "I Get a Kick Out of You," 127, 185, 257; "I Got Plenty o' Nuttin'," 141; "I Guess I'll Have the Rest," 110; "I Guess I'll Have to Change My Plan," 142; "I Had the Craziest Dream," 244; "I Have But One Heart (O Marenariello)," 85; "I Hear a Rhapsody," 112; "I Like to Lead When I Dance," 183; "I'll Be Around," 129; "I'll Be Seeing You," 48; "I'll Never Smile Again," 50–1, 53, 80, 162; "I'll Remember April," 165; "I'll See You Again," 165; "I'll Take Tallulah," 63; "I Love Paris," 166; "I Love You," 105; "I'm a Fool to Want You," 113, 151; "I'm Beginning to See the Light," 32, 185; "I'm Getting Sentimental Over You," 179; "I'm Gonna Live 'Til I Die," 130; "I'm Sorry I Made You Cry," 85, 101; I'm Walking Behind You," 120; "Imagination," 49, 179, 186; "In the Blue of the Evening," 180; "Indiscreet," 184; "I Only Have Eyes for You," 81; "I Should Care," 80, 81; "Isle of Capri," 152; "It All Came